The Peregrine Falcon in Greenland

Virginia R. Peterson

THE PEREGRINE FALCON IN GREENLAND

Observing an Endangered Species

James T. Harris

University of Missouri Press
Columbia & London
1981

To Ned Perrin

Library of Congress Cataloging in Publication Data

Harris, James T
    The peregrine falcon in Greenland.
    Bibliography: p. 255
    Includes index.
    1. Peregrine falcon. 2. Birds—Greenland
I. Title
QL696.F34H37   598.9'1   78-67404
ISBN 0-8262-0343-4

Grateful acknowledgment is made to the photographers whose
photographs appear on the following pages:
David Clement, pp. 4, 40, 66, 68, 81, 86, 100, 139, 160, 163, 173,
177–80, 194, 207, 210, 218, 221, 228, 243
M. Alan Jenkins, pp. 26, 110, 119, 121, 128
William G. Mattox, pp. 23, 69, 185, 196
The author provided photographs for pp. 42, 54, 191, 219, 233

This book was published with the assistance
of the Frank Luther Mott Fund.

Preface to the Paperback Edition

Three years have passed since I completed manuscript preparations for the original publication of The Peregrine Falcon in Greenland. During this time, peregrine fortunes have been mixed. But we now have good reason for optimism concerning the future of this species, due to the concerted efforts of many people.

Peregrines have continued their remarkable comeback in Great Britain. Everywhere cliffs are rapidly being recolonized, even in coastal regions that were once almost entirely depleted. In contrast, survival of America's Rocky Mountain population remains tenuous. Reproduction is poor and peregrine numbers greatly reduced. Peregrines seem to be slowly increasing in California and the other Pacific Coast states, but many pairs still experience reproductive failure, due to egg-shell thinning caused by pesticides. Researchers have been removing these highly vulnerable eggs for artificial incubation under carefully controlled conditions. Upon hatching, the young falcons can be returned to wild nests.

Populations in arctic North America show varied trends. Peregrines along the Yukon River have bounced back to pre-pesticide numbers. But in other areas, peregrines remain in reduced numbers and still experience poor productivity.

In West Greenland, Bill Mattox and others have continued the annual falcon surveys. Their data do not clearly indicate either a decline or a strong and healthy population. Pollutant levels in eggs analyzed from 1978 and 1979 are still high, but lower than in other arctic populations. Four of the cliffs occupied in 1972 have not hosted young in recent years. One of these, Ring Sø, was guarded by a lone adult in 1980. First Eyrie has remained totally abandoned. Yet other eyries have been yielding numerous young. Peregrines have been inhabiting marginal cliffs. and a few cliffs that had formerly been occupied by gyrfalcons now support peregrines.

It has become increasingly clear that contamination of arctic peregrines in good part occurs on their wintering grounds in Central and South America. Recent studies have focused on the peregrines and their prey in winter. The falcons are well distributed throughout the habitats one might expect them to prefer, but these hunters do concentrate in certain regions, most notably along the west coast of South America from Colombia through central Peru. Some but not all areas currently receive heavy doses of DDT and other pesticides. The varying trends evident in arctic breeding populations appear to reflect the varying degree of contamination of the winter ranges for each of these populations. The future for arctic peregrines will depend on events in these impoverished, tropical countries.

The eastern United States, where breeding peregrines totally vanished during the pesticide era, presents a less politically difficult situation. Successes in captive breeding and reintroduction offer great hope for the species' return. In 1980, Cornell University's combined breeding programs in New York and Colorado produced an all-time high of 176 peregrines. In the west, 52 of these falcons were released to bolster the remnant Rocky Mountain population. In the east, 67 young peregrines were freed at 14 sites from New Hampshire to Virginia. This brought the total number of released peregrines in the east to over 275 since the program's beginning.

Reappearance of single and even paired peregrines at the release sites has fueled hopes that wild peregrines would soon be hatched, raised, and fledged by free-flying parents. Then in 1980, two pairs of released peregrines in New Jersey hatched their own eggs and fledged all the young. A third pair—possibly with both adults naturally wild rather than released—fledged two young in coastal Maine. These marked the first successful nestings of wild peregrines in any state east of the Mississippi River since the 1950s. DDT and the residues of other pollutants in the prey have reached levels low enough so that the falcons can again reproduce successfully.

Also in 1980, the personnel of the Cornell program achieved another significant success. For the first time, they were able to establish a pair of falcons in the wild by introducing a captive adult bird to a fully wild one on its territory, so that the two falcons took to one another. The newly formed pair raised a brood of young supplied from the Cornell incubators. This method of pairing birds may become increasingly important as more single falcons set up territories and await a mate.

The reintroduction efforts convey a dual message. They demonstrate the extraordinary difficulty of repairing damages we have inflicted on our environment and among its creatures. Yet these labors for the peregrines also reveal an immense, creative capacity we have for caring about our earthly home. We humans can nurture its recovery with beautiful patience. Not only our grandchildren and children, but we ourselves may soon know the day when fiercely wild peregrines will rear their young at hundreds of cliffs that are now silent and that, except for our efforts, might remain without peregrines forever.

J. T. H.
April 1981

Preface

Today overpopulation as well as food and energy shortages force humans to exploit their environment increasingly and in more efficient ways. Economic uncertainties overshadow concerns for wildlife. Yet many of our present decisions will have irrevocable effects on the nonhuman life of our planet. To make wise choices, the general public still must learn a great deal more about the other inhabitants of our earthly home.

In this narrative of a summer's research in Greenland, I have documented an endangered species problem from both scientific and humanistic perspectives. The magnificent peregrine falcon, imminently threatened in both North America and Europe, is loved by an extraordinary variety of people. It is an ideal subject for this exploration of wildlife issues.

My four companions and I visited Greenland to discover whether or not falcons still nested on cliffs rising above the tundra. Three themes develop the narrative. First, the search for the falcon eyries—does a substantial number of pairs produce young in Greenland? Second, the fate of the one falcon family I observed for much of the summer—will the adults succeed in raising their young? Third, the development of my feelings toward the species and the individual falcons—and thus, what is the value of this endangered animal?

The book will provide readers with the scientific information necessary for a thorough understanding of the peregrine's present status and its biological value. All of us can and should comprehend the complex background to the species's problem. For the writing of this material, I have relied upon extensive notes from the field, detailed study of the technical literature, and conversations with many students of the peregrine and of Greenland. Much of this information is basic to an appreciation of other wildlife species and their ecosystems.

However, because the peregrine's greatest values for humanity are experiential and aesthetic, The Peregrine Falcon in Greenland is most uniquely a subjective account of the species. These values are directly discussed during the course of the narrative. Yet they must figure principally as the reader follows and in a sense experiences my encounters with individual falcons. The personal narrative, then, accomplishes my central purpose.

Many people have helped me with the book, and I wish to acknowledge at least the most significant of their contributions.

I am grateful to my friend William G. Mattox, who made my

travel to Greenland possible and assisted me throughout the
field study and also during the writing. I appreciate the excitement
and skills of my companions in Greenland: Richard A. Graham,
William A. Burnham, and my tent mate, David M. Clement.
M. Alan Jenkins, and F. Prescott Ward accompanied us in 1973.
The United States Air Force, the Richard King Mellon Foundation,
and Dartmouth College supported my fieldwork. The research
was performed in close cooperation with Finn Salomonsen,
Curator of Birds at the University Zoological Museum, Copenhagen, Denmark. The Danish and temporary American residents
of Søndrestrøm, Greenland, in numerous ways made life on
the tundra more comfortable.

I particularly appreciate John E. Ross of the University of
Wisconsin for his support and advice at all stages of the writing.
Merton M. Sealts, Jr., and William G. Reeder kindly read and
commented on a draft of the book. Joseph J. Hickey read portions
of the manuscript, answered many of my questions, and generously
made available his materials on the peregrine. Susan L. Flader's
continuing interest in my work has helped me maintain my
own energies and enthusiasm. Lois S. Harris commented upon and
typed major portions of the manuscript.

The library materials of the Department of Wildlife Ecology
at the University of Wisconsin were of great assistance. The
Department of Agricultural Journalism and the Institute for
Environmental Studies at the University of Wisconsin supported me
during the writing of the book. Noel Perrin gave me suggestions
and friendship and lent me use of his cabin, where I wrote
most of the first draft. Mary Dokken, Virginia Beske, and Beverly
Schrag have all spent many hours typing for me.

I have purposely been vague about the locations of peregrine
eyries, to avoid increasing the likelihood of human disturbance.

J. T. H.
14 March 1978

Contents

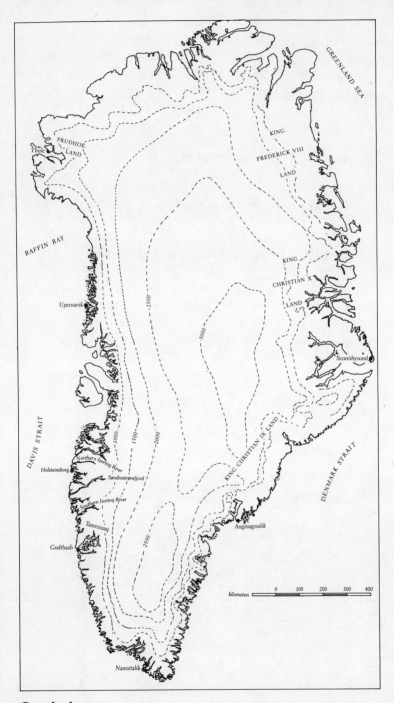

Greenland

Part I.

The First Encounter

It was spring 1972 in northern New Hampshire. The trees
still were leafless in early May, the maple trunks and branches
dark. Through the car window, through the shifting silhouettes
of branches, I saw a black raven twist his extended, wide
wings. He rose beyond the forest's reach and soared. The sable
raven, he gave me all the wish to visit the empty remote
wilderness. I was restless and said aloud, "Do you know how
I can get to the far north this summer?"

My companion thought a moment; he tapped the steering
wheel with his fingers. "Would you like to study peregrines
in Greenland? I know a man who may be going. Bill Mattox
is his name."

Dr. Mattox was a geographer at Dartmouth College. I
climbed three flights of stairs to his office. The door stood ajar,
and he listened on the telephone; he motioned me to enter.
I sat and looked at his books, mainly about arctic places,
and at a map of Greenland on his wall. I noticed he had a
friendly voice with varying tones, he was well dressed, thin,
and he took notes with a sharp pencil. But I was wondering how
a windy cliff side and heavy rough clothes would change
him, and I was imagining peregrines, the swiftly flying falcons.

I think he was busy that morning but when I told him
why I had come, he sat back and looked at me, perhaps considering for a moment whether I had ever watched peregrines,
and, if so, how. He took a book from his desk top and opened it
to another map of Greenland. Dr. Mattox was smiling.
I learned how the ice covers almost all the island except for
narrow strips of open land on the west, east, and north coasts.
He spoke many names quickly, of towns and mountains
and fjords.

"The people almost all live in a dozen towns," he said.
"These are on the coast. The rest of Greenland is empty, except
twice a year when the Greenlanders hunt for caribou. You'll
find hardly any level ground anywhere from ice cap to sea,
but mountains and hills and rocks the glacier left."

Listen. "The peregrines come in May from the south and find cliffs to nest on. Not here"—he pointed to the north—"nor here"—to the northeast. He traced the long western shore. "On this coast; there are many in the south but as you go north beyond Disko"—a large island off the middle coast—"the peregrines are fewer until at Thule only two or three pairs nest. We'll be here, near Søndrestrøm, the U.S. air base."

We were thinking of a large falcon with blue-gray back and upper head; its under feathers are white and buff with narrow black bars on the belly. As it flies, the pointed wings and long tail darkly line against clouds until the falcon swerves, and in the sunlight the pale feathers flash for an instant. The beating wings carry the bird across wind and field; it is gone.

They are crow sized, but unlike crows the peregrines have slender bodies and curved wings that fit the wind and carry them through effortless glides and suddenly up into soaring circles. Their wings beating seem to cut the air, as flapping crows never do; little birds, like blackbirds, will often chase a crow and attack its back and neck, but they hide from the falcon. For almost no bird can match the peregrine's flight speed in the open. And the falcon preys on birds, which it catches in aerial pursuits, often by rising high and swooping abruptly down upon them in a steep dive called a stoop.

"They'll spot us long before we reach their cliffs," Mattox said. "Their eyes see farther than human eyes."

He took out another book and opened it to dark black and white pictures of a barren landscape of sharp rocks and cliffs and mountain crests with grassy hillsides between. No trace of humanity in any of them. "Peregrines nested at this cliff"—an odd mound of black rock—"and at another cliff behind this mountain, beyond a long lake." I asked him how far the distances between cliffs were, and how cold we would be, whether the sun shone at night, and where people were.

After some more discussion, he told me, "I'd like to have you with us, Jim."

The peregrines spend much of their time in flight. They pause on high perches, cliffs or trees, with wide views.

A lake with desolate shores, seen from a helicopter on the way from Søndrestrøm to Holsteinsborg.

The dark feathers form a helmet over the head, passing through eyes and down in what are called malar stripes whose width varies with the bird, to outline the yellow of the beak before, and the white cheeks behind.

We talked of costs. "There's equipment we need: tents, cots, ropes, climbing gear, heavy boots, film, mosquito headnets but very warm clothes also. The main cost is transportation. . . . I think we go to Montreal by bus, and then Nordair can fly us up to Baffin Island. You see Davis Strait lies between Baffin and Greenland. I believe a plane crosses once a week, but that depends on the weather, and we must be prepared to camp on Baffin while we wait. If we can't go this way we must fly to Denmark first, and then north to Søndrestrøm. That will cost more.

"I'm still awaiting news on my funding. I've tried several places. But as you're a student at Dartmouth you may be able to get money through the college. Do you know Dave Clement?"

"No."

"He's a student here and wants to go. You two should get together and write up an application."

I walked straight from Mattox's office to Dave's dormitory

4

room. Five people sat on couches and chairs and floor, eating lunch, even though it was 2:30 in the afternoon. Dave was very casual about trip plans. My hurry of conversation and speculation slowed. Yes, he thought, we should go together. He had already been working on the application for money. We looked over the equipment list. Some of these items Dave seemed to have already. I noticed a large coil of rope behind the door, and a pile of pitons sat on Dave's desk.

"Have you been north before?" I asked.

"Yes. I went canoeing near Hudson Bay for two summers." He continued, "Have you ever watched peregrines?"

"I've seen them a few times."

Dave hadn't. I'm not certain he had known about peregrines before he discovered Mattox's trip to Greenland. He was a rock climber and wilderness hiker.

I visited him several times during the following week and together we prepared the application. I wrote most of the explanation of the endangered falcons and our study while Dave knew what gear we would need and where we could get it.

To my amazement, we actually did go to Greenland. Somehow planning the trip in a dormitory room had seemed entirely disconnected from the reality of walking on tundra. Various parts of our plans had to be abandoned. We ran into trouble with transportation. We received word from Montreal that perhaps no such flight to Baffin would operate this season. And that the destination was at the opposite end of the island from the point of departure across Davis Strait. Next we learned that Mattox's funding had not been approved. One of the members of his party would not be able to go, but Mattox and two others would pay their own way. Dave and I did receive money from a fund at Dartmouth. Finally we learned that the U.S. Air Force had agreed to let us fly from McGuire Air Base in New Jersey to Søndrestrøm.

This news surprised me. "Why are they going to help us?" I asked Mattox.

"They're interested in our study." I remembered that the Air Force with its squadrons of jet planes had chosen the falcon as its symbol.

But Mattox said, "No, that's not the important reason. Do you know about bird strikes at airports? . . . At some of the air bases large flocks of birds gather. They rest on the runways or fly about where the jets come and go. One gull in an engine, and the plane crashes. Men and millions of dollars are lost.

"The Air Force has tried to eliminate the birds. The gulls get used to noise or decoys. There are too many to kill. But at some bases falcons will scare them away.

"A falconer flies a peregrine near the runways each morning. Yes, Jim, a falconer. After several gulls are caught by the falcon, the rest avoid the area."

*   *   *   *

The peregrines are wide-ranging, found on every continent except Antarctica, and through many chains of islands, tropical and polar. People have watched and drawn or written of them throughout the world, as long ago as the ancient days of Egypt, and we have hunted with them for thousands of years. We encounter the peregrine in the lonely wilderness— mountain, plain, jungle, or tundra, the storm-swept coast. Ships meet these wandering birds in the middle of the ocean. Yet they have lived within our largest cities.

The peregrine looks over many landscapes, and the creatures it feeds on vary from continent to continent. Yet everywhere the falcons hunt upon unforested land. And they choose cliffs and bluffs on which to nest, where their young are inaccessible to humans and prowling foxes. The pairs scatter in isolated nest sites with forest or grassland miles wide between.

Traditionally, people have preferred to live in lowlands where the rich, wide soil feeds myriad crops, the flat lands where dirt doesn't vanish with each rain and rocks do not break the plow or, standing high, put the plants in shade. These rocky bluffs and natural fortresses were hardly useful to humans, and laborer or gentleman seldom walked to their sides. But when such men did, they felt the awe of dizzy heights and the hard drop; how strange that swift, large birds should circle, swoop before the cliffs, and scream as no creature ever did in the green meadows.

Too many distractions hurried people past the precipice. But perhaps they carried away wild images. And those who didn't forget might hesitate on odd days, stray moments as they leaned over their tools. Far from daily life or work, far above strange falcons were circling. What did their voices mean?

Near and far, the peregrine has been present throughout human history, almost everywhere we have traveled. Distantly present. It doesn't wait on people, as crows or rabbits do, when we plant or sit before our houses. The peregrine doesn't strike our worldly or material needs. A gap exists between our concerns and those of the touring falcon, in a sense a barrier to remembering that the peregrine is beautiful. Essentially the lives of falcons have passed in the wordless wild, and in their turn they have not altered our hopes, efforts, sorrow. Except that now and then the falcons in powerful flight, wings graceful and quick, do touch us. Certain people carry these pearls of memory. Did the treasured strands start by chance, or are there qualities rare among us that respond to the visions?

As for myself, I can't remember first learning that peregrines exist. I had seen them pictured in books. My first meeting came one day in April when I was fourteen, when it rained quietly through the morning and afternoon until at last the clouds were breaking into fragments and the sun shone. Walking outside, where the breeze caught droplets from birch twigs, I noticed a hawk to the north. It was large and approached quickly with steady wingbeats, deep pumping wings that cannot be forgotten, straight past me and on without a pause to the far horizon. For the moment little birds chirped in alarm from the birches.

Encounters with peregrines usually are brief. We hold the memory quietly until, a year or two later, we have another glimpse. For me, the casualness of my peregrine encounters was transformed; not abruptly, for I have memories of many meetings and many moments. One, of Bill Mattox, with his maps and dark photographs. My transformation began with that odd chance, the question I absently spoke aloud when the raven croaked and shook its black wings.

Pesticides

During the weeks immediately before our departure, I spent much time reading books and articles about the peregrines. Anyone beginning a bird study must learn from those who have already watched. The reading is still more essential when you will follow an endangered species, for you can't understand the plight of a vanishing animal without knowing a considerable amount of technical information.

The peregrine's breeding range once included almost all of North America, from the heated Mexican highlands to edges of the arctic sea. A main limitation for the peregrine was lack of suitable nest sites, and thus the pairs were lonely and scattered across great distances on the plains, and absent from lowland areas of the southeast—most of Alabama and Georgia, and all of Florida. In 1942, Joseph Hickey, a student of peregrines, listed 275 eyries east of the Rocky Mountains, all in the United States, but guessed that there might have been as many as 350 pairs before humans disturbed many areas.[1] Probably a larger number of peregrines lived to the north. Richard Bond estimated that 750 pairs lived in all North America from the Rocky Mountains west, less than half of these in the United States.[2]

While these calculations of peregrine numbers are rough, only rarely do we have such extensive information about a bird species spread over thousands of miles. Both Hickey and Bond relied on many observers as they compiled their lists; neither could personally know all the peregrines and eyries that they wrote about. But in certain limited parts of the breeding range, students have located and intensively watched the peregrines. In each area the watching reveals different secrets, for as the landscape and fauna and the human population vary, so do the falcons.

---

1. Hickey (1942).   2. Bond (1946).

Even where humanity has most thoroughly consumed and recreated the country, in and about New York City, the peregrines have nested on cliffs over the Hudson River. Richard and Kathleen Herbert watched them at eight eyries located in the Palisades Interstate Park. The northernmost was 55 miles north of the city, on a tall cliff rising 400 feet. All eight overlooked the wide river. Richard Herbert visited these eyries through thirty years, and his wife for almost half that time.[3]

This part of the Hudson once was occupied by large estates whose owners kept people away with no-trespassing regulations. In the 1930s these estates were bought up to form the Palisades Park, where it became illegal to disturb the falcons. Creators of the park conceived of it as a wildlife sanctuary, and the peregrines' safety had been an argument in favor of taking over the estates.

But these well-known eyries were a dangerous place for peregrines. Egg collecting was practiced as a hobby into the 1940s; falconers visited the cliffs to obtain birds for their sport; some people shot falcons, and even the park police disturbed the adults by target shooting below the cliffs. With the opening of the park, more people walked below and above the rock. Despite all this, the adults would nest or try to nest at the eight eyries year after year, and each time an adult disappeared, another would soon replace it. The prominence of these cliffs and the wide views they provided partially explained the attraction they held for peregrines. The male could sit on a cliff point or a dead tree at cliff top and survey the Hudson, where birds would fly across the shelterless water.

The Herberts witnessed the abandonment of all eight of the eyries. Cold, harsh springs followed one after another in the early 1950s, and at last the Palisades Interstate Parkway was being constructed along the whole length of the river. No efforts were taken to shield the falcons during their nestings from the disturbance of blasting and construction. In 1951 two young hatched at the second to southernmost eyrie, the last young ever to hatch at any of the eight. One of these

---

3. Herbert and Herbert (1965); Herbert and Herbert (1969).

was soon taken. Over the next decade, dwindling numbers of adults attempted to nest. In 1961, only two lone birds were briefly seen, never to return.

Eight eyries, fifty-five miles of river shore, are tiny parts of the peregrine population and range. Elsewhere in the eastern states, local peregrines were disappearing at this same time. Joseph Hagar in Massachusetts had watched falcons at fourteen sites until all were abandoned late in the 1950s.[4] The last Pennsylvania peregrines were seen at their cliffs in 1958 and 1959.[5] In Wisconsin the last pairs raised their last young in 1962.[6] To the south, grim reports began earlier, where for example, the last active eyries in Tennessee were noted about 1948.[7]

Individual watchers of peregrines were unaware of what was happening in the many parts of the eastern states. Hearing only of isolated misfortunes, they generally assumed they were the fault of local causes and only wondered at rumors of similar disasters elsewhere. But in 1964, Joseph Hickey organized a repeat of his 1939–1940 survey of peregrines in the eastern states. Two men spent three months visiting 133 cliffs; they failed to find a single peregrine![8] Information from the west indicated that the peregrine was endangered in California, the Great Basin, the Rocky Mountains, and southern Canada.[9] In another part of the world, far away in Europe, peregrines were vanishing from many countries. Finland, estimated to have held long ago a thousand pairs, retained only nine known pairs in 1965.[10] In West Germany in 1950, 320 to 380 pairs bred, but by 1967 less than 90 were estimated to remain.[11] In 1967 for the first time no young peregrines were found in Switzerland.[12] No known active eyries remained in Austria in 1969.[13] A decline of such extent

---

4. Hagar (1969).   5. Rice (1969).
6. Berger and Mueller (1969).
7. Walter R. Spofford II, in Hickey (1969).
8. Berger, Sindelar, Jr., and Gamble (1969).   9. Hickey (1969).
10. Linkola and Suominen (1969); Bijleveld (1974).
11. Mebs (1969); Bijleveld (1974).
12. Herren (1969).   13. Bijleveld (1974).

and speed had never before been witnessed for a bird species.

Oddly, peregrine numbers through the years had been noted for their stability. Joseph Hickey in 1942 felt that the peregrine population in eastern United States had declined by just 10 to 18 percent through a very gradual process—only at the low-lying cliffs in more settled regions did the peregrines experience too much disturbance and abandon the sites. In wilder regions or at the larger cliffs peregrines had remained essentially as always.[14] Similarly, in Great Britain, there was little evidence that the peregrine population had decreased from the beginning of this century until World War II.[15]

The cliffs are remarkable for the long periods during which the peregrines occupy them. One Massachusetts cliff, which had falcons early in the nineteenth century, still had a pair in 1950, while a second whose eggs were collected in 1861 had a pair in 1951.[16] In 1625 the nobility of Berne, Switzerland, ordered protection (for the sake of falconry) of an eyrie at which 21 broods of peregrines fledged during the 30 years 1935–1965.[17]

Strangely, also, peregrines may persist despite heavy human disturbance. A falconer, Sir Hamon Le Strange, took 87 peregrines near one eyrie from 1604 to 1654; the site was not abandoned until 1818.[18] The eyries on the lower Hudson remained occupied into the 1950s despite heavy disturbances for decades. But the most striking instance of persistence and resiliency in peregrine populations occurred in Britain after World War II. During the war peregrines were considered a threat to Britain's safety, for the falcons caught and destroyed pigeons carrying messages for British military forces. Systematically, the peregrines in southern England were exterminated until toward the war's end only one pair was known from five counties normally holding more than 80 pairs. By 1955, the population was restored to its prewar size.[19]

Various reasons have been suggested for the disappearance

---

14. Hickey (1942).   17. Herren (1969).
15. Ratcliffe (1962).   18. Hickey (1969).
16. Hagar (1969).   19. Ratcliffe (1972).

11

of the peregrine.[20] Most of the suggestions could possibly explain a local decline but are inadequate in accounting for the crash simultaneous across two continents. Some animals will prey on the eggs and young—snakes, ravens, perhaps the horned owl, and where the nest ledge is accessible, raccoons eagerly creep. But predation at the nests did not suddenly increase—predator populations had not expanded, and no new predators appeared. Nor did human activities, those same disturbances the peregrines had withstood for years, abruptly increase, and pairs at the remote or well-protected eyries suffered the same fate as the rest of the species. One man, Frank Beebe, suggested that food resources were insufficient to sustain the peregrine population.[21] But the multitudes of pigeons, flickers, and jays that the last falcons had caught quickly and without difficulty still streamed past the failing eyries as they always had.

Two possible causes seemed consistent with the circumstances of the decline. A disease might have developed or been introduced toward which the falcons were hopelessly vulnerable. Or secondly, in recent years the volume of human pollution of the world had grown, including dispersal of certain chemicals that might be poisonous to peregrines. But we know little about animals and what can affect them. To confirm either the disease or the pollution hypothesis the details of the peregrine's trouble had to be examined.

In eastern United States we were hardly aware of the danger until the peregrines were gone. In Britain the falcons faded slowly enough that they could be studied again and again. Derek Ratcliffe, a longtime student of peregrines, was noticing broken and missing eggs at the eyries in the 1950s. At one time this had been a rare event, but as he looked through his notes, he discovered that egg failures had occurred at 14 out of the 49 eyries he had recently visited.[22] At some locations a visit later in the season would discover fewer eggs than did an earlier visit. "Depleted" clutches of one or two eggs, fewer than normal, became frequent. At some nest scrapes

<hr>

20. These causes are fully discussed in Hickey (1969).
21. In Hickey (1969); Beebe (1969).
22. Ratcliffe (1958).

where the eggs had vanished, he found tiny shell fragments
in the dirt. Most astonishing, he watched a female at her scrape
through his binoculars. She was eating or breaking an egg,
and when he climbed the cliff he found the tiny pieces.

In 1962, Moore and Ratcliffe published an analysis of the
contents of one peregrine egg that addled in its nest in Perthshire.
Residues for a certain group of chemicals called organochlorines
totaled 4 to 5 parts per million (ppm) of the egg by weight.[23]
These chemicals resemble compounds naturally occurring
in animals (thus the term organo-) but artificially created
by scientists to control insect pests. They kill insects by
interfering with the central nervous system. The most famous
of these insecticides is DDT. DDT was used in Britain against
pests of orchard and field crops and occasionally against forest
pests. In the egg they found p,p'-DDE, a compound animals
metabolize from DDT. Dieldrin is another organochlorine,
used as a spray and particularly as a seed dressing to combat
soil pests. Dieldrin is also a metabolite of aldrin, another
organochlorine used for similar purposes. The egg in addition
contained heptachlor epoxide, a metabolite from heptachlor,
another poisonous seed dressing. Results from this analysis were
disturbing—3.3 parts aldrin to 1 million parts body weight
had previously been shown to cause death in adult quail.[24]

A male peregrine was found dead by its eyrie on Lundy
Island. He contained a total organochlorine concentration
of 77.5 parts per million in his liver; this concentration was
deemed sufficient to have caused the death.[25]

By the late 1950s, the peregrine obviously was declining in
many parts of Britain. But large samples of the population
were not counted until 1961 and 1962. Out of 718 territories
known to have been occupied before World War II, 488

---

23. Organochlorine residues can be expressed in ppm wet weight,
dry weight, for the whole body or egg, or for lipids. In this case the concentration was estimated for the wet weight of the whole egg. The exact
methods for measurement of pesticide residues or shell thickness are beyond the scope of this book; these details are very important and explained in each of the articles cited.
24. DeWitt (1956), cited in Moore and Ratcliffe (1962).
25. Jefferies and Prestt (1966).

were visited in 1962, and only 68 eyries (13 percent of the sample) held young. In 1963 the situation was slightly worse. In 1964 reproduction and territory occupation were marginally improved, and the population remained stable in annual samples through 1967. This halt in the decline gave hope that causes of the trouble could be determined in time to save the peregrine.[26] Between 1966 and 1971, there was a slow recovery in inland areas north of Wales, but little improvement in northern coastal areas, or anywhere in Wales or southern England, where in 1971 only 22 percent and 13 percent of prewar populations remained.[27]

Ratcliffe and others have assembled convincing evidence pointing to the hydrocarbons as the major cause of the peregrine's decline.[28] This evidence falls into several arguments.

First, the peregrine did not vanish as thoroughly or at an equal rate from all of Britain. It has almost entirely disappeared from southern areas. Northern England and southern Scotland did not suffer peregrine losses so quickly or completely. The Highlands of Scotland have been least affected, particularly the central portions, where falcons retain their normal breeding densities. This geographical distribution of the decline closely correlates with the distribution of agriculture in Britain and the intensity of DDT use. DDT wasn't used in the central Highlands.

Second, timing of the peregrine's decline was closely correlated with the extent of use of organochlorine pesticides. DDT was first used in 1946–1947, then the organochlorine γ-BHC. During these years reproductive failures were first noted. Dieldrin, aldrin, and heptachlor were introduced in the mid-1950s, at which time the actual size of the breeding population began to drop. In the early 1960s, when the peregrine numbers were at their lowest, many wild birds, species smaller than the peregrine, were killed, and for this reason a voluntary ban on the use of the various organochlorines for spring-sown grain began in 1961, and the ban was extended

---

26. Ratcliffe (1972).   27. Ratcliffe (1973).
28. See Ratcliffe (1969, 1970, and 1972).

in the years following. At the same time that the use of these chemicals became less widespread, the peregrine decline halted.

Third, the peregrine was proven contaminated by organochlorines throughout even the remote areas. Between 1963 and 1965, eighteen eggs analyzed contained an average of 14.8 ppm organochlorines, and every one of them had residues of p,p'-DDE, dieldrin, BHC, and heptachlor epoxide. Four adults found dead also contained all four poisons. Eleven eggs analyzed in 1967 contained only slightly lesser concentrations, but eggs from the central Highlands where peregrines were least affected showed significantly lower residue levels of 4.9 ppm.

The correspondence between population decline and the presence of organochlorines has been extremely close. Scientists have also been working to establish the precise mechanisms of the insecticides' disastrous effects on the peregrine. To accomplish this the myriad complex interactions between the peregrine and its whole environment, living and nonliving, have been explored. Study has been limited because the precariously surviving falcons could not be disturbed and their safety risked in efforts to obtain evidence. And no extra peregrines were available for carefully controlled laboratory experiments. Scientists were forced to gather all of their information from what naturally occurred about them. Furthermore, many chemicals were involved, presumably each varying as to the exact details of its effects.

The contribution of DDT to the decline is most thoroughly understood.[29] As we have released more DDT into the environment than any of the other hydrocarbons, its unexpected impacts have been most serious.

While DDT was intended to control insect pests, it is poisonous to most other animals including birds and humans. The concentration of the chemical determines what animals it will kill. Very small amounts are fatal to insects but harmless

---

29. My discussion of the characteristics of DDT is based upon the testimony of Charles F. Wurster, Jr., in *Transcript of the Wisconsin DDT Hearings* (1968–1969). See also Wurster (1969a) and Harrison et al. (1970). Read Wurster (1969b) for an account of the hearings.

to people. Therefore, we believed there was no harm in dispersing DDT through the environment in very small concentrations.

Two other characteristics of DDT are important. First, many insecticides, some that are highly poisonous, quickly break down into chemicals that are harmless. Thus they will cease to have poisonous effects after a short time. In contrast, DDT and the other organochlorines do not break down quickly but remain poisonous. Even animals cannot make the chemical harmless for they metabolize some of the DDT into p,p'-DDE, another poison that they cannot further break down. Second, DDT does not stay where it is put. Water can carry it. It evaporates in the air. It clings to dust particles and follows the winds, even across wide oceans. These two characteristics explain why DDT is widespread, found through the world even where it never has been used. For these reasons, also, we have no means of controlling the effect or the location of DDT once it has been released.

Despite its longevity and dispersal tendencies, DDT might still be harmless to larger animals except for an additional characteristic. Although water will spread the chemical, it is rather insoluble in water. In contrast, it is highly soluble in fats. Fats occur primarily within animals. Thus DDT will concentrate exactly in that place where it can do harm: in animals.

Animals take in DDT with their food. Insects or larger animals that eat plants will ingest the very small amounts of pesticide that cling to the plants. Sometimes, usually where it has been sprayed, DDT will cause the deaths of the insects, because only a little DDT is fatal to such small creatures. Other contaminated insects are eaten by birds and mammals. Larger doses of DDT are required to harm these larger animals. But the insects already contain DDT in higher concentrations than were present on the plants. A bird eats many insects, and much of the poisons in these many individuals remain in the birds. Some birds concentrate so much DDT that they die. They may hold concentrations of the poison hundreds of times higher than does the environment generally.

The birds that have not yet died extend DDT's effects to the peregrine. For one peregrine will eat many small birds and retain many of these moderate doses to further concentrate the poisons. Over fifty prey species of the peregrine collected from all parts of Britain showed organochlorine contamination.[30] Therefore, all peregrines were endangered. While it requires more DDT to harm a peregrine than an oriole, a peregrine will concentrate much more DDT than was present in any of the prey species.

DDT's solubility in fat causes it to concentrate at each step of the food chain. Thus it threatens not only peregrines but all other predators who feed on birds, mammals, or fish that in turn feed on the insects or other tiny animals that initially gather DDT.[31]

DDT has been traced from the vast fields and forests to the peregrines' brains, livers, and other organs with fat tissues. What does DDT, or more often its metabolite, p,p'-DDE, do? As observations accumulated, it became clear that reproductive failure in any of several ways—failure to lay, egg breakage, egg infertility, death of embryos or young—typically preceded territory desertion by one or more years. For this reason observers believed that the decline developed when no new peregrines were produced, and as years passed and the adults died, no replacements came to the old territories.

The suddenly common occurrence of broken eggs in eyries—a dramatic symptom of trouble for the peregrine—has been most carefully studied. Egg breakages could be caused by disturbed parental behavior or by weakened eggshells, or by both. Ratcliffe took eggs from failing eyries, emptied, weighed, and measured them. He thus obtained a shell-thickness index. He compared these recent eggshells with eggs collected before 1940, before use of the organochlorines, and found that while egg size hadn't changed in almost all cases average weight and therefore thickness had decreased. Thin eggshells

---

30. Ratcliffe (1969).
31. In Europe, where organochlorines and other chemicals were heavily used as seed dressings, predators consuming seed-eating mammals have also been drastically impacted (Bijleveld, 1974).

would easily break. Volumnious evidence has since been collected demonstrating the shell-thinning effect of DDT on peregrines and other birds of prey.[32]

Shells are made primarily of calcium carbonate, and thinness seemed due to insufficient amounts of that compound. Thus, a next step in tracing DDT effects involved determining the female peregrine's ability or inability to metabolize calcium. Evidence gathered from laboratory experiments on animals much commoner than the peregrine points to several mechanisms for changes in calcium metabolism in birds, including hepatic enzyme induction and disruptions of the thyroid and of the carbonic anhydrase system. It remains unclear whether one of these mechanisms is the primary cause of shell thinning in the peregrine, or whether several act in combination.[33] Hepatic enzyme induction has been most frequently discussed with regard to the peregrine and provides an example of the complexity of the bodily functions involved.

As in other animals, birds contain systems for dealing with poisons. Dangerous substances are excreted in urine through the kidneys. However, there are some poisons, including DDE, that are insoluble in water and which the kidneys therefore cannot eliminate. Fortunately, the body has another defense mechanism: these chemicals induce the release of certain enzymes in the liver; the hepatic enzymes cause the poisons to be metabolized so that they can be passed through the kidneys and out of the body. At the same time the enzymes destroy sex hormones, including estrogen, that are in the body. The effect is temporary, for the enzymes soon break down; therefore, as soon as the poison is removed and no more of the enzymes released, sex hormones will no longer be destroyed. The enzymes succeed in metabolizing most poisons, but DDE does not metabolize. Furthermore, DDE remains in the liver fat itself, the enzymes are constantly induced, and the sex hormones are thus indefinitely inhibited.[34]

Interference with the female's estrogen can disrupt any

---

32. Ratcliffe (1967 and 1970); Hickey (1969); Jefferies (1973).
33. Jefferies (1973).
34. Testimony of R. W. Risebrough in Transcript of the Wiscon-

portion of the breeding cycle. In particular, it causes her to form imperfect medullary bone. This special bone the female lays down early in the breeding period within the hollow spaces of her other bones. It then provides her with some of the large amounts of calcium she must suddenly muster to form her eggshells. Without normal medullary bone, the female may lack sufficient calcium for eggshell formation. Hepatic enzyme induction, a body defense mechanism successful in the natural conditions under which it developed, appears to have become destructive in a human-created situation, the introduction of an artificial insecticide.[35]

The other organochlorine pesticides are chemically similar to DDT, are widespread, and also collect in fat tissues of animals. In west Scotland, reproduction in the golden eagle declined with the same pattern of egg thinning and breakage.[36] Analysis of egg contents revealed that the species contained more dieldrin than DDT, the reverse of the peregrine situation. Reproductive problems appeared as dieldrin began to be used in sheep dips in west Scotland. The chemical on the wool and skin protected the livestock from various pests. Eagles frequently fed on dead sheep. When use of dieldrin in the dips was discontinued, residues of dieldrin in the eggs decreased, and reproduction improved.[37]

Dieldrin induces liver enzymes more powerfully than does DDT.[38] The different chemicals vary in their toxicity, and species vary in their response to each chemical.[39] Yet it generally is believed that effects of these residues in bird tissues are additive.

Eggshell thinning is a sublethal effect of DDT. It is difficult to obtain conclusive proof for causes of death in a rare species scattered through the wild. Yet now the circumstantial case against DDT as directly lethal to adult peregrines is

sin DDT Hearings (1968–1969); Simkiss (1961); Peakall (1967); Risebrough et al. (1968); Ratcliffe (1970).
35. Testimony of R. W. Risebrough in Transcript of the Wisconsin DDT Hearings (1968–1969); Simkiss (1961); Ratcliffe (1970).
36. Lockie and Ratcliffe (1964).
37. Lockie, Ratcliffe, and Balharry (1969).
38. Peakall (1967).
39. Ratcliffe (1972).

strong. Many eyries were abruptly abandoned after the adults unsuccessfully tried to nest. Presumably, these adults died in greater numbers than during the prepesticide era. At one time, an eyrie abandoned by one falcon would speedily be reoccupied by another; suddenly this no longer happened. The decline occurred too rapidly to be attributed to reproductive failure alone. Furthermore, several dying adults that were discovered tremored in the manner characteristic among smaller bird victims of DDT.[40]

Two scientists examined two lanner falcons, close relatives of the peregrine, which had died in captivity apparently from pesticide poisoning.[41] Comparing the residues of heptachlor epoxide and dieldrin in them with wild peregrines, they concluded that levels of only 5.2 to 9.3 parts per million in the liver for these two substances combined could be lethal for either species. A falcon eating only a few heavily contaminated prey individuals, like pigeons, might thus die. While dieldrin and heptachlor epoxide are more toxic than DDT, DDT has been much more heavily distributed and more heavily concentrated in the falcons.

In 1971 two peregrines died when they crashed into obstacles as they pursued prey. This is an extraordinary accident for a healthy falcon, but both individuals contained substantial organochlorine residues, chemicals that disturb the nervous system.[42] The accidents suggested that contaminated individuals not only are likely to suffer accidents, but also may lose the coordination necessary for hunting. Some adults may starve.

The reasons for the peregrine decline were much the same for North America as for Britain. The decline spread temporally and spatially with the spread of organochlorines in the environment. Reproductive failure occurred in the same way as in Europe, and organochlorine residues appeared in adult peregrines and in the contents of their thin-shelled eggs.[43]

Species of birds differ in the extent to which their diets and distribution expose them to DDT. Experiments have

---

40. Jefferies and Prestt (1966); Hickey (1969); Ratcliffe (1962, 1969, 1972, 1973); Bijleveld (1974).

41. Jefferies and Prestt (1966).   42. Ratcliffe (1972).

43. Hickey (1969); Cade, White, and Haugh (1968).

also shown that while DDT has the same effect on different species, one species may be more sensitive than others to the same levels of contamination. Probably vulnerability in all these ways combined to make the peregrine suffer first from organochlorine pollution. Its fate, and the spread of its decline into new parts of its world range, has served as warning for what is happening less abruptly to other species.[44]

Other pollutants recently released into the environment may add to the problems caused by the organochlorine pesticides. Among these are organomercurial pesticides and polychlorinated biphenyls (PCBs), used in plastics and paints, which also concentrate in animal fats.[45] While the PCBs do not appear to cause shell thinning, they are heavily toxic to avian embryos.[46] These other chemicals have been much less common than DDT, and DDT levels alone are high enough to endanger the peregrine. Yet their presence further threatens this falcon and other birds, and without strict controls throughout the world, they may cause worse troubles in the future. We humans still hardly know what we do to this earth.

The peregrine in Britain quickly responded to decreasing uses of the organochlorines. There is hope that the peregrine will remain. But by 1972, as we prepared to leave for Greenland, only in Britain had the decline been halted and the species's status improved. The environment still carried a heavy burden of DDT. In North America the falcon continued to become rarer in the western states and southern Canada.[47]

The American Arctic, from Alaska across to Greenland, is the breeding place for hundreds of peregrines. In the 1960s these populations seemed intact.[48] Their good health was expected, for pesticides had never been used on their breeding territories. Yet each fall the falcons leave the north for warmer regions, so that the organochlorines reach even these arctic populations. By 1970, reproductive failure appeared in several parts of Alaska and northern Canada.[49] On the Colville River in Alaska, eggs were thin shelled and breaking.[50]

---

44. Hickey (1969); Ratcliffe (1970); Anderson and Hickey (1972).
45. Ratcliffe (1972).   48. White (1969).
46. Peakall (1975).   49. Cade and Fyfe (1970).
47. Cade and Fyfe (1970).   50. White and Cade (1971).

The number of breeding pairs on Ungava Peninsula dwindled.[51] Alaskan eggs, adults, and the bodies of many prey species, also migratory, contained DDT residues.[52] The future of these falcons was no longer secure.

One large area had never been studied. Peregrines lived on the west and southeast coasts of Greenland. Were they also endangered? These falcons pass down the Atlantic coast in autumn. At some locations where the wanderers have been observed for decades there were fewer migrants appearing in September and October.[53]

West Greenland, 1972

I think often about the explorers of birds and of the world. Two hundred years ago adventure meant discovery, extending human knowledge of the wild. Ships far away on the ocean looked for land. Peregrines appeared from out of the limitless waves. New peregrines, they did not look like any of the peregrines Europeans had seen before. It was a many-marveled unknown world.

No longer can we live as fully lighthearted. A myriad of discoveries do wait. But more beautiful than the flash of a strange wing, a plant hitherto unknown, more beautiful, challenging, fragile are the fates of plants, creatures, places that we know well and love. How can they remain, in spite of all that people do?

We were traveling to Greenland to learn the status of its peregrine population. Our work had two main portions. Mattox and the two other members of our five-man group planned to survey a sample area of West Greenland, locating all peregrine pairs within a thirty-five-mile-wide strip running one hundred miles from the Greenland ice cap to the sea. By locating falcon cliffs they would know the breeding density of the species; they would climb each eyrie to count eggs and young and collect addled eggs and shell fragments for analyses. The reproductive success, the number of young per

---

51. Berger et al. (1970).
52. Cade, White, and Haugh (1968); Lincer, Cade, and Devine (1970).
53. Ward and Berry (1972).

Lakes and hills of Greenland within our inland study area.

eyrie, would indicate whether the population was still healthy. Changes in status would be apparent if information on breeding density and nesting success in this area in future years were collected and compared with the first season's data. Eggs and shells could give more direct proof for pesticide contamination.

Such a survey could be performed only with constant traveling over the tundra. No one eyrie could be visited for long. Therefore Mattox could not collect detailed information on the nesting peregrines. Yet we wished to know why Greenland peregrines were affected or unaffected by the organochlorines. For this we would need information on diet and behavior of the falcons. And if reproductive failure occurred, we wanted to know how: were behavorial disturbances or sterility of the adults involved as well as shell thinness and breakage? For these reasons Dave and I would camp close to one or two eyries and watch behavior at the nest cliff.

We hoped our research would help in efforts to control use of the organochlorines. We must know the desperate peregrine well if we are to act and save it. We must know its problems as well as what preserves some individuals from destruction.

Traveling

Bill Mattox, Dave, and I drove a rented car to McGuire Air Base. There we soon joined the other two members of our group: Dick Graham, a lieutenant-colonel in the Air Force, and Bill Burnham, a student working on hawks in Colorado. Burnham was impatiently waiting for us outside our hotel; he was broad chested, dressed in a tie and a broad coat. While Graham gladly greeted Mattox (they had previously traveled together to study falcons), Burnham was already asking Dave and me if we had worked with raptors before—his chief love.

We ate at what I considered a very plush officers' club. Dave and I wore borrowed trousers, coat, and tie with our own hiking boots. I remember our praising the dinner, but that was the only time during the entire evening that our conversation left peregrines or Greenland.

"What will we do when we first arrive?" Dave asked early in the meal.

"Yes, we ought to discuss that," Mattox said to Graham.

"I think we should check into those aircraft first," Dick began. "We'll want to fly over the tundra before we actually hike out into it." Graham was a pilot. Mattox had told Dave and me there were two small planes at Søndrestrøm that could be rented. "I hope we can get out Wednesday."

Dave wanted to know how we would use the planes for our study.

Mattox explained that, although we couldn't land near any of the peregrine cliffs because the land isn't level, he hoped to spot all possible sites from the air and mark their locations on maps. "That will save us when we travel on foot. We'll know exactly where we need to check for the falcons, and not waste time covering tundra without cliffs.

"You don't know yet how hard that tundra is for hiking," Mattox warned.

But I wanted to know how we would identify which were peregrine cliffs from the air.

Graham told us, "Sometimes you see the falcons flying before the cliff. You fly as low and slow as you can."

Mattox added, "Although some falcons won't fly when the plane passes."

Burnham, "Do you know what mute spots are?" We

didn't. "White stains on the rock from peregrine excrement. They're on eyrie ledges and perching spots. Visible from a great distance. All you have to do is spot them."

And Graham continued, "In places lichens grow on the mutes, and their orange color is another falcon sign. We'll be able to see both the orange and white from the plane."

"But don't other birds leave stains?" I asked, thinking of ravens.

"Yes, you're right, Jim," Bill Mattox answered. "Other cliff-nesters make them. So that until we visit the cliff we won't know that it has peregrines."

Graham and Mattox apparently disagreed on how useful the planes would be. Graham felt we could cover the entire area and then follow our marked maps on foot, while Mattox thought we must take several flights, then check them against a ground survey before flying the rest of our area.

This conversation was unlike any Dave or I had heard before. Dave knew little about any bird, while I had enjoyed all varieties but had never singled out hawks. I was reminded of the passion with which bird-watchers speak, only these three men had more focused interests. For Burnham the little birds disparagingly became "dickey birds"—all the sparrows and swallows and orioles. Burnham was explaining to Dave what falconry was and naming the various hawks that were used. All the favorite species, the swift ones spectacular in flight, mainly caught birds. At that moment I thought I would rather hunt with a slower red-tail or mouse-catching harrier that wouldn't kill the singing birds but instead slay dusky rodents I seldom saw.

I discovered another way that raptor people talk as birders do not. Burnham was speaking about peregrine eyries he had visited in the west. I asked him where.

He said, "Colorado," with an odd tone, or a suddenness that made me continue.

"Where in Colorado?" Even though I knew no places or parts of the state and wouldn't understand his answer.

He laughed. "Don't expect me to tell you that!" He looked away but I stared at him.

Gyrfalcon eyrie with heavy mute stains below the ledge.

Mattox was looking at me. "Jim, locations for peregrine eyries are secret. Or else something may happen to the falcons."

Burnham looked back at me. "I'm sorry. But there's no reason for you to know where they are."

We flew on a cargo plane, the great C-141 with huge round nose and long wings that drooped in their weight and magnitude toward the runway. We entered a tiny door that was low before one wing. Outside we heard the whine and roar of engines warming, but inside they throbbed and beat against out heads; we felt the vibrating of metal and floor, the air around us. We sat on trembling benches, held by tight, red seat belts, and we stared at oxygen masks and read the cabinet labels until the crew members took their places. One man slammed the door shut, but we could not hear its bang over the leaping engines, as fiercer the plane shook and moved, then descended the runway.

The aircraft had been so loaded with supplies for the base that our luggage placed to the front seemed a trivial addition. We were the only passengers. By crawling over our luggage we could peek out a small porthole on either side.

I remember what Mattox had told us of Søndrestrøm. It is the main airport in Greenland. The island has so little flat land that only two jet airports exist, with no additional sites near any of the towns. People must travel by helicopter or boat, or in some areas, dogsled. Søndrestrøm is at 67° north, on the Arctic Circle, at the head of the long, deep Søndrestrømfjord where a plain has been created with river sediments. Overland it is eighty miles to the sea, although by boat down the fjord one must travel one hundred miles. This is the widest section of open land on the west coast, with twenty additional miles between Søndrestrøm and the ice cap. To the north the coastline curves east toward the ice. South, the ice cap approaches the sea.

I remembered seeing Labrador, halfway between New Jersey and Søndrestrøm. Its shore was broken into a thousand tiny bays and scalloped inlets, and, inland, myriad lakes and pools with connecting channels and rivers. On land, a thin forest of evergreens. Somewhere on this coast a research party using plane and boat found only two pairs of peregrines in 1970.[54]

Dave saw Greenland first. He called to us, and we all crowded round the tiny porthole. White mountains stood high behind the sea with clouds scattered over them. As we approached we saw the gray, broken shore. Tumbled rocks and snowy cliffs fell into the sea while long reaches of water inland divided the mountains. We passed over land, dreary gray and white, where mists and snow clouds seemed to snatch away the sun. No sign of life, not plants nor animals nor people. I sensed the chill. How could creatures survive, or we survive, seeking a way over the rocks and ice?

One of the crewmen told us we must sit down and fasten seat belts. We soon felt the plane descending. We could see only the cargo poised above us and the darkened floor.

After the heavy landing and the slower roll along the runway, the plane stopped. A crewman opened a side door and spoke with someone below. I felt the rush of wind before I had reached the opening. The wind I noticed first outside the plane, also, chill and strong, funneled down the airstrip. For within a mile on either side rose cliffs hundreds of feet

---

54. Cade and Fyfe (1970).

tall. On the north, one of gray rock in many shelves and
ledges blocked the sky entirely along that quarter of the horizon.
To the south a darker cliff fell without pause from top to
bottom. The wind rushed between these walls from the
northeast. There the rivers came down from the ice cap,
although all we could see were brown hills and mists. To the
west, levels of sand with narrow river channels. "To the
fjord," Mattox pointed.

I was turning to see all directions and held my binoculars
out because I looked at the two cliffs mostly and did at last
spot dark specks moving against the rock; but these were ravens.

Two Danes drove us in an Air Force bus to the bachelor
officers' quarters, a long rectangular building that the
wind cut against as it did against all the other buildings, and
we gladly hauled everything into the warmth inside.

We took three rooms. When all the luggage had been
placed between the beds, we sat on top of it. Restlessly.

"Let's get outside," said Dave.

"Bill, where's that nearest peregrine eyrie?" asked
Burnham.

Mattox had visited one peregrine eyrie in this part of
Greenland years ago and knew about several others. Already
it was 2:00 P.M. but we didn't worry about the dark catching us
far out on the tundra. We could walk all night if we liked.
Mattox and Graham felt they should visit the base commander
and several of Mattox's old Danish friends. The rest of us would
go. Only one of the old eyries was at all close to the base,
and we could probably reach it by evening. The cliffs we could
see from Søndrestrøm had only ravens; the dark cliff was named
Ravneklippen.

*　　　*　　　*　　　*

We packed small suppers, put jackets on, and left.
Walking, we became warm. Dave and Bill liked a fast pace;
they had brought ropes to climb the rock face when we reached
it; like mine their eyes scanned the hills. Quickly the pavements
and buildings dropped behind. The land had odd, pointed

shapes, and views changed quickly as we rose or descended, or passed hill corners.

The ground rose gradually. We saw brown grasses perhaps a foot long but the continual wind prevented their standing upright. Stunted bushes grew on some of the hillsides, their tops reaching hardly higher than the grasses, except in several places where the hill rose steeply to the north, or great boulders sheltered them. We seemed to have left the strong wind of the airstrip; only the grasses wavered. But the air was chill; I felt alert and sharp.

Small birds with stubby bodies and wings occasionally flew from bush clumps. The first ones flew silently and far away. Then two flushed at once chuttering in strange burry notes and trills, heading toward a distant hill. The next one I saw I followed to the lone bush where it landed, and I watched it on its twig perch, shaking its feathers. It had many black and gray streaks over all its body and a trim black mark at its chin. The more I looked, the less plain he appeared, with a red cap and rosy on his breast. When he turned I found his white rump at last with the faintest black streaks, just before he chuttered in answer to a flying kinsman and flew. A redpoll.

Dave and Bill were atop the next rise, and then down again. I meant to hurry after them but I saw several more of these tiny birds. I remembered them from certain winters in New England, not always the coldest, when roaming flocks descended from the north. Always the redpolls had chattered, but their winter call lacked the buzziness and variances of these summer redpolls. I thought maybe it was their voices that now gave these birds a subtle startling quality, that made me examine their rosiness and streakiness intently through the brief moments while they and I paused until they flew and I walked on.

I noticed that Dave and Bill were farther off than I would have liked, on the next gradually rising hill. Beyond them, a mountain. It was more than a hill because the ascent seemed tumbled with rocks, so many that they bore against each other heavily, and beyond a rock wall pressed upward the last hundred feet until atop all an odd, pointed crag broke over the horizon. Were there peregrines on the cliff ahead? I stared at it. Where on the rock would they be? I couldn't quite believe that the rare peregrine might actually nest here, before us. I looked at the grasses, bushes, the rock heaps close by. There must be peregrines. The landscape seemed marked by their presence. Not because of the wariness of the redpolls; their chatter seemed too full of redpoll to hint at peregrine. Maybe it was the sky, wide, free of treetops, or maybe my eyes.

Only a few slopes separated me from the rock tumble, or so it appeared, but the cliff remained distant as I continued. Still early evening and not dusking yet, this was the year's second longest day, and I was curious whether the daylight would remain into the morning. But clouds covered the sun, and I guessed only that it hung somewhere north of west. I decided I would turn around and head for the base. I called to Dave and Bill, yet they didn't hear or look. I ran to catch them but quickly noticed that they too ran, only a short way before me but hopelessly beyond reaching them without a long pursuit. They were eager. And I was thinking of this our first walk in the wilderness, where hikers must remain together and one person shouldn't walk alone or abruptly select his own personal direction; but Dave and Bill continued to run, and I guiltily turned around.

My way was clear and seemed much shorter. Although any direction I might have selected had all ups and downs, this overall descent lightened my boots and almost encouraged me to turn back toward the cliff and find the falcon. But the clouds began to lose their luminescence and the tundra quieted. Redpolls and other small birds flew less often. The cloud-filtered light declined imperceptibly: I could see well even in the distance, but the contrast softened between the grays and browns.

The change was gentle, one that I could best sense by standing still and listening. Now that my boots didn't brush grasses I felt the silence, at first absolute to accent the hill edges against the sky and the distant, mottled boulders, until I heard wind stirring grasses close by, and a trickle of water somewhere on the tundra. I heard high, tinkly notes from some hidden bird on the hill.

This was the faint promise of night that in the south would create glimmers of lights in cabins and homes. Only the dusk never deepened. At last I reached the sandy areas near the base. I took my boots off, and pulled socks off and stuffed them in my pockets; then the myriad sand grains cushioned my feet. Pebbles too, and as I paced, a prostrate grass stem would press my toes; and behind I saw shallow prints, and they didn't form a straight progress but wandered. I stood near one of the rivers. The sand cooled and chilled until I felt little with my numb feet.

Dave and Bill returned to the base two hours after I did. They had reached the cliff and walked all along its bottom without flushing a falcon or hearing one call, and they saw only old mute spots from some past year. This cliff appeared to be abandoned.

*   *   *   *

Dave and I awoke early, when the sun was still close to the hills north of east. We walked outside. The same chill wind came down from the ice cap. Heavy shadows stretched from the buildings and only a few airmen walked the streets, stumbling, half awakened, to their breakfasts. Mattox, Graham, and Burnham already sat in the mess hall.

To live even for brief periods on the tundra required many preparations. Mattox and Graham would remain on the base, assembling gear and examining maps with several of the Danes. Hopefully they could arrange our use of an airplane. Bill, Dave, and I would visit for the day a more distant cliff that Mattox remembered from ten years earlier, where he saw peregrines on a blue-skyed July afternoon. We took a different direction than we had the previous day and soon passed over a low ridge. Here we saw sodden tundra with pools of still water and sticky, dark earth. We came to a long lake whose far end was vague before us. Our course lay all along the shore and beyond. The ground steeply rose from the lake to a ridge high over our heads, often crested with rocky buttresses and cliffs. It would be hard work to balance as we walked across the sloping ground with the cold lake below us, but we found narrow level trails close to the water and in places branching into several parallel tracks ascending to higher ground where the shore curved. Odd, I thought, how fishermen should travel this lake so heavily that the grass would entirely disappear from their footpaths.

One rocky head larger than the others reared above us on the ridge top. The rock had irregular white streaks, the mute spots we had hoped to see. But a large-winged bird flapped from the rock, veered out into the wind, quickly turned, and vanished around the cliff end. Here was a raven cliff.

Ahead the ridge curved away from the lake, and the tundra by the shore was wet, low, and faintly green. We had to pick our way carefully, or take quick, long steps when the ground sank with our weight. At a higher spot short bushes with their many crooked twigs caught at our feet. The tiny leaves were so few and small that I wondered if the plants were dying. From under one close before us a brown bird flushed. I stopped instantly. These northern birds almost of necessity choose ground spots for their nests, and a quiet bird late flushing in June probably has waited by her eggs as long as she dares when the footsteps approach.

"Wait! There's a nest here!" I called. "Watch where you step! The eggs will be hard to see."

We found the nest under the bush. I had to twist a branch gently to see it, made by a longspur, tiny companion of the falcon on the tundra. I always watch nests with interest, but in this new unpeopled landscape I felt we explored, and I drew my notebook from my pack as if my knowledge was more than a matter of personal interest, and wrote, "grass with caribou-hair lining—eggs—six in two rows of three light brown with dark brown speckles (small)."

We drew near the end of the lake. The ridge that had held us close to the lake descended gradually; but beyond it rose again much higher than before, crest after crest and a cliff spread half a mile across with ledges at various heights, but some parts sheer for hundreds of feet. Beneath the cliff small outcroppings lay bare, with piles of talus rock fallen from above.

We passed the marshes by the lake end where the mosquitoes chased us. Quickly we left the lake below as we clambered over boulders or up gravelly slopes. We came to a level shoulder that paralleled the ridge. Bill sat on a rock and scanned the cliff with the spotting telescope he carried mounted on a gun stock.

"Take a look here," he said suddenly. Dave and I clustered near him. "I thought I saw something move against the rock."

The rock face seemed vast. "Where?" we asked.

Bill pointed. Dave and I hurriedly searched the humps and cracks and grassy ledges with our binoculars. Nothing at all moved.

Dave mentioned that he didn't see any of that whitewash. All three of us hoped that by looking long enough we would find it. Bill pointed out several rather dull patches. As the minutes passed I felt less hopeful, more discouraged, for surely we should have seen some motion, some sign, if the large falcons were present. Greater than the cliff seemed the empty grassy slopes in all directions, and more still the sky, pale blue and white. The one eyrie had been empty the night before, and this second cliff would prove equally barren. I did not wonder why or how, or consider what two abandoned eyries hinted of peregrines and pesticides, but only felt the loneliness. I looked over the colorless landscape, bent to touch the lichened boulder where I sat. How could a splendid falcon resist the vastness of the physical and inanimate that pressed so heavily, and live? Here we would find only lichens and small brown birds under bushes.

Dave and Bill stared at the cliff. I could not tell from their faces whether their thoughts followed mine, or whether their light calm purpose matched their erect postures and Dave's quick hand that brushed a mosquito from his forehead. Perhaps I wait less well than others. Bill looked at me.

"Let's get closer," he said.

We followed the level ground until we stood opposite the near end of the cliff. Dave and Bill climbed the last grass and the talus toward the foot of the cliff while I perched atop a boulder. I was to see the falcon flush, because they needed to watch where they stepped to maintain their balance and might miss the peregrine if it quickly winged out of their view round a cliff corner.

Their climb was longer than we had expected. My friends

went so far that I couldn't even see dark-shirted Dave. I glanced at the lake behind me, near and yet many steps away. My mind wandered. I don't know how many minutes swiftly passed.

First I heard their voices that hardly carried the words to me except "peregrine." I heard their voices, and then I heard a high scream off the rock, echoing, "kaa-ka-ka-ka-ka-ka," and I stared at the ledges and cracks and overhangs; it was such a big mountain, and at last I saw tiny Dave, "ka-ka-ka-ka-ka," but I couldn't see, and I started running walking running up those hills. All the way panting at last tumbling to a seat beside the other two, among the rocks.

But no more falcon cries. We stared, and searched with our binoculars but the peregrine had disappeared.

Bill pointed out where Dave had climbed ahead, and where he had stood, still no sign of the peregrine, when abruptly Bill had seen her. "She popped out of the ledge." He tried to show me which but wasn't certain any more. "I could see her white breast, and she stared down at Dave, and when I called to him she cackled." He didn't know where she had gone. Dave had returned to sit behind Bill. The peregrine might be sitting on her eggs, or perhaps had flown away.

Dave was smiling. He looked eagerly for another glimpse of the falcon.

That ended our first encounter. We didn't try to flush her again, for this was egg season, and we didn't want the eggs to chill while the falcon left them to scream and fly at us. We turned to go. We were standing at the base of the cliff. I watched the ruffled patterns the wind made on the lake we had passed, shifting blues, aquamarines, and whites, now a long walk distant through a stream-cut cleft in the mountain slopes. The shore was irregular, following steep rises and falls of the land, and beyond, lower, I saw the head of the fjord, and then more mountains, and tall ice-covered peaks and blue sky. I hadn't expected my first tundra peregrine to be such a tiny speck in the wild that I couldn't even see it as it circled home rock, low, while I heard its echoes.

Part II.

*The Tundra
for a Home*

When I awoke the next morning deep gray clouds darkened
the day, and snow lay on the higher hills. A few snowflakes
fell nearby, quickly melting on the ground. The five of us
stood outside staring at those white hills.

"How much more of this can we expect?" I asked.

Mattox had talked with the weather officer the day before.
"They've just had the hardest winter in recent years. Usually
it's very dry here, with little snow, but more fell this season,
and it's still deep on the farther mountains—not these hills—
you'll see the mountains soon." The land already looked
rugged enough to me, rocky, steeply sloping, and barren.

Mattox added, "He didn't know when it would warm up.
He hopes very soon. Just hopes."

Mattox and Graham thought the cliff beyond the lake
would be a good place for Dave and me to set up our camp
and watch that pair. Despite the cold, the nesting season
already was well advanced, and we wanted to begin our observations as soon as possible. Bill Burnham knew from the voice
of the falcon the day before that we had alarmed the female.
Her appearance only when Dave had approached very
near, and her quick disappearance as he withdrew, strongly
suggested that she was incubating eggs and reluctant to leave
them exposed for long. Probably her mate had been away
hunting. Bill seemed to know or guess many details about
this falcon, even though he had seen her only briefly and hadn't
been in Greenland before. I trusted his speculations. He was
guided by hours watching peregrines in hot Colorado.

Yet Mattox wasn't certain from our account that we had
discovered an active eyrie. Sometimes a lone falcon, often
one in its first year, will guard a cliff through the whole
summer. In places south as the peregrines gradually vanished
from their old cliffs before the pesticide poisons, solitary birds
were particularly frequent.[1] Mattox and Graham felt we

---

1. See Hagar (1969) and Herbert and Herbert (1969).

should visit the cliff once more, find both members of the pair, and locate the eyrie ledge. We decided that I should stay in the base to gather food while the others hiked out to the cliff.

Just before he left, Graham said, "When you talk with people, Jim, be vague about what you will be doing. Don't mention peregrines, or where you will camp."

I was not unhappy to stay near the warmth of the buildings. The others returned in the early evening. Both falcons had flown over them as they paced the cliff bottom, and they had seen the ledge where the female had flown from and later disappeared. They knew her eggs must be there. They had left the cliff area quickly because of the cold that might kill the embryos.

The next morning all five of us prepared to leave the Arctic Hotel. Each of us felt stiff from our hiking. The clouds remained and another snow lay on the hills. The discussion about the airplanes had been useless—one of the small planes had been damaged on recent landings, and the other required an overall servicing and maintenance check before it could fly again. Thus the whole of the survey area had to be covered on foot. Mattox and Graham were quietly discouraged. "We won't be able to do it all."

Roads ran from the base in several directions, but soon terminated at outlying installations. Mattox, Graham, and Burnham rode an Air Force truck a couple of miles west, then continued on foot. They planned to return in ten days. A Dane fresh from Europe drove Dave and me out on another road. He looked at our towering packs as we struggled into them, and at the snowy hills; he was sympathetic and interested in where we were going. He hadn't walked out this way. "Oh maybe someday I will try," he suggested, "when there is sun out.

"Good luck," he said.

Dave's pack towered over him. I hadn't really wanted to walk out all bent over and hurting, to struggle over the still strange tundra. But Dave wanted everything out in one trip so that we wouldn't have to return in several days. He carried the thirty-seven-pound tent on a long box across the middle of his pack frame, a pack tied on above the box, another tied below. I had fuel, stoves, a small tent, telescope, tripod, camera, books, notebooks, food for a couple of weeks.

We cheerily said goodbye to the driver.

The previous day the four had hiked on the opposite side of the long lake. Dave and I followed this route because the lake shores were level, easier for balancing our packs. According to Mattox, normal rainfall was less than ten inches per year. Yet the ground never thaws far below its surface, only some few inches, and the light drizzles that the lowering clouds release are caught in the dark topsoil. We found our low shore flooded from melt-off and two days' slushy snow. The misty rain, chill marsh, and flushed sweat mingled until we were damp all over, and we could watch our frosty breath as we panted.

"We will rest where that cove ahead is widest," said Dave.

We took two rests. The first, with my pack leaned against a tall rock, refreshed me; I bathed my face in the lake surface. But the second rest left me exhausted for the steep climb away from the lake. The cliff hid half-wrapped in mists, solemn and silent. I glimpsed it with my wet eyes but mainly trudged behind Dave, head bent to the ground. When rock reared half across the sky, Dave stopped.

"Here we are." Water drops clung to his beard and eye-brows. He squinted up at the mists and rock. I hardly knew Dave. What did he feel approaching the falcon cliff so wearily, falcons he hadn't even heard of only two months earlier? How did he care for them—was it love of the wild that carried him here, or really some spark of enthusiasm caught from Mattox and the peregrines, or Bill Burnham's voice as he described the falcon cackling?

"I don't think we should stay here. We're too close." To the cliff, he meant, we shouldn't risk disturbing the falcons. "I know a place farther down." On we trudged to where the hill paused again, and then we set our packs down.

"Let me show you that eyrie ledge," Dave said. It was on the part of the cliff closest to where we stood, one short ledge among dozens. Mists had cleared from the seemingly empty cliff. Were we watched? I carefully scanned the rock, but could find no falcon sentinel.

We set up camp—a light tan tent ten feet high amidst all the wild gray and brown. Below us the ground quickly fell to a stream valley—upstream wide spreading into a marsh of grasses; downstream the valley narrowed, and the current quickened. We drank its chill water. Among the grasses little birds must hide from the terrible shadow on the cliff.

My shirt and pants had dried while we quietly worked. As when a cloud parts to bare the sun, so I slowly noticed my warmth, and the freshness and clean moisture of the air.

Far away a peregrine might be calling. Long, thin calls perhaps, or the wind or my hopes. But louder now the voice sought the cliff and I saw the dark form a hundred yards out from the mountain, overhead, rushing, wheeling before the rock. It touched the grassy ledge below the eyrie, wings motionless for an instant, and then it spun round calling once more to land at a white pointed rock just below the cliff's brink.

Such a small and hard-to-see bird. A graceful, swallowlike bird, playful on buoyant wings. Perhaps it had returned with food for its sitting mate. We checked the eyrie, for the second falcon should emerge to take its meal—would it find it on the ledge below, or fly up to the white boulder where its mate waited?

"Dick says that the high voice is the male's," Dave said. I looked toward the male on his perch. The rock lay bare. Already he had flown and left the cliff impassive.

"Where's your telescope?" said Dave. He mounted the scope on its tripod, and placed it in the tent opening toward the eyrie.[2] A cloud-dark dusk was growing, and we planned to cook our supper on the two stoves we had newly positioned. With the tent all unzipped I could lie on my cot and see the eyrie.

Dave left the telescope poised. I kept taking quick looks, and Dave did also; he'd tell me when the mists covered the eyrie, and when they had swept aside.

---

2. For many of our observations, we used a spotting telescope with a zoom lens having a magnification range from 15 to 45 power.

Our campsite below First Eyrie—the tan tent
with Long Lake in background.

"I wonder if the falcons have quieted for the night."

Later we heard a voice deeper and throatier than the
male falcon's, some odd cackle of the female we thought at
first, somewhere off the cliff. We stood outside the tent and
wondered. But it was not far or high enough for a falcon. Then
Dave saw the dark fox. It barked—a whiney, lonely sound.
As we ate our dinner we heard two, then three more. One
close before the tent, with dark fur except for a light grayish
patch on his back and left ear. Below the tent, one mostly
gray was answering; the others were on farther vague slopes.
When the foxes crouched, I could hardly spot them against the
tundra, were they chubby boulders?

Once started, the foxes continued their howling, and
as we sat within our tent—it grew chill outside—figures
watching us would step closer, howl so close outside that we
didn't know whether they were mournful or angry. I had smiled
when Danes at the base told us we would hear the foxes
barking. But these barked more than I liked, too sadly it seemed,
and I wondered whether we would be listening to their conversation every night. Perhaps they were disturbed and objecting
only to this first evening of our tent and scents.

The foxes broke our fragile mood. We had been feeling
not so much the evening or the wind or grass or the cliff
itself, darkening and mist covered, but the falcons there
somewhere above us—breathing, tiny. This was their valley, and

40

we two humans had come to stay. I had sensed a hint of awe
even as I sat in our tan square tent, the feeling had crept in
the opening along beside the telescope, it kept me quiet and
Dave quiet, tensed happy, and listening, it stirred the grasses,
something restless between our feet and the earth.

But now persistent foxes were filling our ears with this
wailing, as they stood close by the tan canvas where we couldn't
see them. Dave didn't like it. Several times he walked out
the tent so that the watchers retreated. But they crept back
with soundless feet and hollow voices as soon as Dave came
inside. Finally he gathered a pile of stones.

"If they keep this up too much I'll get them with these,"
he told me.

I hoped it wouldn't come to that. I liked the foxes, I told
Dave I liked the foxes. Then I laughed at our wry faces—we
were victims of these sly, noisy creatures. Three of them barked
at once, and I added hopefully, "There are so many anyway
that you couldn't get rid of them all."

Dave said he wouldn't do anything unless he was desperate.

After a leisurely supper, Dave lit his pipe. All our gear
was arranged and our wet clothes hung on a rope strung
through the tent's middle. I thought of Mattox and the others,
all wet, huddled in the two-man tent. Without a base camp
and moving on at morning.

I felt restless and went for a walk, chuckling because after
all that long hike I wanted to walk. South and east, low
hills hid the land. I kept thinking about all the empty land.
The day before, a plane had gone down somewhere along
the fjord; but the search parties hadn't yet been able to find it.
The frightening ice cap waited close on the east. Four hundred
miles across. No people. All this country, and we with strong
legs, and cliffs to explore that no watcher of birds had ever
seen. Wilderness.

Dave was asleep when I returned. Just as I crept into
my sleeping bag, a fox started barking. It came very close until
I got up and stealthily unzipped the tent opening. I stepped
outside where the wind touched my legs and arms. A silver fox
hesitated. Ha, I picked a pebble and tossed it toward the fox.

Side view of Ice Cap Eyrie, with ice cap behind.

And the falcons—I gave the eyrie a sharp look as if I knew
its secrets, and turned back and into my cot for sleep.

Species and Subspecies

No two individual peregrines are identical. The thousands
of characteristics vary within the limits that make a peregrine
a peregrine. And they do not vary randomly—falcons tend
to be suited particularly to the area in which they live. Hardly
any of the mammals and birds have world ranges as wide
as the peregrine's. Almost like different worlds are Greenland
and Mexico, Ceylon and Tierra del Fuego and the Congo,
the Fiji Islands or Tasmania. The peregrines from one part of the
range look distinct from the peregrines of another area.

Therefore the peregrine is divided into subspecies, and
at present the whole species is not endangered, but only certain

of the subspecies. Of what significance is this distinction?[3] There is a confusion among scientists, and among those laymen who overhear the disagreements. For among birds some subspecies seem to differ more from one another than do certain species from other species. Are not all peregrines, peregrines? Is the Japanese peregrine distinct from the Chilean? Now there are disputes over whether some peregrines form one subspecies or two, as well as whether several subspecies actually form different species.

All animals die. Each death is somewhat chance or coincidence. But each death is in some respect a result of the animal's own nature: it cannot endure the hottest sun; or when it is eight years old, it doesn't see as well or move as quickly as once it did. All animals die. A landscape doesn't retain the same animals, but one replaces another replaces another.

Each animal is an expression of its exterior environment and individual experience. If it was born where food was plentiful, it is strong and healthy. It becomes accustomed to the companionship of certain other animals. It learns to fear the various enemies it has met. Yet also the animal is unfolding from within. Its parents have endowed it with that array of qualities and potentialities present at birth.

An animal lives a short time or a long time. The longer its life the more it affects other animals from without, as predator or prey or competitor. Yet also it produces more offspring the longer it lives. It creates animals new from within. The new animal, the young, springs from its parents in two important ways. First, it does indeed continue their inherited qualities. Yet, secondly, it is a genetic recombination, a union of their two inheritances; as a total individual it is different from either parent, and becomes a new possibility in the landscape.

Under natural conditions any male of the species can reproduce with any female of the species, but not successfully with members of any other species. The marvelous reproductive creativity within one animal kind is separated from that of all the other kinds.

---

3. See Mayr (1970) for an excellent treatment of species and subspecies.

Reproductive isolation occurs in many ways. One species may be ready to mate at a different time of year than another species, or prefer a different sort of environment. Behaviors leading to copulation may be incompatible, or the physical structure of one species may prevent successful copulation with another. Or perhaps hybrid unions of one kind with another will be infertile, or the hybrid young quickly die, or at least they will be infertile, and never reproduce their strange mix of inheritances. Reproductive isolation results from a complex of physical, behavioral, and physiological qualities of the species.

We often think first of these many other qualities when comparing two species, for example, peregrine and gyrfalcon. They are important, as the ways in which we recognize and react to the species, as determining how and how well it can survive, and how it affects other animals. But reproduction is uniquely significant; it determines at once both the continuity and creativity of all these qualities that are inherited.

While all members of a species are capable of reproducing together, mating does not occur randomly between all individuals of a particular species. The primary limitation is geographical location. Only animals living in the same region will mate. Even birds do not freely roam over the globe or the species's range, but tend to breed, migrate, winter in limited areas.

Scientists distinguish portions of a species by name. These are the subspecies, not reproductively isolated but differentiated according to their physical appearance. Members of a subspecies inhabit the same region and therefore the inherited characteristics of these individuals mix as interbreeding continues; the individuals closely resemble each other in many of their visible characteristics.

The abrupt separation of peregrines into either one subspecies or another is artificial although convenient for human observers. Because frequently visible characteristics vary gradually not abruptly over a species's range. More importantly, physical appearance does not reflect many qualities of an animal that suit it for survival in its environment.

Overall genetic, rather than just visible variability, is significant for reproduction.

In North America there are three named subspecies of the peregrine.[4] These subspecies are distinct from the peregrine race first described by scientists, Falco peregrinus peregrinus of Britain and Europe. The peregrines living throughout southern Canada and the United States were anatum birds, known by the third part of their Latin name, F.p. anatum. On the northwest coast, with seabirds off British Columbia and in the Aleutian Islands Peale's falcons live (F.p. pealei), larger and darker than the anatum. Northern members of both of these subspecies migrated to the southern parts of the ranges; southern members continued near their eyries all year. Until recently no other subspecies were recognized, and the range of anatum was believed to extend onto the tundra by the Arctic Ocean. But in 1968, these pale falcons were described as a third subspecies, F.p. tundrius.[5] Dave and I searched for tundra falcons. Others of this subspecies lived in Canada and Alaska.

Some races of the peregrine still reproduce as they have always done. But the once far-ranging anatum peregrines have disappeared almost entirely, the populations of F.p. peregrinus are shattered and weak, while the tundra peregrines are contaminated with pesticides, and reproductive failures have been discovered in parts of their range.

Despite the visual similarity of one peregrine to another, the surviving races do not replicate the genetic makeup of a sister race that has vanished.

The Tiercel, the Falcon

We awoke to another cold morning when we saw the moisture of our breaths rise, and we touched our numb noses with our fingers. Dave started one of the stoves, and I left my sleeping bag, planning to huddle next to it until we had hot

---

4. For more information on the subspecies of the peregrine see Vaurie (1961) and Hickey and Anderson (1969).
5. White (1968).

coffee. But the tent was unzipped except for a foot at the bottom; grasses showed through the opening, and a leafless branch of the dwarf tundra bush that I could just see if I bent my head. The light was a pale glow. I unzipped the tent, and stepped into the wide air. Where the mists hung low for one morning more, and I saw a snowflake pass. Dave left the coffee also.

"Well," I said. "How will we watch them?"

But Dave hadn't answered, only walked a few paces from the tent, when we heard a falcon voice falling from the high, vast rock. We couldn't tell from where exactly, despite the many times the deep voice sounded, deeper than the high male's cry, somewhere down from one of the numerous stone points, pinnacles, walls, or the sloping irregular ledges with tufts of dead grass. All motionless while the falcon cried, until with silence, I caught the pump of long wings, a peregrine launching from the ledge below the eyrie to fly left, then right, and finally perch. The light belly averted, the motionless falcon melted into its dark background. And Dave had sighted a second falcon on high, which alternated quick wing-beats and glides with leisured turns and soaring. Rising, it vanished among the misting cloud bottoms. And the first bird, unnoticed, had already left its perch.

We looked from the blank clouds to each other. With wind, and the chill that trembled our eyes, the visions just ended didn't seem kindred with the heavy tent, the ground, our hands. The expanse of the tundra—the long lake or the ridge—made the tent seem crowded up under the cliff; the small falcons with their thin cries and the mystery to their flight, the way they disappeared though we knew not when or where, or why they shifted perches by their home—these doubts widened the air between tent and cliff.

To avoid disturbing the falcons, we decided we would remain hidden as much as possible, using the tent as a large, comfortable observation blind by leaving the lowest part of the opening unzipped. Dave watched first, lying in his sleeping bag with his eyes at the opening.

A quiet hour passed. I in my turn lay on the floor and

stretched my eyes skyward. Occasionally I would scan the cliff with my binoculars, hoping to find a peregrine, or to check specks I had noticed with my unaided eyes that might be the white of the peregrine's breast. One more time I scanned the cliff and surprisingly spotted both peregrines, one larger than the other, circling against the sky over the cliff. For a minute they swooped about each other and sometimes even seemed to touch in midair, one beating up from below and behind the other; we could not be certain in the distance. Then the smaller dropped quite quickly below cliff level. I watched the eyrie for a moment but saw nothing. The larger, solitary, still circled—a few wingbeats but mostly soaring—almost directly over the eyrie. She could see the tent, perhaps my binoculars through the opening or Dave's head beside me. Then moving a little more quickly she passed down the ridge with spaced wingbeats and disappeared at last toward the large lake.

*   *   *   *

The weather remained cold with clouds and occasional snowflakes for the next several days. We spent many hours watching from the tent, and even when we didn't watch, we'd listen for the voices, because we liked hearing them, and we often could find them flying as they called. We learned we could usually walk about outside the tent without any reaction from the peregrines, but occasionally they might call, "kaaa kaaa kaaa," a leisurely sound that didn't seem agitated or angry, although still we'd stop what we were doing and stand motionless, eyes up to the cliff. But we found it unpleasantly cold to sit outside the tent for more than a few moments.

The second day I awoke hearing the peregrine voices. Dave lay on the tent floor watching the cliff.

Later Dave left the tent, planning to hide by a huge boulder uphill where he could watch more easily. I sat in the tent writing. I heard his footsteps pause on the hill. Then I heard them continue away; a falcon quietly called. The tundra was empty and silent and the cries descended, like shrill whispers out of the deep mountain but swift on the air, like falcon flight, called me to the tent opening. Not until Dave reappeared above did the peregrine cry again. Dave hurried down the slope.

"Where's the telescope?" he said.

"Inside here," I pointed my arm vaguely behind me as I tried to see the falcon.

Dave then was fumbling with the tripod beside me and squinting through the eyepiece and focusing the lens. "It was the male," he told me even as I repeated, "What did you see?"

"I saw the peregrine on that round rock below the eyrie ledge. When I kept walking it flew left, then—here he is!"

"Where?" I asked. Always we had frantic direction giving and taking when one of us saw the falcon before the other did.

"Left of the eyrie. One hundred feet . . . just as high. He's preening."

"Where, Dave?"

Dave looked over the scope. "Do you see that white band of rock?" Pointing, "No, over here, an overhang above it," back to the telescope, "he's still preening."

I found him and soon Dave let me have the telescope. The male clenched a rough out-jutting of rock with his talons. He faced south, away from the cliff, toward us. I could see his very light underparts, and as he turned his head his white cheeks flashed between the malar stripes and the helmeted top and back of head, all gray-black. His dark wings and back contrasted with the white of the belly. He scratched his head with his foot. He ruffled his shoulder feathers with his beak. Small against the cliff. We still had a good look—the best ever.

Before long a fox barked from the foot of the talus. At the second bark the falcon looked up briefly, then out and west toward the lake, before he continued his preen. His marks did appear to be those of the tundrius peregrine: very white breast with only moderate barring on the white belly; a narrow malar stripe that left a wide and obvious white cheek. The anatum falcon had buffy over most of his underparts and a wide malar stripe that left little white on the cheek. The tundra falcon also is smaller than the anatum of New York

48

and Minnesota.[6] These Greenland falcons looked tiny, not the obvious, large presence I had expected, although probably the landscape would have dwarfed any falcon, no matter how large.

He called, flew back and forth before the cliff, spiraled up to depart quickly north over the ridge. We had watched him for an hour. For another hour we both watched and waited for him to return. Something I felt, something that Dave and I shared, reminded me of Bill Burnham as he had talked to us on our two hikes. He had told us about the peregrines, what we would see when we camped by the eyrie. He was feeling the days he had spent by the cliff, under the falcons, in dusty Colorado; a wealth of love in his voice. Some of the words he used were strange to me, and Bill had to explain them.

"What's the tiercel?" He smiled, "You'll get to know him. He's the male peregrine. The female peregrine, she's the falcon. Tiercel and falcon go for any of the falcons, but the other species have their own names too. The gyr, she's the boss, the female gyrfalcon, and her mate is the jerkin."

"Gyr, and jerkin. . . ."

"And do you know the small merlin?" A delicate and gray falcon, only twelve inches long. "The female is the merlin. Guess what the male is. The jack. The name fits him. He's spunky and quick."

Dave complained that not only did you have to learn so many different species's names, but for each species you must call the male and female by new words also. How would we ever know when falcon meant peregrine, and when it meant the female?

"You'll learn." Bill was pleased. Either he enjoyed telling about the hawks, or he liked our puzzlement. "There's lots of other words. I better not tell you all of them now . . . well you call the peregrines something different at every age."

"At every age!"

"Well, they are different at every age. When the peregrines are young at the eyrie, and haven't yet learned to fly, they're eyasses, in the eyrie," he repeated. For clarity,

6. White (1968).

or for the sound of the words. Fledging is the time that young birds first fly, just after they leave the nest. "After they fledge, the young peregrines hang around the cliff, calling for their parents to feed them. Then they're branchers. And there's haggard, the adult peregrine.

"When you go to the sea coast in the fall, and see the peregrines migrating, many of them are the young of the year. Their backs are brownish-black, and their breasts heavily streaked with brown. We call a peregrine like this a passage bird."

Bill's voice filled these words as if they had personal meanings dear to him, but he hadn't made them. Falconers of old Europe had spoken of their birds with these same words. People endlessly name what they love. It is poetry.

I have followed birds with friends but Bill shared his watching with thousands, for the tradition from falconry, the names, the association of these birds with humanity and with the hunt, gave Bill an intimacy with those scattered across the world, or long dead, emperor, kings and queens, the minstrel and tapestry weaver.[7] I looked at Bill carefully. He had a noticeable western drawl, and praised, boasted of the dry western states, his home, to the exclusion of other places. Yet how cosmopolitan he was!

Some of Bill's names soon became very easy to use without thinking. Occasionally I would realize that I had uncon- sciously picked up another falconer's term, like mutes for the excrement stains on the cliff. But at other times Bill or Dick Graham would drop an incomprehensible word not realizing that I was fresh to falcon watching. The vocabulary clued me to that difference between superficial and deep contact with an animal, a difference that seems subtle or intangible when

---

7. In the middle of the thirteenth century, Emperor Friedrich II of Hohenstaufen wrote his long work *De Arte Venandi Cum Avibus* (*The Art of Falconry*), remarkable for its scope, its detail, and its biologi- cal accuracy. The translation by Casey A. Wood and F. Margorie Fyfe, published in 1943, serves as an excellent portrayal of the sport in me- dieval Europe and of Friedrich himself, preeminent among Western falconers. But in the Near and Far East, the tradition of falconry extends back thousands of years before Friedrich.

we first meet and recognize animals, when we don't need or want the special language.

Some falconer's words are or have been understood by the general public. Many know the eyrie as an eagle's home on the precipice. Haggard also has come into general use, distorted, however, and unrecognized. The captured haggard falcon was unruly and wild, a difficult bird to train for hunting. The public's familiarity with an animal's intimate names probably reflects that public's degree of contact with the animal. As hawks vanish from all but the loneliest areas, the rare falconry words will be spoken less.

As Dave and I attempted a general study of behavior of the peregrine pair above us, we planned to write down everything we saw of the peregrines. We had two hard-bound yellow notebooks for our notes. But on those first cold days we wrote hardly anything for all our hours watching. We saw little. Not only did the peregrines seem hidden or lost on the cliff, but we didn't seem to notice much, about the way they flew, or when they fed, or which peregrine was which. This last we decided we must learn well and quickly.

Mattox had told us how the male and female differed.[8] Plumage is identical for the sexes. But for the peregrine, as for many hawks, the female is larger than the male. The falcon is generally one and a half times the weight of the tiercel. This difference is noticeable whether the peregrines are perched or flying. Size influences the manner of flight—we needed especially to learn this distinction for we usually saw the adults alone when size was hard for us to determine, and either sex seemed small against the vast cliff or the empty tundra. But only when the two flew together did I know tiercel from falcon, not by flight but by size. I quickly learned to distinguish their voices—the falcon's was lower pitched and harsher. But though I knew the voice I could seldom decide which bird on the cliff had actually called.

The large falcon is also swifter and stronger than her mate. Thus usually the falcon dominates in the pair relationship,

8. Cade (1960) discusses male-female differences and interactions in the peregrine.

choosing her favorite perches and limiting the tiercel's access
to the eyrie.

The peregrine is a solitary bird, wandering alone through
all the year except at nesting season. Only at the eyrie cliff
will two peregrines come together. The peregrine is fiercely
aggressive toward all other birds, whether prey or other falcons
or even intruding eagles. Traditionally, falconers have seldom
housed two peregrines together—the smaller usually will
be killed. And while occasionally two females can be hunted
at the same time, if male and female are released at once,
the female will pursue the male rather than smaller prey,
and the male will flee away and be lost to his human keeper.[9]

Perhaps the elaborate courtship on the nest cliff serves to
weaken antagonism between the mates. Pairs differ markedly
in how well they cooperate with each other. The male
catches food for both the young and the female during the
first weeks after hatching. Quarrels usually arise when the
male provides insufficient food, or even balks at the last minute
in delivering prey to his mate. Or the male may enter the
eyrie when he isn't welcome. The female's dominance
surfaces at these moments, for the male almost always yields
to her, or else she will force his submission. But some pairs
seem so well adjusted that the female never reveals her
supremacy. Perhaps this adjustment takes several seasons to
achieve; while the pair separates at the end of nesting season
often the same two will return to their cliff the following year.
Differences in disposition may also be significant—one member
of the pair may be particularly irritable, and then the two
are forever quarreling.

One evening when I walked elsewhere on the tundra,
Dave saw a falcon return from the direction of the large lake.
It soared over the ridge then dove almost to the ground
below the cliff. Returning swiftly to the cliff top it dropped
once more past the eyrie to the ground, and up again to
turn small circles. On the fourth pass for an instant it touched
at the ledge below the eyrie. The fifth time it touched rock
again, only two peregrines came off instead of one. Suddenly

9. Cade (1960).

they screamed and flew together west. Two hundred
feet out from the eyrie the lead falcon suddenly swerved
round. Dave watched the falcon rush west, high and far, then
he stared at the eyrie for over an hour. No falcon approached or
left the ledge.

Bones and Feathers

The tundra and and its inhabitants are significant for
the watcher of peregrines not only because they affect the
falcons, but because they change the watching also. Rich
experiences arise half from the exterior world, in this case the
falcons, and half from our own hopes and joys and a thousand
fractured thoughts as we watch and respond. The tundra
changes us. No human on the tundra sees peregrines as he or
she would from a rowboat on the Hudson River, or from
a road just departed from houses, barking dogs, and playing
children. From our viewpoint, it is the setting that most of all
distinguishes the nesting tundra falcons from their lost kind
to the south. The watcher in the north thus has a distinctly
different encounter. Money, time, and a long jet flight
cannot procure an experience that has passed away from our
own land.

Even sheltered in the tent Dave and I were cold. The rock
and the uneven ground, the light all through the night, and
especially the falcons made us restless. As we didn't dare
disturb the peregrines in such cold weather when eggs quickly
chill, we looked other ways out on the tundra.

I took the last watch on our first day in the tent. After
lunch Dave packed a few items in a small knapsack and prepared
to leave. At last he said, "I'll be back before dark."

But we hesitated together before the tent. I felt sorry
to have him go, and I think he felt the separation also, for
he turned after he had walked several paces, and said goodbye.
Quickly without seeming effort he grew small and difficult
to see.

The cliff was silent. I too prepared to leave. I would
walk east so that I could climb round onto the ridge without
disturbing the falcons, then back along the ridge top to

A secluded cliff we nearly overlooked in our survey because of
the surrounding higher ground; in 1973 it held nesting ravens.

try seeing down into the eyrie. When I looked back I saw that
I also was vanishing effortlessly from the miniature tent, my
home.

I climbed a south-jutting spur of high ground. Here
bushes grew two feet tall where the rocks sheltered them from
the north. I passed farther east on the spur than necessary,
hoping to catch a long view of the land beyond. But the
ridge stretched far east and its main peak reared not over
the peregrine cliff as we had assumed but entirely out of sight
of the tent atop its own cliff. That way, the ice cap. Boulders
perched above the new cliff—the ice cap's glare might
reach them. But I stood hesitant. The tent had passed out of
sight behind me, as had the peregrine eyrie. Don't walk alone. I
felt the loneliness of all the grasses and stones and the sky,
no people, how would Dave find me if I slipped and fell?
Where was Dave wandering now? This wilderness made my
head light so that my thoughts rushed and I hurried east.

Here lay a still pool that mirrored clouds. The ridge now
close above me and all the rock ledges and lesser outcroppings
pointed toward the ice cap, leaving grassy avenues between.
Atop the ledges lie boulders and stones and pebbles balanced

in long lines that reached east. One, larger than an ox could drag, sat atop four fist-sized rocks. Another leaned heavily over the cliff brink above me. I was following the fresh trail of the glacier: it had set the boulders down as it melted and it had carved the hills.

I saw it. First the ledges had gray clouds behind them. Closer and the ground hid less of the sky—whiter clouds appeared. Then their bottoms seemed glossy, hard, icy along a barely perceptible line. They had a hard texture, too bright and strong for clouds, the ice cap smoother than any plain, even for all the miles I could see, east, southeast, northeast, north, south-southeast almost half across the horizon as at last I reached the ridge's east end. Ghastly. Lifeless. It didn't lie low on the horizon like the sea. Mountains stood at the edge, and black cliff faces—the ice rolled over them, or leaned heavily upon their crests, and beyond steadily rose. No animal walked for five hundred miles to the far coast. At its center it thickened to two miles of ice.

I stood half panicky, waiting for the heavy ice to slide the short distance that separated us, engulf the grasses, engulf the ridge just as it swallowed now the black cliffs.

In my fear I felt drawn as if I faced a serpent's mirroring eye. All the sky above me and behind me had a dull gray cast, but the clouds brightened in the east, not to rosiness and warmth where sunlight peeps but to the glow of ice as cloud reflected glacier reflected cloud.

The ice, how close was it? Too close. So close that I felt I might quickly run to touch its smoothness: the ground fell long and slowly before me. The tundra had its browned wintry look, but was jeweled by a dozen small lakes and half-hidden pools. No cliffs close by, except this falconless one by which I stood. Farther a lake stretched long, thin with undulated shores, and entirely frozen. Its ice had a dull gray whiteness unlike the ice cap, but it gave me a lonely feeling for this was late June and still the lake lay imprisoned, not a resting stop or home for ducks or loons or a wandering human. At its southeast end a brown, straight cliff waited. It might hold falcons. Then the ground ascended chiller heights into ridges of mountains bare and exposed with cliffs, but shadowing these, before the ice cap, grim blue-gray peaks formed a line with snowy shoulders and treacherous passes. Dead and threatening. What shelter could I possibly find?

Enough. I swallowed one last look and turned.

I came upon a pond enclosed in a valley by small rock faces. Now a dark fox with spots of gray near his tail and on one ear was accompanying me. Its rounded face had none of the leanness of a red fox, but it perked its unpointed ears as if it wondered what I could be and crept several feet closer. Only five yards separated us. Suddenly my body tensed—could this creature have rabies? Mattox had warned us of the friendly fox who will act curious and mild before his lethal bite. The fox and I eyed each other. I yelled tentatively. It backed only a few paces. It advanced again. It gave a little snarl, sharp from its dark tongue and pointed teeth. I hurried to the near hillside, scrambling for loose rocks. When I held a handful I tossed several at it to widen our distance, and then I ran between the pond and the hillside where the animal trailed me until I passed the next rise.

I looked ahead to pick out my easiest route. I had to climb over ledges and boulders onto the ridge top; then I could walk along the cliff brink and peek down to the eyrie below.

A hare bobbed among rocks. It had pure white fur that gave it a clean appearance or aged, like an old man snow-white but agile, and its long ears pointed straight up. It sat on its strong haunches to watch me, then stood, with its forelegs drooping and its back straight. Two feet tall to the ear tips. It bobbed up and out of sight.

The hare had chosen a more difficult route than I took. Once I saw it ahead of me. Its size and whiteness made it figure prominently as a rabbit never should, a clear target for the foxes that must chase it.

I walked a short distance back from the cliff brink, and at last crept forward to poke my head out and over, not certain what I would see but careful not to silhouette myself for the falcons to notice. First, the speck of tan was our tent. It didn't appear to threaten the peregrines at all, but sat far out from and below the talus, hardly higher than the long lake. With my binoculars I could see its front entirely zipped. Had Dave returned?

The cliff had grown different rocks and ledges and textures than had been visible below. I found the eyrie. The ledge was narrow. I lay on one of the few spots that looked deep into that well-protected cleft. By squinting until my eyes watered I tried imagining that an oval stone was the falcon. No; either she had wedged her way toward where the ledge met its sloping roof or she had left the eggs uncovered.

I waited an hour and a half without seeing either peregrine. I grew suspicious that we had guessed the wrong site for the eyrie. Only once had a falcon touched that short ledge. Perhaps the falcons had preferred a long ledge immediately beneath. We had seen them there, even both departing at once.

From my perch more of the hills rolling southward appeared, but nothing beyond them. Dave returned from almost due south. He was striding halfway down the last hill, and his dull blue shirt blended with the rocks. He paused beside the pond he had told me about. I hadn't noticed it before. From high the tent looked as though it rested by the shore. Odd.

Several snowflakes fell. The sky still looked ivory to the east. Although the mountain chill had come up into my feet I didn't want to leave. I sat alone. Dave didn't know where. The world had frightened me that afternoon, and I doubted that the air ever again would feel so fierce. I didn't want to leave. The size or strength or chill, these alone hadn't shaken me: I had been a child of the earth as never before, an offspring loosened of all the contrivances my ancestors and relatives had built around me. This time I walked without help. The weight and lightness of the landscape, I had to sense them, for nothing separated me or made me sacred and invulnerable. I breathed remarkably like the foxes or the hares. We would all fall the same way.

*   *   *   *

Dave welcomed me to the tent, and we gladly talked
together. He too had seen the ice cap, and then had turned
south. On his map two large lakes lay among those hills,
each with many contour lines bunched close to its north shore.
He had reached the closer of the lakes. As the map suggested,
a cliff ran all along its nearest edge. He had walked its top
but hadn't descended to the water.

"We better check this carefully for an eyrie," he said.
Our Danish map labeled all the places with long Greenlandic
words like Angmalortup Nunâ. It was curious that the Greenlanders knew the inner tundra so well that they named
everything, but we looked carefully at the various lakes, and
found three all Taserssuaq. This means simply "large lake."
The two lakes south had unpronounceable names. Dave had
seen an island in the closest: Island Lake. The other we
called Al's Lake for the beginning of its name.

*   *   *   *

Our next walk we took together, to visit the cliff on
Island Lake. Several times as we climbed the first slope my
boot struck against brittle ground. I stooped to spread the
grasses: this dark, smooth substance was ice. The ground was
slow to thaw.

From each hill we saw yet another higher hill. Although the
sea flowed eighty miles away, the fjord reached almost to
the air base, still at sea level with the large lake only one step
higher, our tent and valley one more, and everywhere beyond
the land rose. Without trees the shape of the land overwhelmed
the landscape. As desolate as the tundra appeared, the higher
elevations knew greater barrenness where the two- and
three-thousand foot peaks with snow had a blue-black color
and I feared that no vegetation at all grew there; on the many
cliffs no peregrines could live, nor other creatures.

We did at last find a highest hill, two hours' walk from the
tent. The next rise lay distinctly below us, and we had a
wide view once more, of similar hills that resumed the climb
in the distance.

To my surprise Dave said we were almost to the cliff.

That next hill didn't roll down its far side. We suddenly stood on the edge of a precipice. Below lay an irregular lake with a single island, a dull white icy lake bordered with darkness where edges had thawed. Narrow places to walk bordered the foot of the cliff. Two loons fished, by necessity close to shore, one or the other diving at intervals. They had long sharp bills and bodies longer than ducks', floating low in the water.

Dave climbed around the near end of the cliff to reach the lake shore. He would walk the bottom while I traced the cliff brink; he would yell and clap to flush the falcons while occasionally I would roll a rock over. Both of us were impressed with how easily falcons blend with a cliff. Our search would be thorough. But if we discovered a falcon pair, we could quickly leave them in peace and return another day to locate the eyrie and wait until warm late summer to visit the ledge itself.

This was a short cliff and Dave soon appeared below. We began. We passed slowly along the lake. Dave banged clappers made of rectangles of plywood. The noise echoed from the rock. The loons ignored us. I rolled a stone over the edge, shouting "rock" just before to warn Dave, then listened to it on the ledges. I heard Dave's electric distant cry "Peregrine!" I leaned over the brink looking everywhere. No cackling. No falcon flight. No movement.

At last, "It was over here," Dave called.

He added, "Try to see onto those ledges. Do you see any eggs?"

I could look down onto five or six inaccessible ledges. Many of them had small rocks or grasses but as carefully as I stared, and as often as I shifted my position nothing more appeared. The peregrine doesn't build a nest of grasses, sticks, and branches like the bulky eagle's home. It usually lays its eggs on a sandy or gravelly spot where mammals cannot walk. As the eggs roll, the falcon must find soft sand where she scrapes a hollow to hold the eggs safely.[10]

From my height the scrape would not be visible, only

10. Hickey and Anderson (1969).

clustered eggs. I could not find them. At last by Dave's direction
I rolled another stone, and then a last one over the edge to
flush the falcon.

"I don't know where it went, why don't you . . . ," Dave
called.

Too high a cliff for us to talk across. And we had disturbed
the falcons enough already. I would climb around the end
of the cliff and join Dave by the lake.

Dave met me halfway up the slope. He had found small
white feathers scattered under a rock, where the falcon
must have plucked its prey. Dave wasn't certain whether he
had seen a peregrine or a gyrfalcon. Half hopeless of success from
his shouting and clapping he had glimpsed a flickering of
wings, light feathers pointed wings of a large bird that whisked
around the rock corner.

We stood below the cliff at the spot where Dave had
seen the hawk flush. "I'd like to stay here," I said.

Dave pulled out his fishing line. "I'll walk along the shore.
You catch up when you get cold."

*   *   *   *

Always the chill comes when you stay in one spot on
the tundra. I put all my clothes on from out of my pack and
pulled my poncho down about my legs and feet. I stared
at the smooth, gray cliff. Occasionally I glanced behind me at
the frozen lake. The loons had departed.

On the tundra I had lost my sense of distance. Often the
farthest mountains beckoned as if I could reach them in
minutes, and certain quiet lakes or heaps of rocks seemed close
enough for quick sprints. Places where I stood quickly shrank
to insignificance as I left them. But a hill ahead might take
an hour or two to reach and disclose another hill identical
behind it. Another hour. The constantly sloping ground
and the bare frame of the earth (the rock bursting through
grass), which no vegetation softened or hid, gave the tundra
a vast scale. My confusion had many causes. My excitement.
And the air held no dust or dirt, wasn't as dense as at lower
latitudes—I could see far. But strangest, no houses or roads or

humans marked the landscape. It hadn't been fragmented
into myriad pieces but stretched one continuous fabric out
to the horizon where one might wander a year, forever,
as free as caribou. Without people, somehow a hill was more
like all the other hills, a lake mirrored all other lakes, the sky,
unbroken unmarked by roof or telephone wire. You had
to feel the more subtle qualities of place, not how far to the
highway or how trampled the path, or whether you trespassed
or not. Learn again to see. The vegetation superficially
seemed continuous—grasses, fragments of bushes, a moss or
two if you looked closely. Watch the curve of the ground.
Note the rock patterns, or how the mountains, range behind
range, follow nearer rocks or lakes. But these signs shift
strangely as you move. Look, look, or you are lost. I felt a vague
tingling or puzzlement whenever I tried to discover one spot
a second time.

Where no one restricts or turns your footsteps, yet no
human or machine speeds you on road or track or through the
air, where only the strength of your legs carries you, then
also only your own weakness holds you, and you must know
always you are weak, where always the crooked mountains lure,
and dim cliffs that might hold falcons.

Yes, the emptiness did stir me. No people, no shelters
where I might warm my feet. Even the animals were few and
scattered, apparently only because they had few places to hide.
Three mammals: the fox, the hare, the caribou. I considered
each in turn.

We saw many foxes. Mainly they prowled about during
the twilight night, or by evening or early morning. On a certain
mound near our tent we had to walk alertly, for among the
bushes and also where the soil lay bare twenty burrows had
been dug, sloppily with varying widths and some with the
dirt straggling out from the opening. But more evident
even than the holes were dozens, scores of bones. These littered
the mound everywhere. The sun had bleached most of them
white, but dried bits of flesh clung to one or two where sharp
eager teeth had missed morsels. Many of these were caribou
bones, the smaller ones such as lower legs and hooves that

could be dragged. This was a fox warren. Its owner had barked because we camped so near.

Two fox cubs would lie on the ground between the holes, or clumsily scamper until one blundered into the other, and they both fell, or sat. They idled in the dirt. A full-grown fox with a lame leg would lurk in the bushes near them. Perhaps it savagely watched us. If Dave walked toward the cubs, the parent never appeared; the young did not scuttle into the convenient holes but instead tottered and trotted to farther holes and watched Dave and yawned.

Now that it was summer, the foxes had young hares and bird nests to find. But these foxes lead miserable, hungry lives through the winter. Perhaps many clustered at the air base dump with the ravens. Yet the vast majority must fend for themselves, gnawing on dead caribou. And they stalk ptarmigan and hares, the abundance of which varies from year to year in the population cycles that seem to hold many arctic animals.

The long-legged hare is a difficult animal to catch. It feeds while on hillsides and, if the fox appears below, it will race uphill with a speed the stubby fox cannot match. The latter has a better chance if it can stalk a hare from above, for it may swoop down so quickly that the hare hasn't time to gain its full run. For this reason the hares usually feed facing upward on the slope, and if they spy some leafy willow sprouts downhill they will hop below and turn around to face uphill again.[11]

I never saw the burrow of a hare. Unlike the foxes, the hares rely on hidden homes for survival. From a distance, their white fur shines across the tundra, resembling round rocks of pure quartz. Perhaps hares also stood on the patches of still unmelted snow; I never noticed them. Hares are warier than foxes or ptarmigan. If one notices movement, he sits upright on his hind legs with elevated eyes and ears. If he drops to bob several steps, he'll stop and resume his upright pose to have another look. He has a curved back and he looks like an old man hurrying on the cliff.

---

11. Cahalane (1947).

The caribou don't have specific homes on the tundra, although they may choose favorite meadows with good grass for grazing, and chill water nearby.

They are remarkable for their antlers, which vary from small prongs of bone to the wide thick racks of the largest stags, perhaps even five feet from the foremost point to the hindmost, and a horizontal spread of nearly four feet. Their weight makes the stags run with heads arched over their backs. The females also have antlers, much smaller, but in this species alone among American deer are females so weighted.

The sets of the males already had grown large in June but were furry brown, velvety. Although in other areas they are a defense against wolves, in western Greenland the antlers serve little purpose except at rutting reason.[12]

Now a redpoll chuttered near my head and flew beyond to land below the cliff. I shifted my position to reshuffle the cold in my legs. All the tundra animals lived intensely for me. A sense of kinship had crept upon me, a feeling that we shared the difficulty of living, and their presence, their successes, even the humming of mosquitoes, encouraged me. A kinship because I felt it, but Dave and I ran slight risk of death with tent and stoves and down sleeping bags while a day's walk would take us to the air base. Yet danger and kinship were real for me then because I felt them.

I reacted toward these mammals differently than toward birds on the tundra.

For wherever creatures live they give particular attention to their own kind. Dogs greet dogs on the street. The squirrel saves a special chatter and scurry after nuts until other squirrels approach. With people as with animals this special recognition varies. In the city we feel located and content because friends live there also. Where we are strangers we look for people out of the crowd who resemble us in their dress or manner. A man living abroad responds to his countryman with a momentary eagerness not shown toward his new perhaps highly valued acquaintances. And where people are few,

12. Kelsall (1968).

we greet every person we see and never pass one by eyes slanting to the ground or sky. On the tundra the mammals were my closest neighbors and relatives.

The mammals and I seemed to share an immediate recognition. An illusion took hold of me, that we had a mutual understanding of and interest in our parallel lives, because we all had fur or four-chambered hearts or some bond. These mammals all adjusted to my presence: the fox walked more stealthily, the hare sniffed the breeze for my scent and delayed eating to watch me, the great caribou hesitated in their trails at the dim, wide tent, at the quivering air rich with more than damp grass and muds. A human is a stranger to this tundra community, a blank entity that becomes defined as he touches and alters what he meets. To know myself I would watch my neighbors respond. In them I would find judgment of my character, good or bad, and I needed their companionship or else I was alone.

My mind, not resting as I awaited the falcon, fabricated mammalian responses plainer and more human than the subtle realities. The foxes despised me because they were sly, envious creatures. While always in summer fleas chewed at them and miserable they ran for meals to quiet their imperious cubs, they could see me—idle, furless, and itchless. They were powerless in their enmity and therefore irritable. They glared at me with flickering eyes. I liked the foxes and smiled in return. In contrast, the caribou were as friendly as they dared to be: they kindly left winding paths everywhere that eased walking and offered passages among precipices. But shy. If one carelessly blundered near me, saucer-eyed he'd frantically whirl about, hooves scraping, breath blowing, and he would charge off cross country, his skull ringing with astonishment and terror at slender two-legs. The grizzled hares had aching backs and crooked ears, they had grown disdainful of youth, the human purpose. They chose to remain neutral and distant.

Dave had rambled out of sight. I packed and followed him. I found a bird's body by my path. One of the small birds that the falcons hunt. Something had torn away the head and much of the body, leaving delicately feathered wings stretched out over the mud. Did a falcon choose this cliff for his eyrie? Why then had he fled so precipitously and never returned while we waited nor defended against our lingering?

I found Dave, trying his line in deep water close to shore. He had caught nothing. We returned to our peregrine cliff.

The Eyrie

Late the next afternoon I left our camp to climb the ridge. The peregrines were continuing to use the ledge below the supposed eyrie. I would take a position on the cliff brink where I could see both ledges in question and watch while Dave climbed from the tent as far up the cliff as he could without a rope. When the peregrine flew from the scrape it would betray the eyrie's location.

Then Dave would hurry away, and I, hidden, would watch the falcon return to its ledge. Unnoticed, I wouldn't anger the peregrine. These extreme precautions against disturbance of the falcons might have been unnecessary at cliffs visited once or twice briefly. But by camping beneath an eyrie the whole season we heightened the danger to the eggs and young; we felt obligated always to extremities of care.

The moment I peeked over the cliff brink a dark falcon dashed past the rocks far below and cackled. I saw no more for I pulled my head back, marveling at the peregrine's watchfulness or at the coincidence, but he (it was the tiercel's high voice) continued calling for some minutes more. Later I caught sight of his movement level with me, dipping and rising by the horizon as the tiercel soared before me, whirling on the wind so smoothly and swiftly that he hardly flicked his wings at all but stretched them against the air currents to turn and rise while he covered the earth with his gaze. I shrank under the sharp hawk's eyes that were ten times more powerful than mine, and I scarcely moved to risk the breaking of his glorious dream and progress still rising over the cliff sailing rushing toward me and the ridge-top, but now with an abrupt turn he whisked over the mountain. He left the falcon's view spread below me.

After awhile Dave came out of the tent. His climb up

Adult female perched at edge of eyrie ledge.

the slope seemed leisured and delayed (this peregrine's view!).
But when he reached the cliff foot he shouted and clapped
to warn the falcon. Dave received no shrill answer. I saw
nothing move on either of the two ledges. Dave walked beneath the sheer rock discovering the easiest route up and he
shouted, with echoes. He climbed, and still no peregrine appeared. He was moving slowly—I think he had trouble
finding footholds—and several times he paused and looked
up at the ledges. No answer to his shouts. He reached the far
west end of the lower ledge and looked fully down its length.
He raised a leg and stepped upon the ledge. Now, now out she
came from the lower shelf beneath an overhang. "Kaaak
kaaak kaaak kaaak." She dove over Dave, once and again and
again. Never to touch him, but in her turns her dark back
and white lower parts alternated and contrasted until Dave
reached the grass, when silently she landed at the brink of her
ledge. Dave was rushing away. She watched him intently. When
he had departed far down the slope she glanced back over
her right wing, then scuttled out of view beneath the overhang.

The Black Cliff

Joyous with what I had seen, I left the ridge top on its
north side to seize a quick view of new mountains. I saw a
river far below me. I saw a dozen cliffs beyond spread among
the many mountains; the sight would quicken my feet for the

rest of that evening. The river cut the base of the closest cliff, a symmetrical arc tallest in the middle curving evenly down and out to the ends, where on each side the river turned. The rock was black, rough and sculptured into many shapes. Clear against the black, many mute spots shone where they trailed under a dozen ledges. Could more falcons live so near?

I circled the whole ridge that evening, returning to Dave and the tent from the west. Dave had supper ready. We discussed plans for the coming days. To help Mattox and his party, probably long weary from their hikes, we would survey the hills south and east beyond Island Lake. Before departing for the two to three days, I would hike to Søndrestrøm to leave Mattox word of our trip so that he wouldn't travel out to our camp during our absence.

The following morning I walked west along the cliff base. Where the way was easiest I hiked north and approached the river valley I had seen the night before.

The near slopes fell away to reveal Black Cliff. The distance still hid the mute spots, almost a mile away, when a tiercel peregrine screamed not near or overhead but from the black rock in a voice thin and vague carried all this way on the wind. He continued to call through the next minutes when I must have been a far speck, but he had quieted long before I reached the river bank opposite the cliff. Only the passing water sounded and the steady, unmoving rock betrayed no watchful presence. I shouted "Boom!" that hit the arching cliff in its center and echoed many times. The female peregrine cackled, but I had to shout again so that she cackled longer and appeared flying against the sky, then alighting on a boulder atop her cliff. The tiercel flew and cackled over her until she too rose, and the two flew up high directly south toward the massive ridge and I lost sight of them. Here was a second pair only two miles from the first, but the chill river and its sucking muds posed a barrier that might prevent our ever locating the eyrie on its ledge.

Late that afternoon I arrived at the air base that felt crowded with buildings and Danes.

Bill Burnham with rubber raft used for crossing river
to Black Cliff in 1973.

The treaty between Denmark and the United States
that provided for the air base at Søndrestrøm also stipulated
that the Air Force would employ Danes for many jobs normally
performed by airmen. Most of the Danes worked in Greenland
for short periods of several years, at Søndrestrøm or the
coastal towns, for their government exempted from taxes all
money earned in a stay of at least two years, a sizable incentive
as taxes normally consume half of a Danish citizen's income.
Danes came for the two years, although they disliked winters
and left their families behind. Some never visited the
wilderness.

I met a man that evening who was not an unusual case.
He had no time for the landscape because he worked sixty
or seventy hours every week. He regarded his Greenland stay as
two years wholly sacrificed so that he could buy his home in
Copenhagen. Somehow he had already heard of Lieutenant
Colonel Graham's expedition for birds. It was curious
how the thousand residents of Søndrestrøm—Americans,
Danes, but only several native Greenlanders—knew of everyone
and talked of everyone. But more curious how many isolated
themselves with overfull thoughts of home and hot Europe
or New York, cut off from everything beyond the Søndrestrøm
roads.

Black Cliff.

Mattox, Graham, and Burnham were not huddling in
their tent by some nameless lake but strolled into the mess
hall for supper. After our surprise at meeting, we fired questions
at each other. They had just returned. They hadn't found
any peregrines but did have news of a gyrfalcon pair. The
adults were both white, and Bill had roped down to the eyrie
ledge to find three eyasses. My friends hadn't covered as
much ground as they had hoped. Although the cliffs they had
seen were small, and thus not likely to be occupied by falcons,
they heard about the peregrines on the Black Cliff with evident
relief, because constantly as they walked and walked they
had wondered whether many peregrines were still living in
Greenland, or would we find only late, lingering pairs? Mattox
told me that peregrines would not act with such aggressiveness
as the ones at Black Cliff unless they guarded an eyrie.

And Dick Graham would have to leave Greenland
immediately. At supper he was quiet, sad, and he looked worried
also. In Colorado he kept twelve Spanish peregrines that he
was trying to breed in captivity—these birds would be difficult
to hold healthy in their cages, and I wondered if something
had happened to them that Dick must leave. He hoped
to return in two weeks. The next day the two Bills would
begin to cover another section of tundra.

I didn't leave the base until early evening, when already electric lights shone, and their light so dimmed my eyes that the tundra was darkened.

Dave awoke and talked when I returned almost at midnight. The tiercel quietly called from the cliff as I lay falling asleep.

Population Surveys

The peregrine has successfully claimed most of the world for its nesting range.[13] But two requirements have limited the species's spread: the tall cliff and a level soft surface for the nest scrape. In some areas of the world the peregrine will lay its eggs in an old nest of a raven, hawk, or eagle, species that make the hard rock habitable with their stick structures. In North America the peregrine has rarely done this. In a few cases people have set boxes or baskets out, the bottom sand covered for a scrape, and watchers have even dug ledges for falcons into the rock of bare cliffs.[14]

Most cliffs have good ledges. Most areas that have not had nesting peregrines do not have cliffs. The favorite ones are the tallest, with a grand view, and water somewhere below. Yet rocks as small as dozen-foot-tall outcroppings in a hillside have held eyries. The shorter precipices remain inhabited only as long as humanity, and the roads and disturbances we bring, do not approach too closely. The decline, or retreat, in the 1940s of the peregrines that inhabited civilized areas was due to their abandonment of these marginal locations.[15]

The peregrine has ventured away from cliffs to nest. Most of these experiments have been temporary or on a limited scale. In Alaska and arctic Canada where human disturbance is low, the peregrines frequently choose the shifting cut banks over rivers.[16] On little, predator-safe islands peregrines have nested on the ground. Oddly, in Finland peregrines also took to the ground to nest, where bog eyries probably once

---

13. Hickey and Anderson (1969) review what is known about pere-grine nest sites throughout the world.

14. Hall (1955); Fyfe and Armbruster (1977).

15. Hickey (1942); Ratcliffe (1969).   16. Cade (1960).

outnumbered cliff sites. We do not know why this population
so successfully adjusted to lowland homes, or why on the
Eurasian tundra ground nesters are frequent, when in most
other areas of the world such records are extraordinary. Ground
nesting is restricted to portions of the peregrine's range where
few people live; but many lonely countries have no ground
nesters. Peregrines have also taken to trees. Very large trees lose
their tops or great branches in certain storms; holes are left
in the trunk. In central United States where cliffs are
absent, pairs chose sycamores, cottonwoods, or bald cypress.
Now both the giant trees and the falcons are gone. More
often, peregrines take abandoned tree nests of other raptors.
This practice is exceptional in North America but common
in the Baltic region; thus in Finland, cliffs, ground sites, and
trees all held eyries. The pairs in some territories alternated from
one type of site to another.[17] The northern part of East
Germany is a plain. Only one cliff eyrie, on an island, was
inhabited, but throughout the area peregrines chose trees. This
population then nested thoroughly free of cliffs, and some
pairs still survive the pesticides.[18]

Most astonishing of all, peregrines have chosen man-built
fortresses, with erect walls that resemble cliffs. Falcons were
hatched on Salisbury Cathedral[19] and also in downtown
Manhattan where millions of people passed far beneath the
eyrie, and the roar rose at morning and night to hide the falcons'
screams.[20]

*   *   *   *

Most important for the future of a species are the numbers
of pairs that nest and the success they have in fledging young.
Thus the breeding survey is the key tool we have for assessing
the effects of human activities upon a species.
For a bird as widespread as the peregrine, single studies
can never focus on the whole species nor even on any of

17. Linkola and Suominen (1969).
18. Schröder (1969); Bijleveld (1974).
19. Morres (1882).
20. Herbert and Herbert (1965).

the far-ranging subspecies. Yet just as individual peregrines can be separated into subspecies, so individual tundra peregrines belong to various local populations. Students will survey a population, defined as the group of potentially interbreeding individuals. Ideally, any two members of the local population have equal probability of mating together (assuming that age and sex are balanced).[21]

Real populations only approximate this ideal. Among any group of individuals, one individual never has a random likelihood of mating with any of the other suitable members of the group, and always some group members will mate outside the group. Nevertheless, within a species, individuals primarily breed with individuals near them. We designate a group of peregrines as a population on the basis of their separation from other peregrines. Thus Greenland peregrines are not only distant from Canadian peregrines, but also are separated from them by the Davis Strait.

The significance of a population lies in the fact that its members reproduce together and recombine inheritances. The genetic variability of the species interacts with a specific environment at the population level, rather than within the widely scattered subspecies.

Populations still are too large for all the nest sites to be visited and studied. Because a group of peregrines seldom forms the ideal, totally distinct population, and because members of the group survive and reproduce under varying environmental conditions, it is important to distinguish the particular sample of the population chosen for study.

Ideally for science all population sampling and studies of the nesting peregrine would be conducted in a standard way so that results could be compared from one area to another. For many practical reasons this ideal hasn't been met, and the variances in survey method require a cautious interpretation of findings.[22]

---

21. See Mayr (1970) for a discussion of populations and their significance.

22. Hickey and Anderson (1969) briefly discuss methods for population surveys. I also talked with J. J. Hickey about some aspects of this topic. Reports on population surveys include descriptions of methods.

One major factor that varies in a population survey is the extent to which all the peregrines of the area are studied. Of course, the greater the percentage of the whole population to be observed, the more definite our knowledge of that population. The smaller the percentage, the more important it is to survey a representative group of all peregrines present. For we want to learn about all the peregrines, not a few of them, and there may be many characteristics common to a small sample of falcons that the overall population does not share: diet, prey abundance, cliff exposure, cliff accessibility to humans or other animals, local climate, competition with other hawks or cliff nesters, disease, and so on. While these surveys attempt to discover only the number of breeding pairs (present abundance) and their reproductive success (a clue to future abundance), any of the varying characteristics may affect the researcher's two primary measures in ways difficult to foresee. After the researcher has minimized biases, he should estimate what potential sampling problems cannot be avoided, and suggest these when he interprets the survey results in order to alert other scientists to their presence.

Because the peregrine inhabits many regions, each with its own natural characteristics and human population, half a dozen different census methods have been applied to the various situations. Two methods yield complete or nearly complete peregrine counts. If the area is small, such as an island, its whole extent can be surveyed. Secondly, some observers have tabulated lists of all previously located eyrie sites for a region. The researcher must correspond widely with all living persons who might know of present or former eyries in the area, and must cull all sorts of ornithological writings and even accounts of travel and exploration to fill out the historical record. Two primary problems appear: the difficulty of locating precisely the oldest or vaguely described records, and the question of whether some of the reports refer to accurately identified peregrines, and not to some other falcon. Once the list has been completed the researcher then visits all of the eyries during the nesting season.

This method is most adequate in areas with extensive

records of peregrine observation—usually where many people live, as in Europe or eastern United States. When human population is sparse or a great many cliffs exist, some peregrines will be missed and those pairs observed may not be typical of the total population. For the eyries on the list will probably be those at the cliffs most vulnerable to human disturbance, thus less favorable for raising eyasses and perhaps sooner abandoned than those on isolated cliffs.

In the wilder regions of western United States, or the Arctic, especially where people know of few eyries, researchers must locate eyries entirely through their own efforts. Since visiting only cliffs that are accessible will result in the same bias just mentioned, and pairs on those cliffs may be atypical in other ways, some small part of the region is chosen as representative and all possible eyrie locations checked by the researcher. Where all peregrines are known to have coastal eyries, perhaps because no suitable habitat exists inland, a section of coast may be traversed by boat, foot, or car. In large areas of Alaska, Tom Cade found that the only cliffs and bluffs lined rivers where the ever-strong currents had cut steep valleys. His survey party chose several rivers and drifted down them in rubber rafts, stopping wherever they found cliffs.[23] Most difficult of all is the survey of an inland area where boats cannot help and no roads exist. This task faced us in Greenland.

To complicate differences in survey methods, observers do not all have the same amount of time available either for each visit to an eyrie or cliff or for repeated visits. Different researchers also hold different opinions on how much disturbance one location will tolerate before eggs and young die, or the parents abandon the eyrie. Survey results can be affected in several important ways. Less frequent or shorter visits to cliffs leave greater doubts if the cliff appears abandoned or if one or more adults are seen only briefly. Some females incubate their eggs very closely and if the tiercel hunts elsewhere—he may be absent for one or several hours—she may not aggressively appear until the scrape is imminently threatened. Our falcon waited until Dave set foot on the nest

23. Cade (1960).

ledge itself. Furthermore, adults sometimes defend a cliff
even though they don't attempt nesting. A lone bird may never
have found a mate or one member of a pair may be too young
to reproduce. Only careful watching can determine whether
the eggs are well hidden or simply not present. The stage
during the nesting cycle at which the eyrie is visited may influence an observer's conclusions. After an early nesting failure
the adults may abandon the cliff for the rest of that season.
The observer coming late would decide the cliff was unoccupied that year, or if the pair remained near, he would
believe they hadn't attempted nesting.

The timing of visits to the eyrie especially influences the
data on reproductive success. Visits at four weeks after
hatching may reveal fewer young than at one week. The later in
the season eyass data are collected, the closer they approximate
the number of new peregrines added to the species's population that season. This is the figure most vital to the continuance
of the species, and therefore of greatest interest in a population
survey. But visits to many cliffs cannot all be planned for
just before fledging, and young leaving the eyrie early may
depart the cliff before the observer's arrival and so be missed.
Also, visits only at fledging yield no information about the stage
in the reproductive cycle at which failures occur, a key element
in documenting pesticide effects—the number of eggs laid,
how many hatch, and at which age the young die. When
comparing figures on reproductive success the reader must
note exactly when counts of the young were made.

As the peregrine over most of its range selects cliffs or bluffs
for its eyries, a survey usually can be completed by checking
all rock faces. Thus the peregrine population can be studied
more thoroughly than other hawk species that nest in trees
or on the ground, species for which thousands of sites are
available. It is even harder to find all of the huge and bulky
eagles' nests. In areas where the peregrine nests in trees or
on the ground, locations of the eyries vary more from one year
to the next than with cliffs. Yet even these nesting territories
are traditionally held. In Finland local people had seen
peregrines nest at a particular bog for sixty years, and their

fathers had found them earlier.[24] Observations of these birds are less frequent than of cliff-nesters, and surveys more difficult to complete. But in Greenland ground-nesting falcons have never been found, either on the open tundra or at the tops of cliffs as in Alaska.[25]

The population surveys when closely examined seem confounded by an assortment of factors that will distort the results. But the many scattered surveys, often taken without knowledge of other efforts, confirm each other's general findings, and the work of different observers in the same area match up well. The surveys help us to know about the peregrine if we interpret them cautiously, remembering that the details of data are insignificant beside their overall tendencies. Here as always, we must be satisfied with an imperfect knowledge.

*   *   *   *

The days and nights of a thousand paired peregrines, the fogs over their cliffs, the chill, feathers of prey drifting from the rock and the tiercel scream, the terror, all fade into many-yeared, many-miled surveys. So too the hopes, the weariness of hundreds of watchers, and those meetings of human and falcon, they lie mute melting behind the rows of data. Science sifts a wealth out of the world so that we may take the remains and turn, twist, compare. It yields a handle for our understanding, that we may manipulate at will. Science takes the simple and plain upon which to build its order. Art also, in its own way, constructs order out of experience, and each person is somewhat scientist and artist. Our thoughts seek an order. We must listen to the scientist's voice to understand the loss of a species; also we must hear the poet.

Over Angmalortup Nunâ

Early in the morning Dave and I left our eyrie for a three-day exploration of Angmalortup Nunâ, the gently rolling land south and east of our camp. The weather was foul, with cold, clouds, and frequent rain. We saw not a single falcon,

---

24. Linkola and Suominen (1969).   25. Cade (1960).

primarily because we reached no sizable cliffs in all our hiking, except the one we had previously visited at Island Lake. This site we concluded was empty—Dave must have glimpsed a wanderer flushing from a temporary perch.

I remember looking down into the deep valley that marked the end of the gentle hills. A thousand feet below, a river ran between meadows actually green where the hills so sheltered them. Beyond the river, mountains rose with jagged, mist-covered cliffs. Other rivers cut their smaller valleys through the rock. It was a perfect falcon's kingdom, with vast views of ice cap, water, mountains, the southern exposure that caught the sunlight, the rivers and lakes that drew birds for prey.

Dave and I hastened east, eager to find eyries, and carelessly separated to walk above and below a forty-foot tall ledge. The rock didn't end past its first bend but ran ahead farther than I could see. We lost each other for over an hour. We had no meeting places, and I could only guess where Dave might be. I wandered for a time high above the silvery river, then sat upon a boulder.

I had walked far enough east to see a desolate mountain taller than all the rest. It had a cruel top, similar to those the children draw for their mountains, pointed, abrupt, a triangle of rock, the mountain and its shoulders blue-gray less from the distance than from the continual winter of thin air and altitude that kept the ground forever barren. I was wishing I might see a fox, or caribou, some animal nearby.

"Hey! Jim!"

Dave's voice. There he stood, two hundred feet west of me, wildly waving his red raincoat. I hurried toward him, heavy pack over my arm.

*   *   *   *

I bumped my knee against a rock early the second day, and soon it stiffened and was fragmenting my strides. I moved more slowly as the afternoon passed, and Dave had to wait for me. I remember we took a short rest by a stream where we drank water.

Two ptarmigan were flying from rock to rock and Dave
tried with rocks to kill one for supper. I lay on my back
and listened to the stones clatter, and touched the strength of
the ground. Not fully until now as I write have I felt the happi-
ness of that chill wind and even the grass stems brushing
close to my ear, rattling as they bent toward me. Does the
smile now come despite that stumbling leg, or did the pain itself
make the moment precious? What part did the cold and
wearying ground have in our awakening on the tundra that
summer? It may be they sharpened senses that otherwise
slumber.

*   *   *   *

Immense excitement held us, alone at the brink of
Angmalortup Nunâ. I felt it at odd moments.
   At the end of the long second day, exhausted and wet,
we set our tent once more, unrolled our sleeping bags, and rested
while our water then rice boiled. But no sooner did I lie down
and listen to wind quivering the tent, then a brightness through
the nylon revealed that the sun shone at last. Suddenly
restless, I popped out of the tent. Where did the stream lead,
down into the misty valley with its possible rock walls and
on through a new landscape we wouldn't cross?
   Ravens croaked and shouted not below but above from
the upper side of the nearby lake. Boulders littered the shore
beneath two rock faces, the larger thirty feet tall. The ravens
with their noise foolishly betrayed their great secret, their
eyrie. I turned from the valley and hobbled over the hummocks
in the lake marshes. One raven flew up and croaked its way
over the lake. Other croaks and screeches came from the cliff,
the clatter rising from two young ravens perched atop a
boulder. They stared at me.
   I decided I wanted to catch one. For no reason. The ravens
sat at the top of the talus. They didn't like my look. They
quieted. Ravens are distinguished by their large beaks. As
I approached I saw these beaks were particularly heavy and
strong. I took off my down parka, its feathers protected only

by nylon, but carried my gloves with me. These ravens seemed fully feathered, and might simply flap away—once fledged, wary ravens are almost impossible to catch.

I scrabbled up the talus slope, over the upper part with an eager, greedy grin because the ravens didn't fly. But I stopped three or four yards away from them. They stared at me directly or turned away to watch me nervously out of the corners of their eyes. One of them had some white feathers patched near its beak. Otherwise they were pure, shaggy black, identical to the adults except for an indecisiveness about their posture and eyes, as if they wanted to leave their boulder and didn't know how. I didn't like the look of them close up. Increasingly their beaks appeared powerful, well suited for all raven businesses including fights with intruders. I wore only thin leather gloves. I watched them nervously.

"Just wait," I called.

Instead one of the ravens spread its wings and flew. The other raven and I stared at each other. Yes, it flew also, but only a dozen feet. While I considered climbing farther, this nearer raven flew again. One peered at me from the cliff top, the other from a nearby ledge. We might have fumbled about the cliff the rest of the evening, silently tilting our heads right or left to spot new perches.

On a rock below, a ptarmigan sat. Probably it had been watching me. It held an erect pose, its tiny, seemingly mindless brown head alertly turned toward me. The bird did not move as I scrambled down the talus, not until I slid off the bottom-most rock into the splashy shallows of the lake.

The ptarmigan flew. "Croa-oa-oa-ooa-oak."

I returned to the tent, chilled and a little apologetic about about my sudden energy, after limping all through the day.

But Dave looked up at me with an impassive expression. "I burned the rice," he announced.

Flight

Late the next afternoon we lay on our long, dry cots. The sun shone. It warmed the tundra and released swarms of mosquitoes. "Jim," said Dave. I was dozing. "We should visit the eyrie."

The cold had prevented such a visit earlier, but on this mild afternoon the scrape could be exposed briefly to the air. Only Dave would actually climb to the ledge, for my inexperience with rock-climbing would slow us too much.

"I'm going to be roped in this time," Dave said. "I shouldn't risk my neck again on this rock."

Dave would climb with a rope end tied round his waist and leave it attached to the rock to assist our future climbs. He gave me a brief lesson in belaying. I would brace myself at the cliff foot and with the uncoiled rope beside me, play out its length as Dave left me. The pitons Dave carried were metal pegs with single holes at the upper ends. Once the piton was hammered into a rock crack, an aluminum oval carabiner could be attached through its hole; the rope glides through the carabiner, but if Dave should slip on the cliff and I held my portion of the rope securely, the rope looped through the carabiner would break his fall and save him. As he passed beyond the first piton his potential fall would lengthen until he placed another piton and the second carabiner would safeguard him. By good luck the peregrines at this first eyrie had chosen a ledge less than a third as far above the talus as the highest portions of the cliff top. They might as easily have chosen a ledge requiring two or even three two-hundred-foot ropes to reach.

We crossed the grass slopes and the talus. Where the rock began we stopped. Dave arranged the rope, tied himself in, and went up. Almost all the rope had left my hands, and still Dave climbed. I scrambled up onto a narrow grassy ledge and called, "Your rope's almost out!" When the rope end slid to my fingers and I tried to figure how to belay with no rope, balanced precariously and lacking space to sit, the tiercel came out from the rock, then the falcon.

They were beautiful. The falcon cackled most, but often the higher screams joined with the lower. They passed in circles and eights constantly overhead and all the small birds in the valley must have cowered close to the ground. Dave's

Bill Burnham descending the Ring Sø cliff toward the eyrie.

head reappeared, far above. "Four eggs," he shouted. Then he
took to the rope again and hurried down.

"Let's go!" he said, and without a pause he ran from
the cliff; I raced after him. At the grass we stopped and turned.
"You don't know how great it was being on that ledge."
Dave would say this several more times. One peregrine still flew
before the cliff.

Falcons in the wind have given us flight dreams. Could
I ever see enough of their powerful, twisting wings, of that
passionate aerial dance?

*　　*　　*　　*

Their wings are like our arms, but transformed.[26] Each
wing springs from the shoulder, and has two bends. The first
is close to the body on the rear edge, and the second, a prominent
turn on the fore edge that is equivalent to a mammal's wrist.
Because the bones as well as flesh and skin about them are
flattened, and because the feathers lie on one plane, the
wings are thin, flat, and have a top and bottom, unlike our
mammalian forearms. The wing's two surfaces divide the air.

The wings serve the major functions that are the two
parts of flight. The inner wing, to the wrist, primarily provides
a broad surface to lift the bird in the air. The wing ends
gain motion forward.

Lift of course is needed to carry the bird above the earth.
The aviator will rise when the air pushes much more strongly
against the under side of the wing than down upon the
upper side. This difference in air pressure is attained in two ways.
In flapping flight at each downbeat the wings compress the
air below them while releasing air above. At the same time
the bird is moving forward, air is rushing past its wings.
The wings are tilted with the fore-edge higher than the trailing
feathers, so that the air scoops underneath the wing, while
air is blocked from the upper surface by the same tilting.
Thus with flapping and forward motion suction is created above
the bird, and the air below pushes it up to offset the pull of
gravity.

Essential to flight is the maintenance of different air
pressures above and below. Any turbulence in the air flowing
past the bird will disrupt the lift of air. Thus the wings are
streamlined, and the feathers close fitting.

The tail also is essential in flight. Its feathers, spread widely,
provide additional surface area against which the compressed
lower air can push. By ruddering the tail—by bending and
tilting it—the bird steers its progress. And at the landing, the
tail as well as the wings are spread acting as brakes, they

26. For my discussion of flight in birds, I rely on Pettingill (1970)
and of flight in raptors and the peregrine specifically, on Grossman and
Hamlet (1964), and Brown and Amadon (1968).

slow the bird to an easy landing because the air pushes against the strong feathers.

While the wings of all flying birds share the same general specializations, the different species vary in the shape of wing and manner of flight. The flight patterns dominate the appearance of birds when airborne, which is when people usually see them, and determine when and how we shall find each species. The manner of flight suits the feeding habits, the survival, of each species.

The peregrine is formed for power and speed. Air resistance, for this falcon to meet in its movement, is minimized. Its plumage is sleek and close fitting; it doesn't ruffle the air. Its wings are narrow and relatively short, again creating little turbulence, while the pointed, spinning tips cut the air for a speed the wide, notched wing-ends of many hawks do not allow. In the stoop the compact, heavy body slits the air while slender wings are bent, half-folded to the body. Even the nostrils are modified within, into curves and rods to catch and slow the wind which otherwise would pass in the stoop too quickly for breathing.

The peregrine in its speed cannot soar as broader, slower hawks can. The short wings are efficient for stoops but provide small surface area for the air to push against and lift. In compensation the air must always come quickly from ahead to brace the tilted wings, the peregrine must fly quickly to meet a strong wind.

This ratio of wing area to body weight is important for soaring flight. Only light wide-winged hawks easily rise. The peregrine has a heavy wing loading. It cannot fly slowly. For the same reasons—its size and speed—it isn't agile like small falcons and little accipiters who twist after their prey through bushes. It directs a straight, sudden pursuit through the open.

Many tiercels are hardly more than half the weight of their falcons.[27] Thus the tiercel, while smaller winged than the falcon, still has a significantly lighter wing loading. She is swifter and stronger, he more agile.

27. Cade (1960).

Late that afternoon the falcon flew before the cliff. The tiercel joined her, and the two of them flickered in circles. He appeared more energetic, rising and stooping all while the falcon glided, roller-coaster flights and fancies with wings held straight until the upturn, and then he'd whip them, beat the air, and zip skywards once more. The falcon coasted. She made turns with corrections only from her wing ends, air flowing certain past her feathers, and her wings looked wider, heavier; I knew she was powerful. The tiercel exercised; she merely stretched.

But now, as we stood at the grasses' upper reach, both falcons had settled on the cliff. "Four eggs," Dave said. "Three stood on end and one was fallen over."

We still do not know how or why the number of eggs in a clutch varies among peregrines. In North America, clutches of three and four are normal, with five eggs occasionally found.[28] Several females have laid six eggs, while one falcon in Wisconsin laid seven eggs, and some weeks after these were taken from the eyrie, six more were discovered. As one moves from temperate North America north to Canada and Alaska, clutch sizes of four become less frequent, so that the average number of eggs per eyrie in Alaska is significantly smaller than the average for southern California or the eastern United States before the pesticides were used. This variation is not simply related to a north-south gradient, for eyries from northern Mexico again hold fewer eggs on the average than in more temperate regions.

Two and three eggs are the normal for Australia. Clutches of one and two have often been observed in North America, but one never knows whether the count represents the total clutch size for that female, because more eggs may be laid after the count has been taken, or some eggs may already have disappeared, through one mishap or another.

For this reason also, unless counts are taken several times, the egg data leave many uncertainties about mortality in the eyrie. But each climb to the eyrie risks the success of that

---

28. Hickey and Anderson (1969) review the literature on peregrine clutch size.

breeding pair. One observer could assign as a cause of mortality the sudden flushing of the incubating falcon, for several times he had seen an egg knocked out of a scrape by a falcon during her hasty escape.[29] After reading this account, we always approached an eyrie noisily.

Formerly, many persons collected birds' eggs as a hobby. They were called oologists, because they were interested in all sorts of information related to eggs or clutch size. Some oologists took pride in the quality of their work, keeping careful records of all egg sets they took, and additional notes on the distribution and behavior of the birds they pursued. But for some it was a fanatical desire, and the nests of favored species like the peregrine were robbed far too often, without regard to the welfare of the species. By the 1940s the hobby was declining in popularity; eggs were disturbed less often.[30] Most oologists alive today are aging retired men with rich memories. Their collections still yield scientific information. Most measurements of eggshell thickness for prewar years have been taken from oologists' eggs.[31]

The variation in egg laying is yet another example of the plasticity of the species as it has adjusted to the scattered continents and islands.[32] A study of the peregrine's egg laying across the world may reveal subtle ways that environments alter falcons. The thorough understanding of the intricacies, the million-faceted dynamics that relate clutch size to climate or landscape, or perhaps to some other characteristic of the peregrine that itself reflects the environment, directly as clutch size may not, this understanding can tell us of more than of the peregrine. For the widespread, many-formed species bears testimony about evolution in general that the highly specialized inflexible species cannot give us. Most species have limited ranges; they have adapted to very particular circumstances. Their clutch sizes cannot be compared across the extremes of landscape or climate. The peregrine, that held

29. Cade (1960).
30. Hickey (1942); Herbert and Herbert (1965).
31. Hickey, personal communication.
32. See Lack (1947–1948) for a general discussion of clutch size in birds.

The scrape and four peregrine eggs at First Eyrie
on Dave's first climb in 1972.

within the limits of reproductive isolation as it spread through
the world, allows these comparisons. It provides as unique
an opportunity for scientific study as that famous cluster of finch
species that Darwin found long ago on the Galapagos Islands.
How has the varied peregrine remained a single species?
Clutch size is one way that it has flexibly tuned to its dissimilar
environments.

Our research had mixed goals. We were applying the
knowledge and methods of study for raptor populations and
behavior, and for pesticide effects to the problem of saving
the peregrine in North America. The new information
we sought on the breeding falcons would serve a specific
purpose. Yet also we attempted as thorough an understanding
of the peregrine as possible, attempted it on faith, perhaps
that knowledge is desirable in itself, or perhaps that knowledge,
even of clutch size, that will clarify in its small way our view
of species change and development, will one day serve a
specific or practical need. And also, Dave repeated happily,
"Four eggs; behind the grasses."

Part III.

Peregrine Days
and Nights

During the next five days we watched the peregrines.
Some of the vague wonder turned to familiar affection. Not only
did we see them at their most active moments—for from
our tent those chill early days we never could find them unless
they called and flew—but we slowly learned how they spent
all their hours. Humans seldom understand how a day passes
for wild bird or mammal, because we're too impatient
to sit quietly, and what time means for a different mind somehow eludes our imagination. How long an hour must be
for creatures unburdened by possessions, a hundred tasks,
or dreams.

The morning after our return (it was July 1), Dave walked
west and then stealthily up the grass and talus. Here we could
walk higher up the ridge without aid of ropes and actually
sit almost on a level with the eyrie only one hundred yards
away. By passing west out of his way Dave hoped the
falcons would not object to his presence when he crept along
the cliff bottom. From this high position we would be able
to watch the falcons more easily than before. After three hours
had passed, I too hiked west and then carefully up and back
toward the eyrie awaiting the tiercel screams and alarm,
but successful I reached Dave's seat.

He whispered, "The tiercel's perched and watching us.
Look in the scope." The tiercel filled most of the scope's field
of view, his breast lined against the dark rock. He remained
motionless, except for his head which occasionally he turned. He
must have noticed my approach.

"'I've seen both falcons, and the tiercel once left to hunt.
This is a good place."

"Will you come in three hours?"

"Yes," Dave answered. "Don't let him slip away without
your noticing." Dave left.

We marked the times for all entries in our yellow notebooks. We hoped that after several weeks' watching we could
distinguish different sorts of activity at different times of day.

A half hour after Dave left, the tiercel flew up in high circles until I lost him in the sky. Two minutes later at 11:30 A.M. he passed low before the cliff, disappeared around a jutting of the rock, to reappear some seconds later and alight just under the cliff top by a mute spot. This day I could watch the tiercel's subtle movements. Perhaps he would react to activity of other birds, for wasn't that his reason in choosing lofty perches? Five ravens flew high over the ridgetop, and later another one croaked. Passerines flew about the cliff, although neither by the eyrie nor the tiercel. The tiercel, ever alert, and watching from side to side, gave no sign he noticed these motions. At 11:45 he again soared in high circles, particularly facing into the southeast wind. After a minute or two he gradually without increasing his speed headed away, first southeast then more and more south.

At noon I heard his call from the southwest. I caught sight of him close to the ledge as he swooped and the falcon came out from the scrape. The two flew up nearly straight thirty or forty feet until she overtook him and seized something from his talons with her beak, then dropped quickly to the cliff. For five minutes the male alone continued calling and circling. Suddenly he zipped around the corner of the cliff just beyond the eyrie. Out the falcon flew, loud with her deeper voice, to swoop once or twice then land on the eyrie ledge, facing in, still cackling, and crouch for five minutes. Did my presence annoy her?—this was the first chance she had had to notice me. I watched her through the scope. She looked one way, another, all directions as if she covered the whole tundra with her cries. For me, only one sharp glance when I shifted my position. She moved slightly in from the ledge's brink, cackled once more. Then she waddled out of sight beyond grasses, presumably to sit at the scrape.

To my amazement the other peregrine flew out from the eyrie, higher voiced. He circled a time or two and returned to his same perch. It is difficult to watch both peregrines at once. When had the tiercel entered the eyrie? Did he actually incubate the eggs or merely stand over them?

At 12:25 a raven croaked—three passed high, to the east,

crossing the ridge. The tiercel soared before the cliff until they disappeared, then passed once over me and returned to his perch. Five minutes later he flew quickly south; then I saw him circling low below me over the talus slope and lower ground; he gradually gained altitude and silently passed over the ridge to the west. I saw him once more during that first watch from the lookout. He approached calling from the west end of the ridge, passed over the cliff top level, called, "kaaa kaaa kaaaa," turned, and glided back along the ridge, passing high over my head and out of sight, west.

The ravens had already fledged and left their cliffs, traveling in families. Did one group scour the hills for food or to spy activity on the tundra, passing the ridge frequently, or did several families wander more widely?

It required twenty minutes to climb from the tent to the lookout. We relieved each other several times a day for two-, three-, or four-hour watches, and thus each of us actually spent the week alone. These days had relatively mild weather. By midmorning the mosquitoes swarmed out of their secret places and hunted us until the chill returned toward late evening. Even in the sun we exposed no skin, and topped our costumes with head nets.

From the lookout the eyrie ledge lay spread its entire length, grass covered and sometimes two yards wide. But these grasses tallest at the far end entirely hid the scrape and the incubating falcon. By the scrape, a rock lichened gray and orange formed the ledge's brink. When either adult perched briefly it was on this rock. But for most of the time the ledge seemed empty. If the tiercel hadn't shifted away from the cliff area he perched elsewhere among the crags. He faced west almost always. We thought he might be facing the wind, but one day the wind shifted, without affecting his stance; probably he wanted to watch us until he became accustomed to our presence on the lookout.

The falcon incubated the eggs so constantly that we seldom saw her. The tiercel brought her food. Dave saw several of the food exchanges similar to the one noted on my first watch, when the falcons would meet in the air. Only twice the female turned upside down at the last instant before they touched so that she took the prey with her talons rather than her beak.

I particularly remember one aerial exchange. At the climax, with cries fiercest and shrillest, the pair rose before the sun that blinded out their meeting. The falcon dropped to land at the cliff top, and it was the tiercel who perched on the eyrie ledge, walked to the scrape, and disappeared. The falcon remained on her rock, evidently eating. One white feather floated off. She bent over her feet, back toward me. Her meal lasted several minutes. At last she returned to the eyrie ledge. The tiercel didn't rush into the wide air—apparently he took his turn on the eggs—and after fifteen minutes the falcon glided in a long, direct curve to the ground near the stream, where she braked to follow the ground then wheel abruptly, and land. Then up again, the air filled her wings, and down, up once more and down. She beat her wings once and glided twenty yards to alight again, but soon slid low all down the stream past the marsh, past the tent and our dishwashing places. I saw her back as she rose and searched the lower talus; then she ascended spinning curves to choose a new cliff perch. I didn't know whether she seriously hunted, unsatisfied by the tiercel's catch, or whether she stretched restlessly after her confinement on the eggs.

The tiercel incubated at several other times, occupying the scrape for seven out of the first forty hours we watched.[1] Once after the adults switched places I heard an unfamiliar call. The falcon had soared before the cliff and landed on the ledge. She watched small birds moving before the cliff; she walked to the scrape. The falcon's feet are not suited to walking as are those of many birds like ravens or ptarmigan— the falcon had an awkward shuffle as she crossed the ledge, as if she walked on her wrists, the tarsi. As soon as she disappeared I heard a high "chip-chippering" lasting several seconds, either from one adult or both, and an adult flew out and swooped round the cliff.

---

1. See Nelson (1970) for a discussion of sexual roles in incubation for the peregrine.

We never learned what signaled the times when one adult would replace the other on the scrape. The falcon seemed strongly attached to the scrape and eggs. But perhaps the male disliked sitting for long. For once as the falcon sunned herself on the extreme east end of the ledge—she sat atop the round boulder half an hour—a deep "hin-chuck, hin-chuck, hin-chuck" came from the eyrie. She looked that way, listened to the sound without responding until the tiercel rushed out of the eyrie "hin-chucking" and departed down the east along the cliff. Only then did she return to the scrape.

Distinguishing one adult from the other imperceptibly became easier. The tiercel's appearance on the cliff gradually impressed me so that if the falcon held guard instead, even on a far pinnacle, somehow I'd sense the difference.

Beyond taking his turn at the scrape the tiercel had two tasks, to secure food and to guard the cliff against intruders. He brought food for the falcon at several-hour intervals, small birds he had caught somewhere on the tundra. These hunts did not occupy all his time; after an hour at his perch he might disappear for a half hour, or an hour or even two. We could not know when he caught himself a meal, and sometimes he may have returned without prey because he had already eaten his catch. Or else he may simply have exercised over miles of tundra or down by the shore of the long lake.

His other task required him only to remain alert on the cliff. I think he kept watch for interest's sake as well as to spy out enemies, as when he looked down at the fox barking far below the cliff, or where passerines called from the bushes. He preened also, briefly or for long thorough periods. I never saw him with his eyes closed and always if he remained motionless for a moment soon his head would turn, he'd be gazing far off at the hills or even the sky. At intervals he'd call, "kaaa kaaa kaaaa." Occasionally Dave or I would be moving, but often nothing at all would happen to agitate him. When he shifted perches he'd almost always call, breaking the two-hour silence, and then his voice might sound off and on for forty minutes.

Probably no amount of watching from the cliff side can reveal that mystery beyond what the tiercel does, how he senses the time pass. What unraveling behind his eyes do the hours bring? The human waiting by the cliff also, strangely seated all the afternoon alert but unoccupied unless the peregrine moves, he busies his mind with embroidering fanciful peregrine thoughts because he has a mind that must be busied. The tiercel himself, intelligent but only as a bird, hasn't this problem, and when his muscles ache he flies. But the falcon undoubtedly has active sensations, that we guess are like stirrings of dim, half-created emotions, and our guesses feed happy wonderings as we sit on the lookout, or the weird loon laughs from the long lake and we feel too, some writhing of pleasure half-formed that we don't understand.

Every perch on the cliff has its particular qualities, and each wind touches uniquely, although we humans hardly notice the differences. The peregrine may have awarenesses we lack, undisturbed by a mind that ever abstracts, recreates, and fabricates. His repose, it is a solemnity, may adjoin the tangible and unobtrusive more closely than we ever can. We dream on the lookout. Does the tiercel constantly feel the rock instead?

I called the falcon repose a solemnity. Is that the proper word for a hawk clutching stone with its rough talons? Solemnity describes the falcon less than the human watching. Feelings hang between human and falcon on the cliff. That the tiercel, hidden because he is tiny, will guard the cliff through the days and let no creature pass unnoticed, that moves me, and each time he warns of his presence—the noiseless wings or his voice even in the dim-lighted night—he hastens my mind; and I quicken also as I write, but who that reads about him and is likewise alerted will not attribute his awe and wonder to the tiercel and not to his own spirit? In this sense solemnity belongs to the peregrine.

When the falcon perched on the cliff, she did not call. But she too would fly before the rock, though her passages seemed more purposeful, direct or somehow heavy, and frequently she would slip into the valley and scour the slopes for prey.

She never left the vicinity of the cliff. If we lost sight of her in flight, always she would reappear shortly. Her favorite perch was the eyrie ledge itself.

The sun shone the day of our first lookout watches. But usually the sky had a uniform grayness, and it drizzled several nights and fragments of mornings. The tiercel liked best to fly with the sun and kept more to the cliff on the cloudy days. We couldn't calculate exactly how long he would leave the valley, for occasionally he'd vanish—we didn't watch carefully enough—to the wide tundra or possibly only to another perch. When both falcons flew at once we'd usually lose the location of one as we watched the other. I preferred staring at the eyrie in these situations, for it was certain that one adult would come.

One afternoon I almost saw the tiercel catch his meal. Once more he had flown up along the cliff top. Where the west slabs protruded, he ducked suddenly out of sight, then after some moments he flew back to perch not far from the high mutes. He faced me but bent toward his feet showing the dark of head and neck. With jerks of his head, he tossed feathers to the air—peregrines pluck their prey before eating. Near the end he turned around—did he turn the body also? Then he had finished, upright watching the tundra only fourteen minutes after his departure hungry from the perch.

The rainy days sent long trails of dark down the cliff, water trickling, and in spots drops broke and fell, catching whiteness of clouds. Water will destroy life in the eggs. One day strong winds came, and the heaviest drizzle we had seen in Greenland. Water in driblets rolled into the grass at the eyrie. We watched intently, but the falcon seemed undisturbed.

Two afternoons later, Dave climbed up to join me on the lookout. "It's warm again," he said.

The tiercel had just finished the meal and shifted from his perch so that I didn't know his position. I told Dave what I had seen.

"I think I should check the scrape again," Dave said. "This time you watch the peregrines from the lookout and see what they do."

Dave left me to cross along the talus tops.

The tiercel left a perch above the eyrie, circled twice with very soft calls, landed. He circled once more. As Dave reached the lower rope end the tiercel screamed. The falcon came out to the ledge brink. As Dave reached the ledge itself, both birds were in the air weaving circles over his head, the loud cackles, and once more the falcon landed on her round rock east of the eyrie. She watched Dave approach, extended her wings, flew and round round, "kak-kak-kak-kak," stoop, rise, stoop, up into the sky and down the tiercel stoops, all while Dave steps to the eyrie, I watch, the cliff echoes. Then Dave leaves. The falcon alights first, on the round rock. She watches him, calls until he leaves the rope, when the tiercel lands. Then she walks forward, stops, looks again, walks, hops to the scrape. There she hesitates; she vanishes behind the grass.

At supper Dave told me the four eggs remained. The dripping water fell on the outside of the scrape where the grass held it. Part of a small wet wing lay there, feathers of the brown longspur or else of redpoll.

Each time I enjoyed the moment or two as Dave and I switched at the lookout. Then we'd tell the news of our watch, what had happened on the cliff, happened invisibly for the one of us at the tent.

On Dave's very first lookout watch he saw an event which I would never see. A haggard peregrine landed on the ledge about fifty feet from the eyrie. Not the tiercel, for the tiercel screamed and dove on the stranger, pushing it off the ledge. Not the falcon, for she rushed out of the eyrie immediately afterward. And the tiercel pursued the intruder quickly toward the long lake, the foremost falcon abruptly sliding to dodge attacks, or twisting upside down to meet the talons above with its own talons. The falcon followed these two for half a mile then glided back to perch above the eyrie. But the tiercel raced a mile west before he returned, and he swept five circles in front of his mate and the tundra before alighting at the cliff's highest point.

Just as we wished to observe the falcons during different parts of the day, we also wished to learn what they did in bad weather. Yet with the worst of chills and rains we naturally found the lookout uncomfortable, so that we each discovered tasks about the tent requiring our attention until conditions improved. On the stormiest day we hardly left the tent at all, but instead shivered in our sleeping bags and read about peregrines in books we had brought from the United States. We only heard their voices through the storm. The human physique is not all that restricts people's movement in the Greenland climate. Our minds are bound to considering how much warmer and drier, more comfortable, we might be.

I wondered what Dave and I might do additionally to learn more in our study. We wished particularly to establish in what ways these falcons were adjusted to arctic conditions, thus differing from peregrines in temperate regions. Of course the endless daylight was remarkable. Several times we had discussed attempting an all-night watch. This effort would require long waits through the cold. Patience.

Tundrius *South*

In May, when we had prepared for our trip, I had realized I would enjoy banding various Greenland birds; for this reason we had obtained the report forms and sets of each sized band from the Danish Zoological Museum in Copenhagen.

In the last fifty years scientists and bird watchers have banded birds in many parts of the world. The birds both young and adult are captured by a great many methods but quickly released unharmed. During the short period of captivity the metal circlet is fastened around the leg. The bander records the identification number on the band, the species of bird, location, data, circumstances of the capture, and other details such as sex or condition of the feathers. If a banded bird is captured, all this same information should be recorded and mailed to the central record-keeping organization, which is also indicated on the band. As birds are recaptured, we have two sets of information about each individual, and as these data pairs accumulate for a particular species we learn where and when the species travels, how quickly the bird travels (when a bird is soon recaptured in migration), and how long the bird lives. Governments restrict who can band, so that correct data are carefully collected and the birds are carefully handled without causing injury or death. Especially the littlest birds panic when caught and may suffer shock and die.

Because so few people live in the Arctic, we know little about the migrations of birds there. More work has been completed in Greenland than in any other arctic area because of a unique arrangement between Danish scientists, the local governments, and the Greendlandic people. Administrators in the various districts of Greenland pick skilled and interested Greenlanders to perform the banding. A set sum of money is paid for banding each species—the exact amount depends on the size and difficulty of capture for the species. The Ministry for Greenland pays another reward for each band rediscovered. Special expeditions from Denmark also band, as well as foreign researchers working with the birds.[2]

The Danish government has justified financing the reward system for banding because many of Greenland's birds have significant economic importance for the people. The sea birds gather in colonies to nest and form great flocks in the winter. The Greenlanders who kill these birds supply feathers for down clothing, mattresses, and pillows and also eat the eggs and meat. About 1,200 tons of meat annually have been obtained in recent years, a significant amount for the population of 40,000.[3] Some species like the thick-billed murre, the puffin, and the common eider duck have been exploited too heavily.[4] Through banding we now know where these species migrate and winter, thus revealing where and to what extent their flocks are vulnerable to hunting. Equally important, most banding recoveries in Greenland are of birds shot. The percentage of birds that die by hunting can be calculated from the total number of birds shot and the total number banded. If the total number of birds banded is large, then

2. Mattox (1970b).
3. Salomonsen (1966) cited in Mattox (1970b).
4. Salomonsen (1970).

the percentage figure will help us decide whether hunting endangers the species in Greenland—we worry when the percentage is high. Banding has helped the local and Greenland governments to decide what laws are needed for the protection of birds.[5]

The small birds that nest on the tundra do not provide food for the inhabitants. As they are not shot and the bodies fall where humans rarely walk, few recoveries are made. However, they all migrate out of Greenland, spending most of each year, thus most of their lives, in regions south.[6] Migrants of the same species leave other parts of the Arctic for the winter. Probably the Greenland longspurs and redpolls and other birds do not widely wander wherever their particular species goes, but journey primarily to specific areas.

Together they form an important part of the tundra ecosystem, and through them what happens in those warmer ranges affects even remotest Greenland. Sadly we had a particular reason for banding these birds, for they represented one means by which the tundra falcons might be exposed to pesticides. These species comprise most of the peregrine's diet. Pesticides may be used in places where many of them winter, concentrating in their fatty tissues, eventually to reach the peregrines. In order to prove this danger existed, it was necessary to collect and chemically analyze specimens of these species. Only banding could tell us where they became contaminated, if they were contaminated, and for this understanding a great many of the small birds would need to be recovered. Thus our banding would only help in a long-range effort by many people. We need to know these details about the Arctic, for the tundra with few varieties of plants and animals can easily be damaged by human activities.

We discovered that watching or searching for peregrines took up so much of our time that we had little leisure for banding. For capturing the birds we had brought with us what are called mist nets, made of many black threads very fine but strong enough that a struggling bird can't break them. These

---

5. Mattox (1970b). 6. Salomonsen (1950–1951).

threads can hardly be seen against shrubs or grasses, and birds fly into them, becoming entangled immediately in the loosely stretched mesh. The longer the victim struggles, the more hopelessly bound it becomes. Anyone who sets these nets must check them often or the birds become so tied that they cannot be freed.

One morning while Dave sat on the lookout, I decided to set up a net below our tent. I planned to put it deep in the valley by the stream. I would have almost two hours to watch it before relieving Dave.

I remember sitting and unraveling one end of one net, eight feet tall, and cutting notches for each of its loops in a bamboo pole we had brought from the air base. I was not concerned that the netting constantly tangled my fingers. At last the loops were tied in place. Then my real problems began. The net was very long. I was dealing alone with fourteen feet by eight feet of clinging threads, while all around me small bushes stretched their gnarled, twiggy arms. My net captured many of them. I paced back and forth with busy fingers. Finally, with both ends attached to their poles, I had to raise the net into an upright position. I had ropes now on each pole, that I would easily tie to rocks. So I thought. But as I could only tie one pole up at a time, the first pole always fell over when I struggled with the second or with grasping bushes. In the middle of this impatient task Dave appeared, down from his watch.

"Hurry up!" he said, "you need to get up to the lookout before the tiercel returns."

"Not now!" And then Dave noticed one pole leaning at a mad angle toward the hillside, the other more or less horizontal, the net drooping between. He laughed.

Together we hastily set the net up. The tiercel's cries dropped from somewhere on the cliff as we worked—we missed that return. Rather than see all my trouble wasted, I left the net up and did not go to the lookout but sat instead by a rock on the level area above the tent, where I might see the peregrines with difficulty. Dave would check the net periodically.

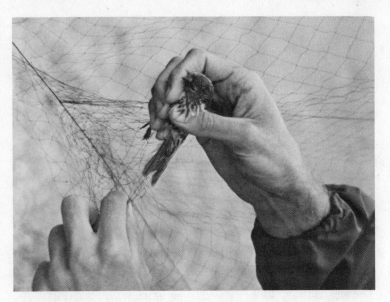

Jim removes redpoll from mist net for banding.

After an hour Dave came trotting, "You caught one. One of those with the red on top of the head. I saw it fly in . . ." Redpoll! We ran down to the net. The bird was a thready bundle dangling close to the ground. Well tangled already, and I made matters worse by trying first to get it out the wrong way. It fluttered as I held it, retangling, and pushed its foot out against the air. I had to enclose it with my fingers so that it couldn't move at all, a tiniest weight hardly felt in my hands so that I might have squeezed it too hard as I worked against the threads. Dave helped me, also, but whichever way we pulled, the threads tightened. At the worst times the bander must cut his net. I suspected this wasn't one of those times but I felt the responsibility of seizing a wild bird against its will and severed the last knots.

Its bib black, and red-capped, it looked even smaller than when flying free. Five inches from beak to tail tip. It had black-brown streaks all over its body, lacking the rosy wash over breast of the male—probably a female. Band number 150 001. Even the smallest sized band hung loosely on its leg. Its heart vibrated under the feathers. I admit I had wanted to band so that I might touch a living, wild creature. I held it high, where the wind brushed its feathers and my skin, and I opened my fingers. Free, it flew right first, toward the tent, and then up the hill. There other redpolls were chuttering.

Where did this bird winter, or where did our only other captive of the summer go, the sparrowlike female longspur, 150 002? Do they still live? To make his effort worthwhile, the mist-netter should have four or five nets up at once, for a single net covers very little flight space. One person should not attempt to set up nets alone.

Greenland peregrines can receive doses of pesticides in several ways other than eating contaminated prey. Wind and water have spread small amounts of DDE even into the Arctic, hundreds of miles from the nearest intentional application of the chemicals.[7] But much more critically, the peregrine like its prey leaves Greenland for most of the year to inhabit regions where human beings, agricultural development, and thus pesticides, are prevalent. The tundrius subspecies scatters widely in autumn. We planned to band as many eyasses as possible, that with luck (only three out of the thirty-five previously banded in Greenland were ever recovered[8]) we might learn more of the Greenland peregrine's movements.

Migration is an important adaptation for many birds whose breeding range is transformed by harsh weather and lack of food during winters. As one would expect with a bird inhabiting so many widely differing climates, the peregrine's migratory behavior varies widely between subspecies. While most peregrines may wander in winter, extensive migrations out of the breeding areas are restricted to the northern races. These also vary in the distances they travel. The anatum peregrines of eastern United States once remained at their eyries even along the Hudson but breeders farther north moved anywhere from several hundred to two thousand miles. The tundra races of the peregrine migrate farther than any other bird of prey. Those in Eurasia even reach southern Africa.[9]

---

7. Risebrough et al. (1968); Lincer, Cade, and Devine (1970).
8. Mattox (1970b).
9. Hickey and Anderson (1969).

*   *   *   *

Many little birds must drown in the ocean. They take, or
the wind takes, wrong directions so that they will never find
resting spots. On ships some alight exhausted. They perch
on the dead structure day after day. The tireless peregrine
appears. Some sailors have seen him on several voyages. He
hunts the small fugitives. When they are gone, he leaves.
Perhaps land is still hundreds of miles away.[10]

*   *   *   *

In Greenland in August when the chill nights return and
lengthen, the eyasses shake their wings and fly. They are no
longer white. They have a fuzzy dark and white appearance. As
the down gradually drifts away, their backs become brown
and their bellies and chests are heavily streaked, unlike the
adults. About the head buffy feathers grow, not the adult white
of throat and cheeks.

When the nestlings are oldest they flap their wings
and exercise. But the first flight is a clumsy, downward drop
through the air. For some weeks the young fly as if they were
practicing, and chase each other; and stoop, at each other or
their parents; the parents stoop at them and scream. The
adults' anger seems to grow, and perhaps they are restless and
ever more seeking solitude. The branchers, the eyasses, cry and
beg, and hunt stones or bushes, dash after prey.[11]

Several Danes told Mattox that the whole family leaves
the eyrie area two weeks after fledging. Soon the branched
peregrines kill their own food. The young falcons may
remain together for a time and run their awkward hunts
in the same proximity, but separately. It is late August. The
adults have left them.[12]

The world is narrowest at the poles. Southward the lands
and seas widen. The falcons scatter among the hordes of
other migrants.[13] How rare they seem. Watchers in the crowded

---

10. See Merriam (1889) and Voous (1961).
11. Cade (1960).
12. Salomonsen (1950–1951).
13. The following paragraphs on migration are based on conversations with D. D. Berger and F. P. Ward, and on Ward and Berry (1972).

States don't know where they will appear, except that even falcons prefer to fly along land where they may stop at intervals and hunt. And they prefer a favoring wind. When the breezes come from the south the peregrines delay. But on northwest- or northeast-winded days the falcons drift. Until they are blown to a shoreline. Here they fight the wind to pass down the coast. Here only they are concentrated, on days when the wind pushes them against the water.

Various people band hawks on the shorelines—in Maryland, on the barrier islands of Texas, at Duluth on Lake Superior, or the edges of Lake Michigan. The number of peregrines observed at a location provide a very rough estimate of population status when compared with totals for other years. However, weather can greatly influence the data. Some years the winds do not push the migrants against the shoreline, and the peregrines pass unsighted inland. Thus conclusions must be based on data averaged over many years, at places where the tradition of watching has been long maintained. Daniel Berger at Cedar Grove, Wisconsin, has calculated five-year averages for migrating peregrines, averaged to offset the fluctuations because of weather. Fewer peregrines appear now than in the 1940s, but migrants have come in steady numbers in recent years.

The peregrines skirting the Great Lakes continue to the Gulf Coast and on through Mexico. We do not know to what local breeding population these migrant peregrines belong— presumably they come from the central Arctic. Falcons at Assateague Island off Maryland journey from the eastern Arctic. Two peregrines banded there were later shot in Egedesminde and Umanak districts in Greenland. Greenland-banded peregrines have been retaken in Montreal and Cuba.[14] Our falcons must pass down the east coast of North America. Peregrines are sighted in numbers at Dry Tortugas, a last stop in North America before the Caribbean Islands.[15]

At Assateague most peregrines are young of the season. The ratio of these passage birds to adults remains eight to one.

---

14. Hickey (1969).
15. Ward, personal communication.

Of course there are not eight young fledged per adult. We don't know why so few adults appear—perhaps they fly over the open water—or why almost none of these are tiercels. For whatever reasons it is eight to one, the ratio is a sensitive indicator of peregrine reproductive success. If it dropped, down to four to one or two to one, we'd have warning that the eyries were failing. Cedar Grove also has more immatures than adults, and the tiercel is rarely discovered. The passage peregrines, only four months old, already contain residues of DDT, DDE, dieldrin, and the PCBs.[16]

Occasionally migrants are noted away from the favored coasts. So seldom that there is no place or time with likelihood of meeting. The lightest weighted of transmitter devices, that send electronic beeps that can be caught on receivers mounted in car or plane, have been set on peregrines. Early tracking attempts were frustrated by the preening behavior of the falcon, who eventually discovered the device delicately attached among her feathers and ripped it off. While an airplane waited, bad weather held a marked peregrine from Assateague almost stationary until the bird found the device and removed it. A Wisconsin peregrine was followed only into Illinois. It was moving steadily south, but in no hurry at a twenty-mile-an-hour pace. More recently, a peregrine was successfully accompanied all the way from Wisconsin to Mexico.[17]

Before the pesticides the anatum peregrines took their own short migrations, wandering vaguely southward in winter, where prey was more common. These larger, darker falcons might appear in the coastal flight lanes, perhaps late in November. Already the tundrius birds would have departed. At Cedar Grove the tundra migrants go through in late September and the beginning of October. At Assateague the migration extends slightly later.

We know very little about these peregrines in winter.

---

16. Risebrough, Florant, and Berger (1970).
17. Ward and Berger, personal communications; Cochran (1975). Radio telemetry techniques are rapidly being refined. Transmitters have become increasingly useful in falcon research.

Winter banding returns occur from Key West, Florida, to the Argentine, scattered through the West Indies—Cuba, Trinidad, the Dominican Republic—and through Central and South America. This is a vast range, and we do not know their favorite places, or how much they move from landscape to landscape. For many years peregrines were observed in Rio de Janeiro; in 1960 one regularly fed at dusk on bats emerging from their roost.[18]

The peregrines return north through the States in March, April, and May. Fewer birds appear in this flight than in the fall passage. Perhaps the migration routes or different effects of weather partially explain this. But primarily, simply, not as many return to the Arctic as departed in the autumn. Most of the young falcons die.

The wandering peregrines die at scattered places and times. Causes of death are seldom observed, and the age or percentage thus dying of the whole population cannot be guessed. Banding provides a means for mortality studies, because many of the birds found dead were nestlings when banded. The lengths of their lives can easily be calculated.

James Enderson has prepared a life table for the peregrine.[19] His data may be biased in several ways. The oldest peregrines may lose their bands before they die and are discovered, causing the life span of the peregrine to be underestimated. In addition, life table calculations must assume that the proportion of bodies recovered to all individuals of a species dying is constant at all ages. Yet many reports were of falcons shot, especially immatures. Immatures may be more easily shot than adults and these kills more frequently picked up by the gunmen.

Forty out of Enderson's sample of fifty-seven recovered peregrines died in their first year. Accordingly Enderson estimated an immature mortality of 70 percent. Shooting might inflate this grisly percentage; but the inexperienced passage birds must blunder down the long coasts and about the tropics without knowing how to hunt well, and starvation must cause many deaths.

---

18. Sick (1961).   19. Enderson (1969).

Thus only a few of the immatures survive to nest; these breeding adults are preciously bought, and precious for the species's continuance. Enderson calculates that the frequency of death does not vary according to age for the adults. Of those alive in any one year, a quarter will die. Many adults live three and four years, while others survive fifteen years or more.

The peregrines that do survive the winter reach Greenland in May, usually late in the month, but in some cases even at the end of April.[20] Then the tundra still is cold, with shifting snows and ice on the cliffs. The passerines are also arriving from their winter places, prey for the falcons. Dave and I had missed those early weeks when the peregrines resettle.

It is cold enough in May that few people have watched the arctic courtships. In regions south the earliest attentions and wooing of the falcon took place a month or more before egg laying, in Massachusetts,[21] and farther south, in California, pair behavior began two to three months before incubation. The arctic pairs haven't this much time; all their courtship at the cliffs sometimes lasts for as little as a week until the falcon lays her first egg.[22]

Those were odd spring days at the cliffs in the States. The tiercel bowed and scraped before the falcon, or wailed enticingly from various ledges where she might place her scrape. The falcon furtive squeezed into the rock cracks and crannies, testing the ground. The tiercel flight was gaudy and magnificent—he was ecstatic then.[23] So I have read. I haven't seen it.

Two peregrines do not come together easily to raise their young. They are fiercely lone hunters, and the transformation to a cooperative pair is intricate and fragile. Where the tiercel will relinquish his own caught prey without reluctance. Where day after day the falcon remains at the scrape; her restlessness must be quelled, she must wait. Courtship is a gradual process where not only must the falcon be enticed and excited, but the tiercel's tolerances and passions must be born, rise, and soar. The bond must be well made, for the two

20. Salomonsen (1950–1951).
21. Hagar, in Bent (1938).
22. Cade (1960).
23. Hagar, in Bent (1938).

will have to cooperate for many weeks, until the young are feathered and hunting.

In Alaska arctic peregrines occupy the same cliffs year upon year, as the species does in temperate regions.[24] Maybe this occurs because falcon pairs simply occupy all the best cliffs of a region. But in parts of North America excellent cliffs have not been used, although they appear eminently suitable.[25] Perhaps the surrounding landscape is poor for peregrines, whether too populated by people, or dry, or cold, prey poor. Thus certain Greenland cliffs were empty, probably as a result of the barren tundra.

Some people talk of traditions at peregrine cliffs, a tenancy passed from falcon to falcon. The pair returns to the same cliff each spring. When one dies, the survivor finds a mate and when it dies, its mate gains a mate, and on, the tradition holds.[26] Or perhaps peregrines may look at a cliff and see signs almost intangible that peregrines have lived there before.[27] This would explain how the same cliffs, often the same ledges, were reoccupied in southern Britain when falcons no longer were persecuted after World War II.[28]

Dave and I below the cliff were witnessing very few weeks out of the peregrine's year. But other studies in the Arctic provide a timetable for the species's northern breeding cycle. With arrival in late May the eggs would be laid in the first half of June. The eggs would hatch in the first half of July. Fledging would occur in August. Then the branched peregrines must quickly learn to hunt before autumn, September, when the small birds leave the island and the hunters must migrate.[29]

The breeding season lasts perhaps ninety-five days. Since that is almost as long as the period during which Greenland is habitable for peregrines, no extra time remains for delays or renesting.[30]

Peregrines seldom nest during their first year. The few

24. Cade (1960).   26. Cade (1960).
25. Bond (1946).   27. Hickey (1969).
28. Ratcliffe (1969).
29. Salomonsen (1950–1951); Cade (1960).
30. Cade (1960).

females that do mate as yearlings do not lay or have small clutches.[31] What do yearling peregrines do for the summer? They are easily distinguished from the adults by plumage, but formerly arctic researchers almost never saw them. Do they have some summering ground of their own—north, south, wandering? Recently more immature plumaged falcons have appeared at the eyrie cliffs in nesting season. Perhaps always they have summered on the same grounds as the adults, but since they are not attached to cliffs they have been swallowed into the wilderness. Rare birds do seem to vanish thus.

The occupation of arctic eyries by immature peregrines is perhaps a warning. If the adults are dying from poisoning as they did in the south twenty years ago, vacancies are created at the prime cliffs. The drifting young birds have a place now, the adults do not keep them away, and steady at their cliffs, we see them.[32]

A biologist, Dr. Howard Young, has taken the information known about breeding peregrines—how long they live, when they breed, how many eggs are laid, hatch, how many young fledge—and he has calculated the number of young that must be raised to maintain a steady, nondeclining population.[33] The figures he uses are reasonable estimates of what actually might occur in a peregrine population. For example, he simply assumed that 60 per cent of the adults were successful in breeding. For a stable population these successful birds would have to produce an average of 2.5 fledged young per pair.

Sometimes Dave and I discussed Mattox's survey. Most eagerly we were anticipating August, when we would learn how many eyasses were raised in the Greenland eyries and know better whether the population was in trouble.

Young's figure of 2.5 is not in itself the significant result of his calculations. Although it does match with the productivity of healthy populations in prepesticide years, it

---

31. Hickey and Anderson (1969).
32. Hickey, personal communication.
33. Young (1969).

depends on all of his perhaps inaccurate assumptions. But he also recalculated reproduction for his hypothetical peregrine population using slightly different assumptions. What if mortality of peregrines increased, or either productivity or nesting success decreased? In all cases, even with small changes, eyries would begin to be deserted within three years. If mortality of adults and immatures were increased by only 10 percent, six out of fifty eyries would be deserted in three years, and a seventh would have a single bird, not a pair. Peregrine populations are sensitive to change.

The Search at Musk Ox Bay

The two Bills visited us one morning. They wanted to know if we wished to travel down the fjord with them to a gull colony. A Dane had told them gyrfalcons lived by the gulls, and we might get a ride the ten miles across water in a boat the Air Force operated to take the airmen fishing. Dave and I decided to go. We hurriedly packed.

"Have you found peregrines?" I asked. I was delighted to see them.

At this, Mattox smiled more brightly than he had on his arrival, the sweat then clouding his face and his feet burning from the hike, "Three eyries! Every one of them a good cliff. Bill climbed down to one, and found four eggs."

"This little tiercel was a zippy brave one," Bill Burnham added. "The wind rushed when he dove on me."

"You and Dave should go see it later on. That pair is much more aggressive than yours here. They started up when we were a mile away."

Burnham said, "But I found a rope leading down to the ledge. Someone has been on that cliff." He was grimly smiling.

"Was it a fresh rope?" I asked.

"It was a fool rope, hardly more than clothesline, but enough. . . ."

Mattox said, "We don't know if it's from this year."

Dave and I had slept late that morning, and we left without seeing the peregrines.

Later, on the hike, Mattox said, "I think we're doing

Two peregrine eyasses at Musk Ox Eyrie, 1973.

real well. We'll find enough eyries to know how these falcons
are doing." Yes, he had been worrying since we learned
the small planes couldn't fly.

*   *   *   *

Almost always when I have come to the sea, gulls have been
crying and their white forms shine before the water. But
now the silence of the fjord, where only windy waves rolled
and the tundra dull-colored and barren met the gray water,
reminded me how closely we approached the top of the world,
the white pole, how near the ice cap massed, the wind it
pierced these fragile living baubles that shiver on the cooling
earth, a wind cousin to the fierce torrents at the top of
the troposphere where no life may hear. And beyond the

terrifying universe. How precious our living companions, we
cling to them. Perhaps we forget in the animal-full plant-rich
tropics. Yet there too the waves often roll, without gulls, the
mighty silence.

*　　*　　*　　*

Eventually, the cruiser did approach gulls, twenty-five of
them with feathers all white, dappled on the water like foam.
They soon flushed and winged around the point in a line.
As we followed we saw more gulls in flight, and passing the
corner we confronted a tall rock face. Grass ramps would
allow climbers to walk by its base. We saw perhaps a hundred
pairs so constantly moving—we had startled them from
their perches—that we could not count them. The cliff had many
points, extensively stained white from the birds' excrements
to a snowy or salty appearance. Where were the gyrfalcons of
which the Danes had spoken?

We passed the main ledges of the colony. Then Mattox
pointed to a different bird perched above high mutes. A
dim shadowish glimpse, a motionless side view of softly gray
plumage and arched back, it looked like one of the carved figures
on a Gothic cathedral. The boat carried us away along the shore.

We entered an open cove. Another small craft lay at
anchor, dingy red and white with a sooty smokestack near its
cabin. The blonde Dane who piloted our cruiser said the other
was a police boat from the coastal town Sukkertoppen, trying to
catch Greenlanders reported to be illegally shooting seals. Our
boat would leave us here for three days. The Dane lowered the
dinghy but couldn't start the motor. At last he realized he was
forgetting the fuel, and then when he tried to pour gasoline
from a five-gallon can, most of it slushed over the sides, to Dave's
laughter that made us chuckle as we shushed him. Two
dark Greenlanders came in their rubber lifeboat and trans-
ported us to shore.

The Danes who worked at the SAS Hotel, where the jet
airline passengers stayed, had constructed a red cabin here
by a river mouth. They had told us we could use it. On
the turfy meadow, fox cubs played. These ran swifter and were

larger than the cubs by our tent, although still they loved to bumble into piles with paws flailing and feigned snarls. The foxes by our tent had abandoned their warren. But by the red cabin Dave and Mattox pursued these half-grown cubs with cameras and never could catch up with them, for although they refused to slip underground always they found a new rock to hide behind.

Later we waited inside for hot water to make tea, sitting on a luxurious crumbling couch. Through glass windows we saw a large and brown bird catching a fish and chased by gulls. Its wings dwarfed the gulls. It had a white tail, it was the sea eagle! We saw him land a quarter mile uphill, the gulls falling away so that he perched in peace. We ran behind the cabin to watch.

"Intermewed eagle," Bill said, using another falconer's word whose meaning I never did learn. The eagle sat for fifteen minutes. Goldish and tawny about his head and neck, with dark and mainly very dark brown body and wings. He had a massive hooked bill that he bent menacingly to the white-scaled fish he held in one talon, but he didn't eat. He looked toward the fjord, as the falcon would gaze, only his bulk, the wide body strong but not streamlined, and a weight of feathers far beyond the sleekness of a peregrine, especially his long head extended from hunched shoulders, these all gave his glare a ponderous rather than fiery power.

The white-tailed sea eagle, close relative of the bald eagle, only reaches southern Greenland from Europe and doesn't pass byond to the North American mainland. Sufficient grass grows in the south of Greenland for sheep to graze, and the sheep farmers fear that the eagle takes their lambs. Banding returns warn that 35 percent of Greenland's eagles die by shooting until today only about two hundred adults remain. From Godthåb District north, the harshest part of the eagle's range, it is protected, but a law cannot be passed to encompass the whole island.[34]

---

34. Mattox (1970b); Salomonsen (1950–1951); Hansen (1977). In 1973, the eagle did receive protection throughout Greenland—but shooting continues to occur.

The eagle lifted his wings, seven feet across, rose, and drifted inland. His long-feathered legs and talons hung down fast to his prey. Søndrestrøm lies far north for the eagle, but no one disturbs the hill country. Had the eagle fled the sheepherders to skulk alone, or had he an eyrie hidden? How often did he come to the fjord?

*   *   *   *

The tides are six feet, and at midmorning the fjord was low. We decided to walk to the gull colony along the water below the cliffs, to avoid climbs and to obtain a better view of the rock. We crossed above a narrow beach the tides had exposed. After a mile the cliff began, usually talus steplike from the water, giant steps, with bushes in between them, and grassy patches also.

Some twigs had a pale brown halo. Mattox pulled off strands of hair that he told us were musk-ox wool, very fine, fluffy, and soft like cotton. The musk ox are not native to West Greenland. The Danes introduced a herd of about twenty some years ago, and very gradually they increased in number.[35] Although the animals scattered sufficiently that one never knew exactly where to see them, they actully remain restricted to a small area bordering the fjord.

The rocks jutted out in one spur after another so that we could never see far. One spur had a thick, local patch of mutes under a cavelikc ledge. Burnham scrambled up to stretch and look inside. Perhaps gyrfalcons had used it a previous year, for bones lay about the stained floor; but none of the traces were at all fresh. Farther on we glimpsed a pearl gray gyrfalcon just as it vanished behind the next spur. Our one encounter in the morning.

Color variation among the gyrfalcons has caused one of the long-standing controversies in ornithological study of the Arctic. Few people travel north to the gyrfalcon's home; if they have seen it at all it is a falconer's bird, or one in a zoo, or with greatest luck, one of the very rare stragglers in

---

35. Steen Malmquist, personal communication.

winter. Most bird watchers know only that it has three color phases—black, gray, and white—and hopefully watch for it in open areas, fields and seashore, in the coldest months. The white holds particular fascination, as Herman Melville generally observed in Moby Dick, and therefore it has acutely been noticed that the white appears least often. Thus we assume it is rarest.

Disagreements over the color phases arise as to where they are found, why the differences in plumage occur, and whether or not they represent different subspecies. The remoteness of the breeding grounds has delayed answering these questions, and as another complication the gyrfalcon lives throughout northern Eurasia—how do these birds relate to the North American three? Recent scientific authorities disagree, but I will follow Dr. Finn Salomonsen's account, as he has studied the Greenland gyrs, and Greenland birds in general, more than any other person.[36]

According to Dr. Salomonsen, the color phases represent three distinct plumages. Within each phase only slight variations occur. The dark birds are deep brown above, some adults with faint gray spots or bars. The gray phase has a lighter back with considerable barring that gives it the shimmery or glistening aspect; the white gyrfalcon has only scattered dark spots or barrings on its white plumage. Birds of different phases frequently mate.

In southernmost Greenland gray birds predominate, interspersed with a small number of darks. The white gyrfalcon comes only in winter. As one travels north, dark gyrfalcons disappear, and grays are increasingly replaced by whites. In the far north white gyrfalcons occur alone. Our area had an intermediate ratio of grays to whites.

The gulls constantly called and flew. We could see their young on the ledges, small, fuzzy-looking creatures with dark down, they tended to sit upright. The adults were revolving above and before us, so many with their narrow wings constantly tilting and turning that we could hardly keep track of one bird's arc, but followed one whiteness, then another,

---

36. Salomonsen (1950–1951).

then another. The larger of the two gull species, the glaucous, was difficult to pick out, but some of them perched on the upper cliff, breasts pointed straight toward the fjord; the Iceland gulls all nested lower—none dared venture near the perches of their cruel cousins—and stood sideways on their narrow ledges. The Icelands feed on fish and crustaceans, but the glaucous will take eggs, or small birds, or drop to lower cliff walls and seize Iceland chicks.[37]

Among the gulls several tall black birds stood like rough pieces of ebony, the thin cormorants, a species common in Europe but nesting nowhere west of Greenland. And among the gulls a smaller, daintier bird flew: another European, the black-headed gull, with its dark head and triangles of white that flashed at the ends of the gray upper-wings.

The cormorants winter in southwest Greenland.[38] Yet each winter some few appear on the rock shores of New England. Perhaps they come from Greenland. And the black-headed gulls, recently colonizing Greenland from Europe, were once very rare on the American coast. But these last twenty-five years individuals are discovered every winter. Do the cold, lonely black-headeds drift southwest in autumn, rather than southeast? No one knows.

While the rest of us watched for a flushing falcon, Burnham walked down a grassy slope along the cliff edge under the colony. Quickly the glaucous gulls leaped into air, and, strangely, the smaller, gentler Iceland gulls awaited Bill's approach. They too flew; they made a loud noise while Bill walked as far as he could under the cliffs, to the water's edge. Frequently gyrfalcons nest near colonies of gulls or especially alcids, the puffins and murres, where they find plentiful food.[39] A gyr can take the young gulls despite the parents' pursuit. But one must watch a gyr cliff carefully. These larger falcons are shyer than peregrines. The jerkin may not scream when intruders approach, and if a person comes too close, both falcons may steal away and wait on the open tundra until all is motionless once more.[40] None of us saw gyrs fly. At last

37. Salomonsen (1950–1951). 39. Salomonsen (1950–1951).
38. Salomonsen (1950–1951). 40. Cade (1960).

Bill returned to us. He had found one snowy gull feather
and several feathers of the gyrfalcon, which appeared soft and
tan as we held them, hardly gray in the hand.

We climbed up over the cliff because the shore was
impassable. Straight below us we saw the gull backs and several
cormorant heads. Past the gulls the cliffs dwindled to outcroppings too small to check. It was late afternoon. We turned
round, doubting where the gyrfalcons could be. We had the
Dane's word, our two sightings, many good cliffs. Very sly
falcons. In the middle of our discussion, I spotted the gray hawk
flying toward us. It was very large pearly gray as it approached,
the gyr female. Silent, never varying from her line of flight,
never pausing. She took slow wingbeats that covered a
wider span of air than the peregrine's wings, deeper wingbeats
that moved her quickly without effort. She passed behind a
distant spur, toward the cabin.

We would split up and hope to find her on our return.
Mattox and I went across the ridge's top while Dave and Bill
would find a way between the rocks and the tide, now just
slightly past high.

As usual in Greenland, "top" could only be applied to
the ridge loosely, and Bill and I still constantly climbed and
descended. We kept merely a half-alert watch for the gyr or her
jerkin. Our eyes were watery in the wind, and we were
calm and easy after a full day and events mixed and new; our
way was short to warmth and food, so we took long strides
but rambled in the evening. The unseen sun even bathed several
cloud gaps in gold.

"When did you first come to Greenland?" I asked.

Quiet the words, his eyes, the pleasure in his voice. Ah,
twenty-one years ago, the summer after he had finished classes at
Dartmouth. A man near his home had come to search for
gyrfalcons and brought Bill along. Yes, then too they had
walked the undulating tundra, until then too their feet had had
a hundred blisters—"Not taped up as well as now," he added,
"I've learned something since then"—and they had dreamed
of firesides and feather mattresses. The gyrs. They lived
on cliffs then, as they do now. They had long wings. "Jim, you've

seen them, oh could they catch anything they're fast, and the white flows in the sun."

We forgot the wind that made our faces red. It really wasn't our words, whether shyness or that inability to speak came between, but some awareness we otherwise sensed: memories of summers past awakened in Bill, I echoed hopes and unshaped prospects. A conversation between a young man and one no longer young, a walk like hundreds, thousands long gone. Some patterns do not pass away, but return and return and return. All things do not change. We have this comfort, we share a multitude of circumstance and desire with even the first humans that breathed. We love the same creatures, we walk sometimes by the old forms, and the feelings, we know they've risen before.

Someday, old, I in my turn will talk with boys. But I am uneasy before the nest cliffs. What changes now? Will the young hopes ever echo my memories?

We came to the cliff brink where the ridge bent away from the fjord. We would not find a way down here. Far below on the shore Bill and Dave neared the cabin. We turned following the ridge a quarter mile until the rock ended. Here we could descend a precipitous grass slope. Beyond and to the left the rock feebly built another cliff, broken up by wide ledges, that we doubted could possibly hold falcons. We had just started down the steep grass when we heard cackling. Peregrine, sounding like a tiercel. Not to our left but to the right, he perched under dark overhanging rock by a mute spot. Another eyrie. We watched him as we went down the slope. He never moved—a frozen, brilliant image of the evening, upright, malar stripes black against his white cheeks and his beak gaped, "kaak-kaak-kaak." This I could remember until I grew old. From a lower angle we saw a heavily muted ledge, only six or seven yards above where we could walk. The whole rock face only reached seventy-five feet tall, but it had a long talus and grass slope below. The ledge looked as though it had been used many years. We couldn't see the falcon sitting.

"Let's leave him alone," said Bill.

We left. From a distance we could still see the white of the tiercel's breast; he hadn't moved.

At the cabin we learned that Bill and Dave also had failed to find the gyrfalcons. We debated whether we should climb to the peregrine eyrie. Mattox was confident the tiercel guarded a scrape with eggs, and wanted to return late in the season when we could count the eyasses, the number that was most important for our study, and band them. Why risk the falcons' safety?

Burnham was saying, "This, with the three eyries north, and the first eyrie make five. And with that pair Jim saw at the Black Cliff, we've got six eyries. That's good."

We decided not to disturb the motionless tiercel the next day.

Hawks in North America

That first evening at the red cabin, after we had seen the foxes and the eagle, we sat inside where the winds didn't penetrate and drank tea. We made a fire in the stove to dry our boots and sit by, our first fire in Greenland. Outside along the shore we had found scraps and boards (even the fjord carried litter to the land), twisted twigs, and one branch too large to have grown in the Søndrestrøm hills. The foreign smokes mingled in our chimney and we breathed scents sealed by the hotter sun to the south. We settled in our chairs, we verged on one of those baked, long evenings when the cold is banished, a conversation and drowsiness fit for winter's nights, except that we would not wait half a year to wander outdoors again but only until morning.

This evening we talked first of the gyrfalcons that we hoped to find soon. These falcons of the north watch the sun for three long months, and some linger through the winter when there is twilight even at noon, when the ice swells and cracks on the fjords and the ice cap thickens for a season, as if the age of glaciers had returned.

Mattox and Graham had traveled to the coast of Greenland one fall several years earlier.[41] "The summer ends quickly,"

41. See Mattox (1969, 1970a).

Gyrfalcon eyasses.

Mattox was saying. "We worked during early September; already the night was deep, and we got up at five in the darkness. The spray of the sea froze, and so did our bare hands.

"The gyrfalcons were following the coastline south. Mostly white birds that would feed on south Greenland's sea fowl through the winter."

"What were you and Dick doing?" I asked.

"We stayed in an old hunting cabin that had a stove but no roof. All day for eight days we trapped for gyrfalcons. We had pigeons we tied to the ground, they fluttered, but flat next to them we set bow nets—they were oval shaped—and if the falcon dropped on the pigeon we sprang the net over it. That's when our hands chilled. Gloves off we banded, weighed, and measured each falcon."

"How many did you get?"

"Fourteen different ones, but seventeen times we recaptured birds, nine times one individual."

"I wonder what he was doing," Dave said. "He must have gotten tired of you and Graham."

What I had trouble imagining were the hunting, winging gyrfalcons in the coldest of winter, arising to the noon twilight not only to stir and themselves survive, but dependent on other creatures still warm for food.

When the sun strengthens in April the white falcons return north to their homes while the low arctic residents take to their cliffs again. The gyr like the peregrine has a scrape but no nest of its own. To escape from the falling snow of spring it chooses ledges beneath overhangs of rock. The companion raven begins nesting even earlier than the gyr and must also place its stick nest to avoid the snow. Hence the gyrfalcons and ravens prefer the same nest spots, and often the gyrs will use abandoned raven nests to support their eggs.[42]

By the fifth of July, now as we sat in the red cabin, the young gyrfalcons grew their feathers, probably to fledge in two weeks. Afterward the family might linger near the cliff, or leave.[43] As late as early August Mattox once had seen branched gyrfalcons near the eyrie.

"There were two males, one a dark gray bird and the other white on the head and front, but with a slate gray back.

"They were quarreling over prey that one held. The second pursued the first lower and lower before the cliff until the white one fell into the lake. I thought he would drown, and I ran to the shore, ready to swim for him; but he flapped his wings through the water, and splashed forty feet to climb out on a rock. I could see the water dripping from his feathers."

Our fire was dying.

Dave asked, "Have you seen the eagle's nest?"

Mattox hadn't. "Their eyries lie in the remotest areas. I've hardly ever seen eagles."

Then Dave added sticks to the fire. Peregrine, gyrfalcon, eagle: these three were the raptors of Greenland. Now our

---

42. Salomonsen (1950–1951); Cade (1960).
43. Jenkins (1978).

Gyrfalcon eyasses.

talk drifted south to the American hawks. We were certain
to think of them eventually, for these were the fauna of our
home, the background we had shared since our earliest
awarenesses. Thus walking in the North we saw northern raptors,
but in a sense we brought the others with us. They too
colored our experiences here.

Joyous is the sight of a new hawk. Yet it is the satisfaction
and relief from those most familiar that surprises and startles
me, that grows with each meeting. I celebrate the life
that leaps within me, the sudden gusts of recognition when the
kestrel hovers and cries, "killy-killy-killy-killy," as I have
heard it these hundred times.[44] But occasionally the kestrel

44. The kestrel is a small falcon, fairly common throughout most
of North America.

so lulls and soothes me that I think I retain vestiges of that awe people felt when they worshiped the animals.

Worship the falcon. The sacred creatures were those remarkable animals that people recognized about their home; perhaps humans were fearful of the mysterious thundering world. Then they always realized their weakness, and the inscrutable comfort that they felt before these animals they knew, this they mistook as the good will and magic strength of the badger or the elk or the kestrel.

By the fire I thought of Massachusetts hawks, Mattox thought of Pennsylvanian, but they were almost the same images because all eastern North America shares the same hawks, and the western states generally have these species also.

Hawks can be divided into several subgroups, the members of which share qualities like build, wing shape, flight, and hunting method. Not only are these similarities helpful when learning to identify hawks, but flight and hunting patterns largely determine how and when you will see a particular species.

For example, the accipiters chase birds primarily, not in the open but twisting and dodging about trees and bushes and only darting quickly past open spaces, blind in the chase to all else but the fleeing, frantic wings. They crash through hedges, and one wonders why they never break their heads against trunks of trees, maybe they do, but oftener the pursuit ends when feathers splash and the accipiter screams triumphantly.

This agility in hunting requires short wings but a long tail for ruddering and abrupt turns. Two of North America's species have blue-gray backs (some call them blue darters) and bellies barred with red but the third, the huge goshawk, has gray above and pearly gray below with a thick gray eyestripe that sets it apart from all other birds.

In recent years, observers on the hawk ridges and on the shores of the Atlantic and the Great Lakes, where accipiters concentrate as they migrate, have noticed fewer of the smaller two species—the sharp-shinned and especially Cooper's,

now totaling less than a third the totals of former years.[45]
At nests that have been watched, the same reproductive failures
have occurred that we witnessed with the peregrine. The
eggs break.[46] Short wings, long tail is the key to the accipiters'
trouble. These hawks are built for pursuit of birds—many
the same species as the peregrine prefers—that eat insects
and concentrate the poisons in their fat tissues. Like the
peregrine, the Cooper's and the sharp-shinned are at the
end of long insect-based food chains. I rarely see a Cooper's
hawk any more. The goshawk alone seems unaffected because
it lives in northern forests where people have little use
for pesticides, and it eats hares primarily, or grouse that feed on
leaf buds not insects.

*   *   *   *

Our voices rambled through the evening. In the strength
of a fire one's awareness of the cool, soft-colored room soon
fades and still more the landscape beyond the windows
will have fled. I stepped outside the red cabin. The wind seized
the door from my hand and drizzle nipped my neck. Mists
wrapped the inland hills in shadow.

The hawks from home warmed our conversation in the
red cabin as the fire heat could not. Burnham dreamed
slightly separate from Mattox and me, as he at last exclaimed,
"When you come to Colorado I'll show you half a dozen prairie
falcon eyries!" His western falcon.

I replied, "You have Cooper's hawks too, don't you?
They are still common? I'd like to see them." You lie exposed
to a particular pain with the loss of a familiar hawk.

More than our own sorrows impel us when we try to
preserve the last local individuals. Children to come will miss
what they do not know. One combination of hawks for an area
is not as good as another. Three raptors suit Greenland

---

45. Spofford (1969); Berger, personal communication. See also
Henny and Wight (1972) and Postupalsky (1975).
46. Shriver (1969); Snyder et al. (1973); eggshells are thinner than
formerly (Anderson and Hickey, 1972).

because it is ice and tundra, short summered with limited prey. But three species for Massachusetts would be tragic, for three do not echo the hills and pine-crowded gorges, the warmth of air and the thousand bird voices raised over our farmland or the long plain that gradually meets the sea. Three species locate Greenland; even one less than Massachusetts's native fourteen is an impoverishment, and we are slightly lost.

I don't speak here of the landscape's health, the ecosystem itself, but of humanity in the landscape. Very few people have the sensitivity directly to perceive the vacancy in the Cooper's hemlocks, but we may read of what once was, we imagine vividly and thus perceive. We don't merely dream that we feel the woods are too quiet without the wolf. Yes, I swallow something more than fantasy when I stand on the hawk ridge with the peregrine view. What losses must our drifting children bear?

*   *   *   *

In the morning several Danes arrived from the SAS Hotel—they had come in a small motorboat with food and beer to spend the weekend. Toward noon the tall Dane from the Air Force cruiser entered the cabin. His boat we could see at anchor in the cove. We discussed our plans with the tall man because we relied on him for transportation to Søndrestrøm. He would soon take Dave and me on board because we wished to return to our observation work. The two Bills would hike from the red cabin for a week's journey to survey the surrounding country. The boat would pick them up on its next return, the following Saturday. I took my pack and walked outside along the shore. The airmen had left the cruiser to fish from rocks exposed by the tide. I dropped my pack, and walked some paces away to sit by myself.

The airmen had made a fire, more for warmth than to cook lunch over—brown paper bags and sandwich wrappers remained half burned or drooped among the wet stones. A drizzling rain had extinguished the flames and trails of smoke seeped from the ashes. There were four airmen, three of them young but the fourth older and heavier. All were dressed

in gray flight jackets and gray pants. The shortest had just
hooked a fish, one foot long. He threw it on the pile of fish
they had previously caught. The new catch and two others
flapped; they jerked in the air so that the plastic sheet under
them rattled.

"How many is that one?" the older man asked.

"Aw seven I guess. He was a miserable fucker," the short
one answered. "Not very big either." The four stood with their
lines stretched in the falling tide. Every minute or so one
would pull his line in and cast it once more.

Two Danes stood back a little from the shore, talking
quietly together. I looked the other way, as far along the water
as the cliffs would allow; perhaps white gulls would come
foraging.

"Did you find any peregrines?" a polite voice asked. One
of the Danes had walked over to me. I tensed, for even behind
him at that moment I saw the short cliff, too distant for the
mute spots to show, but such an obvious wall I didn't want
to give the tiercel's location away.

"Peregrines?" I said. I did smile, hesitating. "Yes,
we saw one adult. A few miles back on the tundra. We don't
know if he was nesting." Almost smug, I avoided pointing
at all as I didn't know where new cliffs might lie beyond the
horizon. "Have you been to the gull colony down here?
We walked there yesterday and found over a hundred gulls."

Our talk was interrupted by the tall Dane who had come
from the cabin, with Dave, to begin our departure. He pushed
his boat to the water and tried the motor. Dead. I looked
at Dave. First the man tried the gas tank, but he had fuel
enough. He juggled the motor, a vague, general juggle, shook
it and pulled the starter, again without success.

The airmen meanwhile were pulling in their lines except
that two got theirs crossed, and another said, "Have we
got to go already?" but none of them noticed the trouble with
the boat as the Dane pushed and pulled various parts of the
engine. The Dane who had spoken with me said something in
Danish but switched to, "Nothing works around here."
Dave and the third Dane, a white-haired man named Ib,

walked along the shore for some reason, bending and rumaging about the drift litter.

"God dammit," said one of the airmen with the tangled lines.

The short one stood over the fish. "What are we going to do with these?" He turned to the others. "Bob?" he called.

"No, I don't want them."

The older one pointed to a silvery, slim fish, "That char will be real good eating. These others . . . not so good."

"Where could I cook them?" the short one wondered.

The tall, powerfully built Dane stood upright by the dinghy. He had a disgusted expression, "What are we going to do now?" The cruiser floated thirty yards offshore. The tall man had new rubber boots on, checkered pants, and a thick-wooled sweater of blue and pure white.

I was beginning to wonder how he had gotten his dark tan when Dave appeared holding a wide board broken at one end, and several thin smaller boards braced together into a square. "You can paddle with these," Dave called.

Dave and the tall Dane got into the dinghy, each holding a wood scrap; one of the airmen climbed in also, and they paddled without undue trouble out to the cruiser. "Would you get my jacket?" Bob called to one of his fellows on the shore.

I couldn't avoid grinning all while the Dane tried paddling back alone. He spun beautifully in circles and toward the shore only by accident it seemed until at last he could step out in the shallows. I dragged my pack over to where he had beached, took the extra paddle and got in, along with the mustached airman. The white-haired Dane gave us a shove off the sand.

Dave helped us board the cruiser, but Bob had already cast his line back into the water. Soon the mustached one joined him. I looked at them hard as Dave and I waited for the next boatload. They hadn't once talked with the Danes, and they had totally ignored the tall man's problems. What did they think of? Anything? The Danes, almost every one I had met, seemed eager to talk, even before they learned of our eccentric research.

At last everyone had boarded and we started up the fjord. I felt tired and stood by the rail to watch the cliffs we had crossed the day before. Soon we were among the gulls.

"One day I saw the gyrfalcon among the gulls," began the same young Dane who had approached me earlier.

We talked over the wave-bursting interruptions and the roar of the engine. He slowly talked of the tundra, of the young gyrfalcons that came in the fall, and the ptarmigan scraping the snow in January darkness, or on the chill days, forty degrees below zero, flying full speed into the snow so that it buried them and kept them alive. He knew the answers to my questions, such as when the snowy owls came from East Greenland, or how many eggs the geese lay. He hunted sometimes on the tundra, and often he hiked, even in winter. The peregrines, he knew them also; he had photographed them in summers past. He told me where I could find two eyrie cliffs, one north-facing and tall, there he had carried his cameras last summer, and another he had just found two weeks ago, on a symmetrical round hill with a Norse name that made it sound like a tower.

The man stood just less than six feet tall, gently swaying with the boat, short brown hair, direct eyes and a smile; he knew what he liked: the creatures, long miles alone, other men who want the same. That knowledge made him serene. He was open and warm.

I regretted my lies to him on the shore of the fjord.

He had come to Greenland from Denmark a second time; he had missed the wilderness. Soon he would leave Søndrestrøm for the north, where there were fewer people.

I gazed behind the boat, brooding over the white curving trails the motor had churned in the water. I hadn't moved when some minutes later, fully an hour since we left the cove, the short airman came out of the cabin with the plastic sheet bulked in his arms, the dark and light of the fish scales showing through. He dumped it overboard where the needlessly killed fish would roll with the beer cans, then float, then rot away.

We were still some distance from the port, and I turned

127

Gyrfalcon eyass perched at edge of eyrie.

from feeling the fish deaths to thinking I could not understand
why these Americans stayed below in the cabin while we
passed mountain and tundra and here the froth of waterfalls.
Why they never strayed from their fishpoles on the shore,
or the cigarettes or beer. What feeble visions; they seem blind
to wonders people have died to see.

Night Watches

It was the third day after Dave's and my departure
from our camp. I crossed the tundra alone. Rough clouds

swirled overhead as they had in chill June, while the rain trickled down the neck of my raincoat to join my sweat. Dave had hiked out from the air base the night before. My errands had taken so long that by afternoon, when I started out, the land was sodden and pools had formed in the mud between hummocks. Whether it was the slippery tundra or the food heavy on my back, or a headache, I stared at my feet almost the whole way, with brooding heavy thoughts. It was the common doubt, when your back aches and the wetness blurs your eyes, to lose the sweeping, inspired confidence and see the closeness, the width of the ground; what worth have your creeping, labored efforts?

I looked up at the cliff often as at last I neared the tent. Most of the rock again was dark with the dripping washes of water. The mute stains stood out vividly. Dave sat in the tent wrapped in his sleeping bag. He said snow had mixed with the rain for much of the day. He cooked dinner for us, although I felt sick and ate little.

He did have news. He had watched from the lookout from 5:30 until 11:30 that morning. The falcons had become fully active even before his arrival. We still had no clue about whether they ever rested during the twilight. The tiercel had stayed near the cliff the whole of that watch so that Dave saw him catch several birds.

The rain tapped onto our tent as we talked. Dave quieted to sleep for the night. I put my boots on for my customary trip outside just before sleeping. As usual the rain sounded harder within the tent than it actually was. It drizzled lightly, it was cold, and the light had its odd quality as well. The tanness of the tent gave Dave and me an even, spread glow by which we could read even at midnight. Outside the tundra had many shades of darkness and light for contrast and a texture that pleased me, while the hidden sun gave the clouds low to the northwest a pale sheen. Vague doubts never yield to reasoned, conscious thoughts, but melt like clouds for the wind or warmth as the day passes. I looked up at the dripping dark cliff. I felt eager to continue my vigil before the eyrie. One must work and enjoy as well as he can, trusting that in the end his efforts will . . . , no the trust isn't simply that efforts will make a difference, but that everything will be all right.

Dave left for the lookout at four the next morning, to find the cliff face seemingly empty; but as he reached his post the tiercel called, already alert. Again the clouds hung low, it rained constantly with drops thickened into slush, but Dave saw seven pieces of prey brought to the cliff. He came down at late morning. By early afternoon, when I planned to ascend, it rained much harder, so that I waited hoping the weather would improve, but at last went to the lookout anyway. No falcons were visible, nor did they call as I took my position. Soon the rain stopped, the clouds broke to reveal patches of blue and the wind changed to southeast, cold but fresh. A dark spot—a falcon—approached from the south and as it reached the cliff it called, the tiercel's voice, "kaaa kaaa kaaa," and he landed on the ledge. The falcon came out from behind the grass to meet her mate and take a small, dark body. The tiercel flew, then the falcon, to circle briefly, "ga-ga-ga-ga-ga," and return to the scrape. She remained hidden behind the grass but I heard a a faint "chip-chippering" noise, almost a twitter, and a very low rattling. These sounds ceased after several minutes.

I saw the beautiful tiercel perched upright as was his custom. He faced me so that always I could see the whiteness of his breast, with the binoculars or without. He looked wet, and his feathers were frowzled and ruffled. He touched them with his beak occasionally, and twice stretched his wings and tail to shake them, rise up on his legs, stretch, and settle once more. When at last he flew he soared gradually up and over the mountaintop for his hunting.

From the first days on our lookout we had noticed a pair of small buntings fly in and out of a deep crack between boulders, only forty feet from our position. That afternoon they were particularly obvious, for I would hear abrupt hoarse noises, a minor uproar from the crack, and always after a bunting would leave. Their young were growing powerful and greedy as they cried for food. These snow buntings, especially the males, have brilliant black and snow-white patterns on their feathers. I could frequently spot the diminutive males when they flew, even at the extreme end of the cliff. Bill Burnham called this nest a bunting eyrie, maybe seriously because it occupied the inaccessible cliff, but with a humorous hint at the comparison of this bird's stature with the peregrine's. The male in his long flashy flights was insect catching; he stooped on flies. But the bunting's oddest habit was to land on a ledge and unhurriedly hop about within a yard or two of the peregrine. We could glimpse the little bird's motion as we watched the tiercel through the telescope. He glanced in the bunting's direction but showed no more interest nor flew nor sought to seize the upstart.

The tiercel's voice sounded in the distance and he again returned to land on the ledge. He had a small bird with gray feathers that he transferred from talons to beak. The falcon walked out to him, wings extended and flapping, "ga-ga-ga-ga-ga," and once a distinctive, deep "clee-chip." She flew a circle and landed directly at the scrape, but I could see her over the grass. The same chips and rattles sounded.

The calls not only grew familiar, but were beginning to convey some meaning to us as we recognized the occasions when they were used.[47] The most frequent was the leisured, "kaaa-kaaa-kaaa," which primarily the tiercel used, at intervals when small birds chipped or Dave or I moved, or often when no particular event seemed to provoke it, perhaps he was restless and changing perches. The tiercel also would announce his return from his hunts, and both falcons would call thus as they exchanged prey.

The next most frequent sound was the quick staccato call repeated in long series, a deeper and hoarser, "kak-kak-kak-kak," for the tiercel and, "ga-ga-ga-ga-ga," for the falcon. This we heard when the ravens fled the tiercel's stoops or Dave climbed to the eyrie ledge. Both falcons pursued that strange haggard with these calls. We considered it their alarm or aggression call. It certainly served both purposes, for

---

47. See Cade (1960) and Nelson (1970) for discussions of peregrine vocalizations.

the whole valley knew when there was trouble on the cliff, and any intruder with ears felt the fierceness and anger poised above its head. We could not say whether a falcon intended either the warning (perhaps to the mate) or the specific intimidation directed and reinforced by its stoops. Perhaps the screams burst out instinctively when enemies approach. Intent, or anger, are vague liquidly notions that humans cannot easily apply to falcons.

Oddly this second call also came during food exchanges, at the very moment the prey passed from tiercel to falcon. Their other vocalizations still puzzled us—the "clee-chip" noise that we now thought sounded more like the voice of the falcon, and the "chippering" from the eyrie as the falcon fed. We suspected and hoped that the rattling I had heard during the last two feedings was made by eyasses begging food as all young birds do. I had noticed that the falcon after the exchange of food did not land on a cliff perch to eat, as she had done previously. Instead today she quickly went back in behind the grasses to eat out of our sight. The eggs probably had hatched during our absence. How many of the eggs? Eyries seldom hold more than three eyasses.

The clouds continued to part and frequently the sun now shone. The cliff was silent. During periods such as this one with no peregrine activity I'd watch the tundra, the long lake, and randomly think about the falcons or breakfast or people at home. Thus this afternoon I was happy with my knowledge of the peregrines. While I waited for the tiercel I thought lightly about our work, as if in oblique, vibrant answer to the previous day's doubts.

On that rainiest day the clouds only once lifted sufficiently to reveal the fjord. I suddenly wondered what humans had wandered this way long ago. Had Vikings sailed up the fjord on their tiny, pointed ships? How dared they venture so far north, where nothing could warm them, give shelter or fuel, except the logs rolled and spewed upon land by the sea? I wondered how many of the Vikings had wished they'd never left their Old World homes.

During my musings I looked constantly out onto the cliff.

Suddenly I saw the tiercel returning from the southwest; he didn't call until he neared the ledge; the falcon walked out to its brink and the tiercel landed, closer than she to the scrape. The two could both see the scrape as they faced each other. The tiercel had no prey as I had expected; instead the two called, "kaaa kaaa," until he walked to stand behind the grass. The falcon called until he returned onto the open ledge. What interest had the tiercel at that moment, and how did the falcon respond at his approach to the scrape? Were her calls friendly or not? How ignorant I was of what held the pair bond strong, or kept the tiercel hunting for the falcon.

The tiercel left the ledge and took a higher perch on the cliff where he was silhouetted against the farthest cliff end. He sat quietly for some minutes.

Research is an activity or excuse that provides the watcher contact with the object of his or her study. Peregrine observers who do not care about peregrines before they begin their study are a small minority who like cliffs, rock climbing, or wilderness instead. Growing affection holds them to their efforts. The contact matters more than knowledge. That quest to understand can allow us humans to relate, somehow, to the strange-speeched animals who will scarcely respond.

I saw little activity the rest of my watch. Shortly before I left the lookout, the tiercel started up, and he soared before the cliff top. Some small bird chipped, and suddenly he turned his wings over his back and twisted almost straight down the rock face. He missed whatever he had spotted, rising west along the ridge and over.

*　　*　　*　　*

Dave had dinner ready when I came down and dished it out even before I got out of my mosquito gear. "Let's do our night watch," I said. "I don't think we should wait longer getting that data."

"Fine with me," Dave replied.

I was eager to return to the lookout. "Why don't I go up right after dinner and stay as long as I can. Then I'll wake you up for a turn. You can get me early in the morning."

"Good."

"I'll try to stay awake long enough that you'll get some sleep."

With idling and dishwashing and the packing of warm clothes, I didn't return to the lookout until nearly 8:00 P.M. The last traces of cloud were gone. I paused several times on the ascent, for I had the feel of something extraordinary happening: it was the departure from the tent until late in the night. We didn't know what the cliff held at night, and it had looked distant and secret the times we had ventured out from our cots and closed, warm air, as if this pile of rock had escaped us once more for its dense, aloof solitude—climb the slopes only if we dared. Maybe the North played with us by day when the sun softened the sky and icy hearts, but late freed from that hot eye the soulless fangs would bare. Wisps of madness might even now curl out of sight behind the mountain.

The light had that stretched appearance of late sun, leaving shadows smeared across the cliff. The little birds sang tinkly songs, but I scanned the many rock perches for the tiercel in vain.

Many minutes later the tiercel swept out of sky, bold as he always rushed boldly at any hour. He carried food, and the falcon met him briefly on the ledge. Brief breaths, and then she had returned to her grass and the tiercel had vanished round the cliff corner. I was alone.

It was July 11. The sun crept north so slowly that the night borders remained constant from one moment to the next. Yet somehow slabs darkened and the rock points held isolated glimmers, then faded into the dimness and slumber. The last sun left the eyrie ledge, the shadow slid smoothly toward me, and then the coolness, growing, touched me. The tiercel called, and I spotted him perched at the cliff top, but too late to catch even there the last sun, nor did high eastern thrusts of stone long linger in brightness.

But below in the jewel valley the sun hadn't set. The cliff alone was blocked by the ridge trailing west. Now the tiercel glided a quick, straight line to the flushed grass beyond

the stream. He stood; then, as he mysteriously had done
on other days, he hopped back and forth on the ground,
not a rapid automatic jerk like the birds who walk more than
fly, but an energetic, leaping stride into the air. Without
warning he reappeared noisy before the cliff, the falcon
clambering also to the eastmost ledges to pluck her prey. The
grey shadows and their speed had hidden their meeting. When
the falcon returned screaming to her scrape, the tiercel swooped
in a vast arc that caught sunlight at its peak, and whisked
himself round the cliff corner. When the rattling and chippering at the scrape ended, the cliff again looked deserted.
The sun left the tent, then the stream. Dusk crawling over the
contours of land. The subtle rises and humps no longer
blended with distance; instead the night edge had leaps and rolly
bumps, it reached toward early captured hollows.

Before long only the farther, southern hills had sun.
The chill that had fallen gradually numbed the mosquitoes
and sent them wherever they go at night. I gradually took
on one clothing piece after another and finally emptied my
pack. The shadows didn't deepen, the sky remained blue,
but the cold reached imperceptibly into my legs. The threatened
northernness of the night did not arrive abruptly—what
does?—but touched so gently that I hardly felt it. I was glad.
I missed the last of gold on a hill.

The little birds also quieted by degrees. Every so often one
would fly or chutter. Then minutes came when none at
all stirred, but I heard a distant waterfall whisper. I wondered
if the tiercel actually slept, or did he watch also? I hadn't heard
or seen either falcon in two hours. I wished I could see him,
for then we would be companions.

Many times in the south, I've wanted to watch birds
or mammals through the night. Now I did, but only with
blackness have the day and night creatures such different lives.
Here in Greenland the hare might prefer no sun, the
peregrine choose sun but neither slept at the others' time; they
remain watchful, waiting. Here sleep and waking almost
seem the same; the two states of life are moving and motionless
instead.

Why had the tundra quieted? The twilight kept light
for any activity of animals. Perhaps all need their period
of relief from hunting and being hunted. Or we carried a habit
from the south. The dim light, not my own drowsiness,
told me I should sleep. Or else, with the cold the mosquitoes
quieted: thus the little birds that seek insects, thus the
ravens, foxes, and falcons that wait on birds, thus I.

After midnight I became so cold that I decided I should
move a little. I took my feet out of my pack and walked
five yards downhill in as excitive and jerky a manner as possible.
From there I looked and saw the tiercel just barely revealed
beyond a cliff corner. I strained to see whether or not he slept.
He looked immobile, but my hands numb and eyes tired
kept the glasses wobbling.

Then he called and flew. He landed above and west of
the eyrie and stared at me. As he slowly called I thought, I dare
not move any more; not now when the rest of the world is
still; if I startle the tiercel and he alarms the falcon, she'll leave
the scrape and her eggs to chill. I waited among the boulders.
Until he flew once more around the cliff corner. Now only
the waterfall stirred. I picked my way carefully from one rock
to another, poised and balanced so that they wouldn't slide
and rumble. To the softer grass below the lookout seat, one
hopeful step but my trailing foot dragged stone. Off the tiercel
came, "ka-ka-kak-kak," and he landed twice, the second time
above the eyrie facing me. Certainly I had companionship.

And at last I decided I might as well sneak up to my
seat, even if he might cackle and bring the falcon out, thus
disrupting their normal night and our observations. He called
only "kaaa kaaa." I sat very still for the next hours, my
feet outside the pack and quickly chilling. The tiercel too was
motionless, but he would call from time to time. First at
me probably, but an hour later, when the little birds began
to move and make tinkly songs, he probably called to or at them,
or because it felt like morning—at least it did to me.

I was curious how his day would start. The redpolls began
to fly at about 2 A.M. Clouds covered most of the sky, but
at 2:15 sun lay on the southern slopes. The rosiness last in

the northwest now had shifted to northeast. The tiercel looked about more intently, especially at a bunting that sang and at the other birds. Shortly before three, he glided out and back to the eyrie ledge. Both falcons called, the female invisibly. Minutes later the tiercel stretched his flight close before the cliff all the way east past the rounded spur, and over the horizon.

Gradually, as slowly as they had advanced, the shadows withdrew. The farthest hills had both the last sun and the first, perhaps three hours between. The loons laughed from the long lake, and at three the falcon flew out from her scrape. She landed round the cliff corner, but fifteen seconds later returned to the eyrie and settled once more. Now a third of the tundra was bright, looked warm; it was time for mosquitoes again. The passerines must waken fully in these places long before those under the cliff—our peregrines had chosen an exposure with the hottest afternoon sun but the longest night. Did the tiercel hunt these sunniest areas first?

At last I packed my things together. I would miss the sun's coming. Stiffly I crossed the talus, feeling a little wonder at the night I had spent, my vigil ending as all other creatures' began, or continued. Still descending I heard the tiercel return, then both voices, saw the tiercel on the ledge. As I reached the tent "clee-chips" and "chipperings" fell from the eyrie. Dave woke.

"It's morning," I said.

I slept well only during the first hours, for soon the sun started the mosquitoes up, a major humming outside the netted entrance, and lone whines within where lucky ones searched for and found my bed. I was up and groggy when Dave returned at noon. I cooked soup. The clouds had disappeared for the warmest day yet, the air probably at sixty-five degrees.

Dave said as we ate, "Let's check the scrape. The sun's hot on the ledge." Both of us would climb!

I couldn't believe we walked up the hill for that purpose. I felt like an observer only, with his notebook, and noted the hugeness of the cliff, the narrow rope, detachedly. I had cord circling my chest with a carabiner attached. I carried a sling rope that would be my safety line. We reached the last ramp of grass. Here Dave fastened my sling rope to the climbing rope with a sliding prussic knot, leaving a circle of cord that I slipped through my carabiner.

"Remember," he said, "slide this knot along with your hand. Don't let it get too loose." One peregrine circling silently.

"Watch where I go," Dave repeated. "Plan out your steps. Okay?"

"Yes."

Dave started. When already he was halfway up I followed. In most spots the hard rock had cracks for my fingers, but dirt round the rocks crumbled and pebbles fell, I took footholds and long stretches I didn't like. Both falcons circled. Dave was out of sight. The cackling began.

It was relief to reach the ledge's end, to unhook the prussic-knotted cord from my belly. The ledge was very, very long. Wide in places, but steep. I hardly noticed the calling falcons, I was intent, was surprised at the length of the ledge and its near presence, what I had watched for so long, with quite normal grasses and mud where I put my feet. Dave walked back, hoping I would be quick. He held a tape measure; he had performed all our tasks at the scrape already.

"There are three eyasses," he said.

"Three," he repeated as I continued my walk. I didn't pause or look at him. Here the grass thickened. Behind, I saw them. The eyasses, all the whiteness of clouds with short down, these tiny downies lay on their bellies, while several of their wing-beginnings, the size of my fingertip, stretched, quivered, and they had tiny gray beaks, they rattled faintly, moved; these, these were the treasure I might grasp all in one hand, all their life and movement, these promised the long falcon wings and the cry on remote cliffs in years to come, the peregrine hope, our joy. "Look, look," I said to Dave.

Behind the white eyasses, the last egg lay. It too was beautiful, bantam-sized and brown, with many darker speckles. I have never seen such a shade of brown, a mixture of clays and deep wood; perhaps it was the texture that transformed it. On its top faint cracks had white edges. The stirrings of life

*First Eyrie scrape with three eyasses several days old
and one unhatched egg.*

within, or else was the barren structure breaking? The
eyasses were tiny but not freshly hatched, all the same age
with eyes open. Would one egg be late?

Now time to leave. Dave started away. I bent, found one
white curving feather, delicate as the others, but larger,
from the falcon's breast. I tucked it in my pocket. There,
at the ledge's end I stood, and Dave already was down. "Hurry,"
he said only once as I descended, and then we both ran
over the talus and grass. When at last we turned the tiercel
still circled, now small and only his light breast appearing.

Dave was smiling and didn't want to continue either.
Eyasses. And an egg. He had taken me to the eyrie.

"Look here," Dave said. He held a plastic bag. Within were two halves of eggshells, with crumbling edges. "This small one," he said, pointing to a smaller fragment, "was buried in dirt at the scrape edge, inside up. I hardly noticed it."

*   *   *   *

Again at evening I joined the tiercel on the ridge, to watch the changing lights and the quiet. At 9:30 he came home calling and landed at the ledge. The falcon came for the prey. When she returned to the scrape, I could see her bending to her feet and then leaning forward—Dave had thinned the grass—I could tell she fed eyasses. The tiercel, still calling, moved down the ledge to the round rock at its east end. There he remained for hours.

The tiercel was crouched, and although he never remained long motionless, he turned his head side to side, to side less vigorously. But the falcon sat where I had stood, I still was fresh from the witnessing. Those eyasses lay timeless, warm beneath her. This was another of the arctic nights for the falcons, like last year's and next year's, yet I was here, I felt nights like these would endlessly content me.

Part IV.

Uneasy Neighbors

Days followed without clouds at any hour. We continued
our lookout watches. At night as I slept I'd awaken with
the tiercel's voice until he entered my dreams, and I never
knew at morning if I remembered real or phantom cries.

The evening following our two night vigils Dave watched
the cliff. For two hours the tiercel was gone. For the first
time the falcon left the scrape not for the food exchange or
for one brief stretch of her wings; now she walked to the
ledge brink and preened or followed little bird motions with her
eyes, or else flew, legs stretched to the air. These breaks
lasted as long as ten minutes. Previously she had kept to the
scrape constantly; she had performed all brooding, and the
tiercel never spelled her so that she might hunt.[1]

During several watches we noted ravens. When they
were far away we might first spot them after we heard falcon
calls from their direction. Or if we heard ravens croaking,
we might see a peregrine flying among them. At these
distances, no attacks occurred. Upon intrusions closer to the
eyrie the falcon did attack, although the raven could easily
depart. This contrasted markedly with the raven's luck when it
approached the cliff face itself, and would end up terrified,
croaking, and trapped in a rock corner, unable to flee the
fierce tiercel for some minutes. The peregrines were always
more tolerant of us, and of other humans, we later discovered,
never cackling or stooping unless we used the rope to approach
the ledge itself.

Other observers have stated the peregrines do not
defend their wide hunting territories.[2] But we very seldom discovered either falcon when we were away from the cliff.
We didn't even see them in the valley immediately below
unless we sat on lookout and actually saw them descend. Their
general presence was felt more than perceived.

---

1. See Nelson (1970) and Enderson, Temple, and Swartz (1972)
on the tiercel's role in brooding.
2. See Cade (1960).

We ran a third night watch, with Dave performing the first shift. I liked this arrangement less well for I slept poorly early in the night, always expecting to be awakened by Dave's return. He woke me and heated water on the stove for his coffee and my tea.

"Better be careful when you go up," he said, "they cackled for five minutes when I got to the lookout."

He was wider awake than I. "When the tiercel got back from his morning hunt he didn't have anything. A few minutes later I saw the falcon in flight, then landing by the bunting nest. When she went back to the eyrie she had prey."

"Did you see it?" I asked. "Was it our male bunting? Did she stoop on him?"

"I don't know. I didn't see it. I don't think she could have gotten a body any other way."

Dave liked watching the sun go and come. "The sun stayed on Sol Gryn all night!" This was the highest mountain west toward the sea. I almost wanted another night watch for that. Not quite. I could see my breath flowing frosty. But mosquitoes also waited. Generally when it was warm we had to cope with insects; without insects there was the cold. But at in-between temperatures we suffered in both ways. I caught myself cursing mosquitoes at the lookout that morning and wishing they all were dead. I wasn't the first to have such a hope, and those who had acted on that threat were one cause for our work in Greenland—the mosquitoes indeed lived with the peregrines.

During this watch I saw four food exchanges on the ledge. Apparently the tiercel gave up food in two ways, at the ledge or as he rose in aerial spirals and the falcon beat up under him with crooked wings, and took prey from his talons. The tiercel almost always would announce his approach, and the falcon on her scrape had better ears than we, or maybe she saw him, for sometimes we would hear her answering calls before his own, or her appearance out on the ledge might alert us to spy the tiercel in quick flight toward the cliff.

The ledge exchanges occurred now that the eyasses were newly hatched. Before most exchanges had been aerial. We wondered if the falcon was now reluctant to leave the scrape but would fly out to meet her mate more often as the young ones grew. The falcon I remember foremost as by her scrape, the tiercel perched upright and calling alone. The two together I imagine rising in their dizzy, clamorous spiral.

The aerial exchange was the most clearly ritual event we observed, although many other behaviors were strictly patterned. Delicate courtship maneuvers, the most formal of all, had been repeated before our arrival. These rituals serve to unite the species, and the unique reaction and action of the courtship must be exactly balanced to let the fiery falcons mate, one peregrine with another while all other kinds of falcons are absolutely excluded. The rituals repeat one spring after another. The years seem to bring no changes. Yet we human watchers live so few years. During the passage of a thousand human life spans the courtship patterns have been shifting. At what point were the ancient tiercels and falcons so different that they were less peregrines, more some strange species? The species concept serves the convenience of human understanding, but a species is fluid, evolving, and multiformed; it cannot be pigeonholed.[3]

The peregrine has always been subtly changing to suit its varying surroundings. Where a breeding population fails to fit into its home, when the setting somehow shifts and the species does not, it dies out. Speciation consists of a multitude of intricate alterations. The extent to which a peregrine can vary and yet remain a peregrine is unclear. Through time we must guess at the many minor changes, and from their totality imagine how the old falcon interacted differently with its prey, competitors, and fellow members of the species.

We know almost nothing of the lineage of the peregrine. Bones of birds are lightened for flight, and thus fragile, quick to be destroyed. Fossils of birds are rare.

The earliest falcon remains date from the Miocene epoch, which began 25 million years ago; these birds were somewhat

---

3. See Mayr (1970) for a general treatment of species evolution.

smaller than present-day merlins.[4] Something very like the peregrine has probably existed for a million years—perhaps much longer, five million years. Earth did not have the same landscapes then. Yes, there were savannahs, and forests broken by rivers where the peregrine hunted. But the details, the plants and animals, large and small, did not exactly match with today's. A million years ago many were subtly older than the present life forms, for many no modern counterpart exists. Five million years ago animals were distinctly older; they stood in different relationships to each other.

The landscape evolves as does the species. All the living parts are tuning to one another for a resilient whole where the many parts can survive and reproduce, continue. The community becomes rich with life. To an extent, it tames and harnesses the nonliving winds and heat and violence, the chemical earth.

The nonliving changes also, and the living system must be retuning or, shaken, must be rebuilt. The individual species matter less in themselves than in the way they relate to the other species and thus all together form the whole community. A species that doesn't adjust dies out. Extinction is a normal event; indeed, all species eventually fail or adapt beyond recognition. When a catastrophe hastens the end, one ice age perhaps, the community is less full of life, and certain relationships are lost. But the impoverishment is temporary. The surviving kinds will adjust to fill the emptiness, or a new species will develop or appear from elsewhere.

The loss is temporary on a geologic time scale. Yet humans and their individual interests live an incredibly short time. From our viewpoint, extinction is endlessly destructive.

The communities evolving at many times and in many places have held the speedy inhabitant of cliffs that pursues birds as prey on the open air and lives most often near water. These communities contained no other creature quite like it. Now, because of events during these tiny last thirty years, some communities no longer have the peregrine.

---

4. Brodkorb (1964); Grossman and Hamlet (1964).

To form a part of a community for long, each species must have its unique way of living. The system is rich with food, and as it develops it can support more life. But each animal has it own share. The species live together because they seek different foods, or the same food in different ways.

The gyrfalcon hungers over, flies over, and dominates the Greenland tundra much like the peregrine. Yet it takes mammals and larger birds as prey, frequently striking its victims as they rest or hide on the ground.[5]

Watchers speak of the peregrine's pursuit as eternally through the air. Thus the careless mammal that might fall victim to the gyr is generally safe from the peregrine. Usually the peregrine strikes its prey with such force that it is instantly killed or crippled. The falcon's speed of descent upon the bird provides the force for the blow, as well as a last-moment jerking forward of the talons. Larger prey, perhaps heavier than the falcon, are knocked down out of the air. But the peregrine hardly slows as it snatches lighter bodies and rushes up again from the momentum of its stoop. For the stoop comes at the end of the pursuit, plummeting down on the target. Because the peregrine seeks a last-minute fall to add power to its blow, it rarely strikes prey from below, but instead will rise higher than the prey to commence chase. On a level course, many birds such as sandpipers or pigeons are agile enough to dodge the talons.[6]

Dave and I saw the long stoop for prey only at the cliff, where the tiercel occasionally followed the steeply falling rock after small birds. When they left the cliff to hunt, both adults would course low over the ground and skim all the rises and dips of tundra. This strategy is probably particularly suited to Greenland where no trees or high bushes stand to interfere with low flight, and where three of the four common small birds (all but the chuttering redpoll) fly near the ground.

The sparse vegetation that provided little cover encouraged another strategy uncommon in the south. If a startled bird sought shelter in a dwarf birch or willow, the hunter

---

5. Salomonsen (1950–1951); Cade (1960).
6. Cade (1960); Mattox and Ward, personal communications.

would instantly rise above and stoop on the spot one or
several times, occasionally succeeding in flushing the bird and
thus gaining another chance for the kill.

Whenever the peregrine appears, little birds are terrified.
In migration, shorebirds will vacate their feeding pools
en masse when a falcon arrives. Most birds chased will streak
for cover. In their madness, ducks dive into bushes or sandpipers into rivers. Once hidden the little birds won't leave their
shelter; sometimes a human can walk among them without
flushing them. The falcon thus is most successful where
it surprises prey, or finds it in the open far from cover. Land
birds crossing rivers are vulnerable.[7] On the Hudson River
the semiwild pigeons sought shelter from the falcons; the
trained racing pigeons died most often, for they would attempt
to outfly the hunter through the open.[8]

Peregrines prey on the full range of birds from sparrows
up to small hawks and gulls.[9] Some falcons may concentrate
on one or two species for food, perhaps near the seabird cliffs,
and at a bridge in New York City one pair lived on starlings
that gathered in thousands to roost.[10] But generally the
peregrine takes whatever prey opportunity offers. Some little
birds, because of their habits or bright coloration, are particularly
vulnerable. In Alaska the female snipe skulks in the marsh.
But the males soar in ecstasies high above the ground and
shelter, they beat their wings for the hollow winnowing, they
are passionately blind to peregrines.[11]

Humans see too few hunts to learn by direct observation
what species the peregrines take for prey. Nor could Dave
and I identify the little bodies the adults brought to the scrape,
gray bundles already stripped of feathers. In addition, we
were not finding remains of prey by the scrape. Perhaps the
adults carried bones and leftovers away, or perhaps, because
the bodies were small, all parts of the creature were consumed.

We did have one means for counting prey. Hawks not

---

7. Cade (1960).   8. Herbert and Herbert (1965).
9. Bent (1938); Salomonsen (1950–1951); Hagen (1952); Cade
(1960); Ratcliffe (1962).
10. Herbert and Herbert (1965).   11. Cade (1960).

only consume meat, but also bones, hair, feathers, and other indigestible tidbits. Everything eaten passes into the crop, and food continues to the stomach for digestion. But bones and feathers are formed into rounded pellets, and these are regurgitated. Pellets will lie below peregrine perching places or on the eyrie ledge. These can be carefully examined, and the remains identified. We collected pellets at each visit to the eyrie and brought them back to the United States for analysis.[12]

For a time Dave and I continued to be puzzled by the strange hopping behavior of either adult; every week or so one of them would leave the cliff and, instead of crossing low over the tundra, would abruptly land and jerk in energetic springs up from the grass and down. Nothing seemed particularly attractive, or playful, about these chosen spots. But one time the tiercel returned cliffward with prey only four minutes after I saw him land and hop (I had lost track of his location while negotiating with the telescope). At last one afternoon the tiercel landed on the lookout side of the valley, I saw him rise and drop, and then he looked at his feet and picked up a brown body.

Dave and I never found a written description of this hop hunting. Apparently the adult would spot a female or perhaps newly fledged young longspurs that liked to skulk about in the grass. Such a tactic would frequently succeed in a landscape as barren as West Greenland's.

While even the female peregrine hunts distinctly smaller animals than the gyrfalcons, our falcon had seldom hunted since our arrival in Greenland; instead the much smaller tiercel did all the foraging. Dave and I could tell that he took only the smallest birds, not ptarmigan, oldsquaw, or the ground-dwelling hare. The peregrine diet at this time was quite distinct from the gyrfalcon's. Later, when the young were older, the falcon would probably hunt larger creatures than did the tiercel.

Young peregrines, the novices, are clumsy hunters.[13] They

---

12. See Cade (1960) for a discussion of methods for obtaining prey counts.
13. Hickey and Anderson (1969).

pursue easy game and don't even attempt many opportunities that the adults would seize. When prey is scarce the young falcons suffer first. For hunting is an art among peregrines, and each adult gradually masters her techniques and discovers new ways to find and catch her quarry. In Queensland, Australia, for example, peregrines sometimes join with butcher birds for hunts. When the falcon pursues the small birds through the air, the butcher birds notice, and they see where the fugitives try to hide. These shrikelike predators burst in among the bushes, because they live by chasing desperate prey around branch ends and through leaves. The falcon hasn't departed; she waits above. When a little bird flushes in its fright at the butcher birds, the falcon stoops, and the little one must return to the shrikes' bushes. It is caught between the two dangers.[14]

The Dilemma

Generally, the days passed for me in uninterrupted eagerness so that suppers were for wondering where the hours had fled and wishing a dozen more would come before twilight then my sleep. But occasionally I felt listless and apathetic, not particularly toward what I did, but toward all I might do, and I hardly cared to awaken from my cot. It was the quietness of the tundra, and the simplicity of our tent and belongings, we had neither people nor things to distract us or fill our days with the patter of activity, slight encounters, and dozens of minor tasks that wouldn't please but wouldn't bore in their briefness. We had nothing but the best of pleasure; we knew what that was. Food and eating gained in importance. These meals were our rituals, when the two of us would sit on our cots and watch the stoves burn and water boil, readying our tin cups and searching for our silverware. We calculated ahead when we could eat each food item, and how much we could afford to consume at one sitting. At the successes in our study, the day Dave saw the four eggs in the nest or the evening after we both ascended, we celebrated

14. MacQueen (1953).

with extra rice or gravy. Afterward we might sit upon our cots and sip India tea or Air Force coffee, with sugar and instant cream.

But what did it reveal, that these dissatisfactions arose even under the peregrine cliff? I had nowhere else I would rather go, nothing better to do than hold the watches. Dave too felt restless, as one day after another passed in our tent and valley. I never asked him how he was restless, but while my emotions sent me into silence and isolation, Dave wished for company, the flutter of words, perhaps at the air base.

Humans must all be cowards when these certain doubts pursue us. Usually when I climbed up the talus slope the peregrines would excite me once more.

*   *   *   *

Dave and I wished to learn what we could of the peregrine as it related to the other wildlife of Greenland. The arctic ecosystem has far fewer species than more complicated landscapes farther south; the peregrine's role would be more important than that of a single predatory species in a more complex system, and its impact easier to assess. Ultimately we wished to know what would be the effects of the loss of the peregrine in Greenland, to understand both life in the Arctic and the value of the peregrine now threatened. This summer we could only begin such a task.

The peregrine's interactions were of two primary sorts. It competed with other predators for food, and with the gyrfalcon and raven for nest sites. And its presence had a major impact on the prey species that lived near eyrie cliffs.

We planned a census of the tundra nesters to learn what numbers of each species were available to the peregrine. Of course we could not count everything over the whole of our pair's hunting range, but by counting on a sample area we could estimate the general abundance of prey species. Furthermore, by the sample count we could know how one species's numbers compared with another's. These figures we would compare with our data on how many of each species the peregrine ate. If the falcons took prey randomly from the birds available, then if buntings were as common as redpolls, equal numbers of each would be eaten. Where discrepancies between abundance and prey figures appeared, we would know that the peregrine selected certain species more than others. Disappearance of the peregrine would have a different effect on each species.

I selected the area immediately before the cliff for the census, partially for its convenience and also for its assortment of streams, wet meadow, sheltered and exposed hillside, and rock piles and cliff. First I made a sketch map of the area from the lookout. I was surprised to discover streamlets I had never before noticed. I copied the map freshly for each walk, and covered the whole area on successive days. Whenever I saw a bird I marked its position on the map with an X and code signs for its species and sex. By repeating the walks, I could compare the X's and learn where the different birds stayed, in essence learning individuals of a species that looked identical, according to where I found them. As the females were secretive and often on the nest, I would outline the territories of each male, and then know how many pairs nested in the area. Using this method, I didn't account for unmated birds. Single males would wander about and out of the valley without a territory, while I would erroneously associate lone females with a singing male who had his own mate. The hunting peregrines contributed to the number of unmated birds.

From the lookout I had underestimated the length of the hike around the survey area. I passed parts of six days, each time knowing better what I would see. The walks cut down on my lookout watches; although I could hear the peregrines, I missed the hours above.

I found four species, the common little birds of central West Greenland. The largest was the wheatear, the only one not a finch, with slender sharp bill and lithe body with long wings. The male was gray backed, tan fronted with black wings, eyestripe, and tail. When he flew for insects he flashed his white rump and long wings. The female was plainer brown, and both adults worried constantly about their

young that fledged early in July and kept a constant racket
for the peregrines to hear.

The young made enough slurry rattles and trills that one
set might have been mistaken for several families in the
same area. They resembled the female except they had faint
streaks about the belly, and they didn't fly when I approached
but looked uncertain and nervous, jerking their tails or shifting
their feet. They flew no farther than necessary, perhaps
to the next rock or bush, and the parents twecked! at me.

Of Greenland's passerines, the wheatears migrate farthest—
deepest into pesticide areas—and thus pose the greatest danger
to falcons. They are common from Greenland to Alaska,
but usually I think of them as European, for they nest throughout England, and the wheatears from the North American
Arctic almost never appear in the States but hasten to the
Old World in autumn. The Greenland wheatears don't touch
at Europe in their migrations but cross the Atlantic directly to
Africa where they winter in the tropics.[15] Few birds so
small have the strength for such flights. Their long wings,
even those of the bumbling young, deserve respect.

The snow bunting is indeed the snowbird, for it is the
first sign of spring for Greenlanders, as Americans wait for
robins, arriving early in April, and some few even in March.[16]
Their song is like the melt water tinkling from ice; they love
rocky areas, and the pairs had divided the cliff into territories,
one after another, to include the peregrine ledges. The
other bunting young were as loud as the ones near our lookout,
and I located several of their eyries. The bunting is one of
the few species to inhabit the barren nunataks, the mountain
tops forever surrounded by ice, and the species reaches far to
the north in Greenland. The last individuals leave in October,
the West Greenland finches to Canada and the northern
prairies of the United States. But the buntings of northeast
Greenland pass north of Scandinavia to the steppes of Russia for
their winter.[17]

---

15. Salomonsen (1967), cited in Mattox (1970b).
16. Salomonsen (1950–1951).
17. Mattox (1970b).

Clearly commonest were the lapland longspurs, the males
brown and white and gaudy with a black hood and reddish
nape. They sang from bushtops or rocks but, unlike the
wheatears and snow buntings, divided all the valley into
territories, even the flattest grassy areas. As the census days
passed, I increasingly noticed males with white splotches
on their necks and heads—already their moult had begun. The
longspurs began to fledge during this same time that I made
my census. Luckily I soon completed the counting, for the
many brown young hiding in grasses would have totally
confused my image of the territories.

The smallest passerine was the rascally redpoll, second
to arrive in spring after the bunting, and these sociable birds gave
me more trouble than all the others combined.[18] The buntings
and wheatear flight colors contrasted with the tundra, and
the longspurs stayed close to the ground, but the redpolls
seemed to fly continually. They wouldn't stay in a particular
area but crossed all happy and buzzily chuttering from one end
of the cliff to the other, or across to Tent Lake or the deepest,
farthest wheatear gorge. Not only that, but the redpolls
didn't stay in pairs; instead three or four would hang together
in the afternoon, and then charge off all in one direction or
separate ways. My chief clues to their whereabouts were the
willow bushes that grew taller than the birches, reaching
a height of three feet in the most sheltered nooks. The redpolls
always alighted in willows, not on the ground or boulders.
They too had young, although they moved about so much that
I was never certain whether the parents fed only their own
young or any of them. The fledglings luckily still lacked
confidence to change bushes often, or fly high in the air, so that
as I located all the young I learned the number of redpoll
pairs.

I don't know if these were the same redpolls to reach
New England in some winters. The longspurs also descended
to America in fall. In Massachusetts they were uncommon,
and we'd look for single individuals among the bunting
or lark flocks. Most laplands pass on to the plains.

18. Salomonsen (1950–1951).

I found no other nesters in the valley. One afternoon three phalaropes chipped from the grassy edge of Tent Lake. These are small sandpipers that do not walk on beaches or sand flats as most of their relatives do, but swim with a jerking motion of their high-raised heads, and spin about in the shallows for water insects and larva.

The phalaropes stayed only one day. Already they were wandering free of their territories as the passerines soon would do. They nested on many of the small pools in the tundra. Unlike all the other sandpipers they never return to shore after they depart the nesting lands, but pass in flocks down the open sea to winter on the tropic ocean where they are lost, and people in boats rarely meet them.[19]

Several other species of birds nest on the tundra but in lesser numbers. In our part of West Greenland there were ravens, white-fronted geese, and loons, which the falcons don't hunt, and mallard ducks, oldsquaw, and ptarmigan. These last three all are rather large for the tiercel to catch, but certainly the falcon hunts them. The mallard lives in small ponds with thick vegetation along the shores, and the oldsquaw in most of the larger deeper ponds and lakes, a rather common duck. The mallards amazingly winter in Greenland at the edge of the stormy ocean itself, where waves threaten to freeze them or crash them against rocks.[20] I could never accept the green-headed drakes that flushed or the plain ducks that quacked loudly as truly arctic and not transplants from the nearest bread-and-pigeons park. The oldsquaw, like so many Greenland animals, has considerable white in its coloration. These are sociable little ducks that flock until mid-June nesting comes, and then the pairs separate; but the mates keep a whistley contact that can be heard while their lake still hides behind the rock corner. She lays a dozen or more eggs, but the foxes search for them, or sometimes the caribou trample them as they drink at the lake.[21] A ground nest is dangerous, and the young that do hatch quickly learn to swim and the nest is abandoned.

---

19. Bent (1927).
20. Salomonsen (1950–1951).   21. Bent (1925).

For the winter, oldsquaw from all of Greenland congregate in coastal waters from Holsteinsborg to Greenland's south tip, where alone the shores remain ice free. Some of the ducks probably pass farther south to the American coasts.[22] Oldsquaw in southern waters do ingest pesticides.[23]

Many of these neighbors journeyed farther than I had to reach the tundra, from Africa, the south Atlantic, South America. A few short weeks after my departure, when the frosts came, almost every bird would leave. For three months the wandering birds form one society. Then each kind scatters, its flickerings of Greenland in black northern eyes, that sedentary people across a third the world may see, may understand or not.

At the conclusion of the census, I had located twenty-two pairs of longspurs, seven pairs of wheatears, five pairs of snow buntings, and four pairs of redpolls. These numbers accounted for one-third square mile of tundra. Because the sample area was more sheltered from the weather and contained more vegetation than average over the landscape, it supported a greater density of nesting birds than did most of the falcons' hunting territory. But if the peregrine limited his hunting to the circular area within two miles of the eyrie—and generally we believe he traveled more than two miles, although not due north where he would have encountered the Black Cliff peregrines—he would have covered a range of more than twelve square miles; he would have terrified hundreds of families of passerines.

When our pellet samples were analyzed in the United States we discovered that longspurs were the primary prey, with ten individuals; but there were nine buntings, and we had one or two victims for each of the following species: redpoll, wheatear, ptarmigan, and phalarope.[24] We expected to find many longspurs, but the flashy buntings bore far more than their share of the burden.

---

22. Salomonsen (1950–1951).
23. Hickey, Keith, and Coon (1966).
24. Roxie Laybourne of the Bird and Mammal Laboratories, U.S. Fish and Wildlife Service, identified the prey remains in our pellet samples.

Observers in many parts of the world have claimed that hawks, including peregrines, do not hunt in the immediate vicinity of the eyrie.[25] Evidence for this conclusion is the noticeable concentration of nesting birds, both large and small, near the eyries. For example, merlins in Norway often have colonies of fieldfares (a northern thrush) sharing the same birch tree with them, and Canada geese nest much more frequently by peregrine eyries on the Colville River in Alaska than elsewhere along the river banks.[26] It appears that the aggressiveness with which peregrines drive off other predators causes this gathering of nests. No raven could prowl near our peregrine eyrie without suffering attack, and the peregrine will likewise drive away gyrs, eagles, and large gulls. Thus the immediate vicinity of an eyrie is relatively safe from nest robbers. The fieldfares close to merlins fledged more young than did other fieldfares without this manner of protection.

But how are these birds safe from their predator hosts? Do the hawks lose all fierceness near their eggs or young, or at this spot is all their attention directed toward their own nest, so that they swiftly come and go high above? Cade in Alaska once saw geese, frightened by humans, also suffer falcon attacks when they tried to fly back to their nests. At last they alighted on the river, and successfully hiked home without harassment. He speculates that the peregrines, who hunt flying birds, will not strike at prey on the ground. The little ones slip safely into their nests by walking or by low flights close to cover. The gyrfalcon, that often stoops on prey at ground level, less frequently attracts these neighboring nests.[27]

In Greenland we found that the immediate vicinity of our cliff, perhaps simply because its rocks and sheltered bushes provided best cover, held slightly more nesters than the rest of the valley. And the buntings did dare even more: not once but often a male walked on the very ledge where the tiercel perched. We never saw one caught at these times; the tiercel hardly noticed him. But it was a treacherous freedom these buntings enjoyed, for we didn't find that the passerines

---

25. See Cade (1960).   26. Hagen (1947); Cade (1960).
27. Cade (1960).

were always secure near the eyrie. Both falcons caught birds at the cliff, and even stooped on them directly from the eyrie ledge. The falcon paid particular attention to the passerine activity at the cliff base, perhaps because she was reluctant to leave the eyrie for long flights such as the tiercel generally preferred. Passerine watching was her chief activity as she began leaving the scrape to perch on the ledge brink. During bad weather, when the tiercel stayed close to the cliff, the closest neighbors bore the greatest likelihood of being taken by either peregrine.

Proximity to the eyrie was not an advantage. The wide tundra, although open to any predator, less frequently came under the peregrine's eye. The falcon's continual presence at the cliff proved a greater danger than would have all the other predators combined.

Most often humans have been attracted to the peregrine for its speed and violence in the hunt. For then the falcon leaves her leisured, restful flight for the long-distance pursuit and sudden stoop. The frantic, vain efforts of her prey to escape, as well as the panic that fires even speedy swallows or sandpipers, dramatize her power. I too admired her splendor. But I focused on the peregrine, not her prey. I had to balance loves for two raging hearts as I thought of the hunts, and I found it best that the smaller remain only blood and feathers. Best for me to remain cliff-bound and watch the world with an eyrie view, the falcons' watch.

Yet I walked the valley day after day and looked among the bushes and gorges, the grassy meadows, until I knew each male in his guarded home plot, and glimpsed his mate more than once or twice, and I counted his young. As I came to recognize the individuals, the tundra ceased to seem plain, or all identical but bloomed as variously as a garden. The cliff shadow at twilight sent less of a chill than another shadow, the eyrie's threat that was thin and long and ever present.

I feared for the male buntings that fluttered in insect flights about the cliff. And the clumsy wheatear children, how could they bear the falcon's shriek, or tottering evade the

talons? I saw the same family each day I climbed the lookout—
each day I counted them. The young redpolls clung to the
tops of bushes, roly-poly like their parents, with clownish,
blank expressions, as if once they lost their confusion they would
match their parents' recklessness. These too I feared for, that
alone lent shreds of stability to their parents.

From the lookout I watched the peregrines fly over the
tundra with their shadows running under them. I had no
resentment for the hunters, only a tinge of uneasiness,
a shifting regret that I couldn't confront, that complicated my
delight at the tiercel's return. I had poor eyes for spotting
him at a distance as he approached, but if he came low, the
small birds chipped from hiding spots; they looked carefully,
always, for the peregrine. They had reason to watch. They
had dangerous blue skies for heaven, and silence but not safety.
The thought that there were many small birds could not
alone comfort me. I found myself watching the tiercel as he left
the cliff, with more than curiosity, to see what direction
he took, how far he traveled to which part of the tundra.
I also had to adjust to the passerines' fatal sky.

The Alarm

The lookout gave us a view of the cliff and valley so that
we could follow the falcons through most of their activities.
But the distance of the eyrie from our position prevented
observation of behavior at the scrape, of either the adults or
young, in any but the roughest detail. As the small eyasses and
the delicacy of the falcon's movements at the eyrie contrast
with the peregrine's otherwise fierce and powerful aspect,
we wished to set an observation blind on the eyrie ledge. If a
blind is well constructed so that no parts of it tremble in the
wind and the occupant's movements cannot be noticed from
without, the birds will return to their normal activity
conveniently close to the blind. At least, that is the theory, for
blinds sometimes prove disruptive, depending on their construction and placing and the suspicious nature of the birds.

Close observations of the young were particularly needed
to assist the efforts at captive breeding of the peregrine.

Because once eggs were hatched, the keeper needed to provide proper conditions for the falcon adequately to feed and watch her young. Tundra falcons might differ from the anatum peregrines which had already been studied. Furthermore, DDT might cause critical abnormalities in behavior at the eyrie that were one cause of reproductive failure; we had incomplete proof for the existence of these disturbances. Only a close watch on the scrape itself could provide such information.

We also wished to photograph the peregrines. We gingerly had packed an assortment of valuable cameras and special lenses, well padded.[28] But even the longest lenses would not magnify the falcons sufficiently for pictures from the lookout, and when we climbed the ledge, the birds of course dropped all normal pursuits to fly over our heads. Dave photographed the scrape, eggs, and young, but to capture feedings or the perched adults we would need a blind.

Pictures from a blind would serve more purpose than merely reminding us of our pleasures, or decorating our scrapbooks. Pictures are the only means most people may ever have to view the peregrine. Preservation of falcons and other wildlife requires certain awarenesses and sacrifices by the public. Its attitudes limit what research or technology can do; it must care if the animals are to survive.

We had been wondering for some time how we would obtain materials for constructing the blind. The night before our three-day trip I had carried light canvas from the base to our camp. Still we needed a frame to hang the canvas on. Then one day Dave went fishing (unsuccessfully) on the long lake and returned with wood two-by-fours that he had found by the lakeshore.

I looked up at the grassy ledge where soon we would be crouching and watching. I felt its privateness, it was not our place but the falcons' home that in their pride they chose to be inaccessible.

During the next days Dave considered how to make

---

28. We used a Nikon F camera; for our photographs from the blind, we relied on two lenses—a Nikkor–Q Auto 135 mm. 1 : 2.8, and a Nikkor–P Auto 300 mm. 1 : 4.5.

First Eyrie ledge with blind frame in place, facing west
away from scrape toward Long Lake.

and place the blind. He had measured the ledge itself; we need
supply only the top, front, and sides, for the steeply falling
slope would form both back and bottom.

He said he would make the frame at our camp and sew and
cut the canvas to fit over it.

He hesitated, then, "I think it's best if we put the frame
up by itself first and wait several days before we place the
canvas. Then the falcons won't mind so much."

I looked up at the ledge. We needed observations from
the blind; blinds have been set on peregrine ledges before,
without bad result. Yet it seemed a risky, threatening act toward
the falcons. I had nothing to say to Dave's plan, only uncomfortable doubts, too vague for words.

The day came when we planned to raise the frame
onto the cliff. During the early morning I sat on the lookout.
I was nervous with thoughts of climbing the cliff carrying
the heavy wood, and with uneasiness about what we were doing
to the falcons. The tiercel brought food several times. Once
when he called on his return the falcon rushed out to
meet him. But instead of joining in their concerted upward
spirals the tiercel whipped straight to the cliff and landed. She

pursued him and snatched the prey, jarring him into the air so that down he landed on the eyrie ledge. She passed him and entered the scrape. An odd friction between the pair.

I prepared to leave my position at midmorning and take a census walk. I was halted in my descent when amazed I heard voices below me toward the lake. Tiny figures walked on the tundra. Two, in bright colors, three more well behind them, and in between smaller forms running. I sat down.

I could hear the voices. These were Danes that somehow had wandered far from the base. What day was this? . . . Sunday morning. They walked straight from the lake toward our tent, toward the falcons. And I felt suspicious. What did these people come here for? I waited some minutes for them to pass, I waited feeling a little resentful at their intrusion, and especially when I heard the children's voices harsh as they roared in imitation of powerful cars or machines.

The long hill separated me from these people. I walked away from them on my census and returned at last only reluctantly to the tent. Dave sat alone outside and saw me coming. The Danes were hidden on the talus slope above. I heard them tapping at rocks. I had lengthened my census walk, and Dave was impatient to take up the blind frame.

Dave told me that one of the Danes had come to see the peregrines. He was a friend of Mattox's that Dave had met once at the base; he had brought a camera and would accompany us on our visit to the eyrie.

Dave and I marched straight up the slope with the frame between us. We passed the rock-hunting Danes, and the children paused, holding granite fragments in their fists; the sky was blue, their mothers smiled.

Dave said slowly, "Where's Steen?" These people hardly knew English.

"Up there," one answered, pointing among the higher, largest boulders.

He was leaning, stealthily, over one of them, and held his camera with its weighty long lens, waiting for the high falcons to fly.

"Steen," Dave said, "This is Jim Harris."

Steen was tall, sunburnt with short hair and blue eyes. He had never visited the falcon's scrape.

"Did you see the peregrine when he brought food in?" he asked.

We walked straight for the cliff bottom. The rocks were hot in the sun, the day was so bright we squinted a little. The tiercel started cackling at us long before we reached the rope end. I looked at Steen. The tiercel flew and circled over us. Was he more aggressive because of the group of Danes, and our direct approach with wood scraping rock, or was it only that his young had hatched? The falcon came off the scrape early also.

On my neck I felt the sun that baked the eyrie ledge and now touched the eyasses. How long would our visit take?

"I'll stay below," I said. "We don't need a third person for this." We were standing at the rope end, and Dave giving instructions to Steen on how to climb and how they would handle the wood frame. The falcons were cackling.

Dave went first, and I lifted the frame up to him. Steen followed. It was a long climb, with the frame scraping and catching on rock points, and dirt falling from the footholds so that I had to turn my face away. Steen had a set expression on his face, and I realized that he had never climbed before.

At last they vanished onto the ledge, and I heard Dave's voice as they negotiated the long ramp and he called to Steen "lift," or "slow." I looked at my watch. Fifteen minutes had gone since the falcon flew. The cackling makes you tense and urgent, you want to rush away, and I had nothing I could do but to watch the falcons stooping, and wait, and hope the eyasses weren't too hot, or the disturbance too long for the tiercel. The minutes passed. What were Dave and Steen doing?

For Steen this was the one day at a peregrine eyrie, his only day ever, and he had climbed the cliff for the few moments, he saw the stirring eyasses with their white down and newly awakened black eyes, he heard the chipping they made and the screams of the parents, he felt all the strength of the falcons' wind rushing, he hardly noticed the minutes vanishing.

The four eyasses at First Eyrie, shortly after the littlest eyass hatched.

And with his camera he was picture taking, again his one chance, and as eagerly as with his eyes and ears he was grasping this experience to hold it and not lose it.

I waited. Finally Dave appeared at the ledge end, and then Steen. Dave quickly descended. When he called up, "You now," Steen was staring down on the rocks, and then he descended. We raced away over the talus and slopes, and panting stopped where a boulder hid us.

The falcons were quiet on the cliff. Forty-five minutes. Well, it was done.

"The fourth egg hatched," Dave said. "There's a new tiny eyass, and he's pressed low in the scrape."

"Four."

"Steen got a lot of pictures. That was a good job."

We looked for Steen's day pack that hours ago he had

set down. The other Danes had already departed toward the long lake. Steen prepared to leave. He was still breathless.

"Well, I . . . at . . . that was good," he said. He couldn't speak English well at that moment.

He noticed cookies in his pack. ""Here, you take these." He was fumbling with his pack and looking at cliff, tundra, ground beneath him.

Then he gave the widest smile. "Thank you!" he said.

"Thank you, for your help!" Dave answered. And a raven was flying high before the cliff. And it passed unmolested down the ridge, black, bulky, flapping, until the light, shining tiercel who caught sunlight overtook it, and attacked from behind. Then up, the peregrine stooped four times on the twisting raven.

*　　*　　*　　*

That evening I sat on the lookout. Neither falcon had called as I ascended, but soon I noticed the falcon perched at her ledge brink. The wood frame dominated the ledge. For an hour the shadows deepened in silence. I was looking south at the horizon where the millions of people live, remembering again how their deeds touched even the Arctic. Chilled mosquitoes were humming about me.

I was tense. What if Dave and I caused destruction of this falcon family?

Something strange happened. Four times the falcon had flown, but the fifth time she went round the cliff corner, and both adults flew out, female chasing male and giving short, high calls. They rushed along the cliff and returned and spiraled, she pursuing. She landed, but then the chase was rerun, and several times the tiercel perched, but at last he left the cliff area. He did bring food soon, and through the rest of the evening called more often than was his habit.

The next morning was another bright day. Dave climbed to the lookout while I took a census walk. On the far side of the valley brown longspurs were skulking in the grass. I thought I heard the tiercel's quiet voice, not from the cliff but overhead. I looked over the wide sky but failed to spot him or to notice whether his shadow passed over the ground. The tundra swallows the falcons, hides them once they leave their cliff perches.

When I reached the tent I prepared for my afternoon watch. But when Dave came we sat awhile on our cots.

"Did you have a good morning?" he asked.

"I finished the last census walk. Just in time. There are baby longspurs everywhere."

"I saw you," he said. "The tiercel flew right over you when he left the cliff."

"How was it on the cliff today?"

"Quiet," Dave answered. I looked at him. "Boring. Only one food exchange in four hours. And the tiercel was away the last two and a half hours."

Later we heard a falcon voice. We stood outside and listened.

"I think I hear both!" I said. Then, "I probably won't see you before you leave for the base." Dave planned to stay overnight at the base and buy food before returning the next day. "Have a good trip."

There were no falcons perched on the cliff but from the lookout I could see the falcon peering my way from the scrape. Just after I sat down she walked out onto the ledge edge. Had I disturbed her?

For the first hour she moved back and forth from the scrape to the outer ledge, several times to sit awhile on the downy eyasses, gaze at the rock or more often over her shoulder at the sky, or perhaps at me far away, she had long-seeing eyes, and then she stood and walked on her long, spread talons to the rock brink. She watched the tiny birds below, or the sky, or the hills.

Now back to the scrape to brood. I couldn't see the eyasses that must have bunched together in that hollow of dirt and feathers. Their eyes sometimes open, except perhaps for the littlest eyass so newly hatched that it wanted only the warmth of its siblings or the dark falcon.

Midway through the hour the falcon bobbed her head at the birds calling from the talus, flew, and spun circles above the valley. She returned a minute later and entered the scrape. Wasn't she strangely restless?

So I thought when she circled again a half hour later. I wanted to know where the tiercel was. The falcon flew a third time, quickly down until I lost sight of her. She returned with a plucked bird and fed it to hungry eyasses.

The sun ran north of west. The falcon perched on other parts of the cliff. She killed another bird and brought it to the scrape. She walked to the edge and looked out.

Where was the tiercel?

The falcon glided long, long sloping into the valley on stretched wings that she didn't move until I lost her in the farther hills. Never had she left the scrape so frequently. Were the eyasses old enough to be left alone? Waiting, I thought about the day before and how long we had taken. I thought of the tiercel. I thought of the reasons he could be gone. It might have been a fierce fight with peregrines from another cliff, or a Greenlander hunter with a shotgun (I had heard shots), or he might have wandered very far, lost. Did he fly from the intruding observers and their bulky frame?

The falcon returned after twenty minutes without any food. She remained on the outer rock. Watching. She preened, little tussles with her breast feathers every now and then. The feathers hid faintly tan barrings. The wind caught them when she roughed them. I didn't know if the falcon alone could raise those eyasses. I looked at all her feather colors.

The eyasses that were huddled in the scrape. The beautiful tiercel who perched upright on his cliff all through the night. And always his voice had announced his return toward the eyrie with food.

The falcon flew quickly down and landed in the valley. She hopped in the grass but was far away, and I couldn't see her well.

The wind stopped and there was a bitterness in that moment that chilled my eyes. I felt afraid and sad, doubting any misfortune and yet unable to doubt.

Dave came out of the tent with his pack on. He was leaving. I didn't know what to do. "Wait," I wanted to shout.

166

Then I leaped down all the talus boulders and ran over grasses and slid past yielding gravel to catch him on the caribou path, and I said, "Wait, Dave.

"The tiercel's gone."

We talked, sitting on the ground. Dave decided not to go to town for awhile, for a day.

He said, "I'll watch from now until I get sleepy. Then you watch."

I realized how barren this tundra would be if the peregrines left.

"Jim. Don't worry so. It can't be helped."

The falcon cackled. She flew east from the eyrie. Then there were two peregrines, the falcon cackling, they circled, no, not a stranger peregrine, the falcon beat up under the newcomer's spirals, took prey from the hanging talons; it was the tiercel. Food given in the air, a long hunt, and when the falcon landed to eat, the gay tiercel whirled circles and called, "kaaa kaaa," had silver underwings. The wind buoyed and carried him.

Humans and Guilt—A Resolution

Dave hiked to the base and I returned to the tent with its windows all open, took my boots off. It was enough, for the time, to sit without boots, not to mind the mosquitoes humming, to feel the relief. I considered the little tiercel in his varying aspects. The evening quickly passed.

The falcon voices stirred me awake in the morning. Outside the tent it was another day unbroken by clouds, another day when the little birds watched the blue sky carefully.

And I had no task the whole day but to watch the peregrines. I never approached the lookout but left the tent to choose a grassy spot a short distance uphill. The falcons too would have a quiet day. I crouched, with my legs drawn high and close to my body. I was humble and lucky; the air felt cold but the sun heated my back and hair.

These peregrines were all right. The young would survive. I could not see the scrape at all from my low position, just the ledge brink. And I had only my binoculars because the telescope remained at the lookout. I stayed for over ten hours. The tiercel brought seven meals, all before mid-afternoon, and each time the falcon rose to meet him in an aerial exchange. She was visible on the cliff about half the time, in the afternoon, but especially in the morning she would be hidden from me by the scrape, probably brooding the young.

The tiercel stayed away from the cliff and appeared only at intervals. At each of his arrivals I realized freshly the beauty of his flight. When people feel little they most easily enjoy and admire the splendor in air. The wind was brisk from the southwest, and he, too restless and quick to perch for long on the rock. The female would drop away from him with new prey, and he would cut deep wingbeats before the cliff and follow the swells and indentations of the rock east west east. But then he'd stop his wings, face straight into the strength of the wind, and bow those long limbs taut in a curve, arced both vertically and horizontally. Such a silhouette, and he hangs motionless. Why doesn't he fall? Why mustn't he hover mightily like the kestrel to keep his position? Effortless he floats, his beak bent down as he watches the far ground—it is far—he actually rises! And I see his long tail is spread into a fan. The rushing air breaks against tail and crooked wings and thrusts him heavenwards until at last the whole cliff and ridge are below, he is a speckle in that blue. His wings straighten, he whips about, and with wind he flashes east so swiftly it is almost a stoop, so high he can fall far and still clear the ridge's sharpest crest to vanish. Again and again I watched this playing pilot.

When he returned, he flew in one way regardless of how he hit the wind. He would be crying with his thin voice and aim straight to the cliff, and never pause in a wingbeat, powerful so that even the strongest gusts didn't affect him. As he met the falcon he'd stretch his wings, and then either his own momentum and the wind at his back, or, conversely, the blow of air against tilted feathers, would lift him. And as he waited for the falcon he loosely flapped his crooked wings, this wide effort to slow rather than speed him so that she could reach his dangling talons.

Similarly, with wings half stretched and only the ends fully spread, the falcon would beat crooked wings in landing on her ledge. Usually she dipped before the eyrie so that for the last yards she would have to rise and lose her speed to make a gentle landing. She would stretch her talons forward for the first touching of rock.

The vibrant air explained so much. I did not see her leave the scrape by leaping up. Always she walked to the ledge brink. Then she could drop into flight, her weight falling speeded her so that with wings stretched she'd catch the muscular wind and zip up, now all the grace and power of the falcon hers.

She was heavier than the tiercel. Late in the afternoon the little birds chipped all about me. Suddenly I spotted her scouring the lower slopes for prey. Into the wind she beat her wings. But at her turns she only waved their tips, and with the wind she hooked her limbs back, and she fit all the hollows and ground rises more swiftly than the little birds could realize or prepare for.

Dave returned late in the afternoon. But I waited until suppertime to join him in the tent. I was all wind blown and wind sensitive.

"Today was very fine, Dave."

"You look like it was."

I laughed. "I wish you had been here. I was sad that you were missing the tiercel on this wind."

"I had a good hike. I saw those loons on my way back."

"We really aren't together very much. You're on the look-out, or I am. . . . Dave, I was thinking how quiet our lives are; that we are sheltered even here. I drank tea today, sitting in the sun. What I feel, I couldn't afford to feel if I had to struggle to live. Do you know what I mean?"

He smiled, "Each of us misses some things." We were quiet.

"Well, I'm glad you had the change. . . . Was there any mail?"

"No. I got a letter. I brought you some cake from the mess hall."

We waited two more days before Dave took up the blind covering. This visit to the eyrie wasn't like the trip with the frame. Instead of climbing over rocks and then leaning at the rope end with neck and eyes strained back, I watched from the lookout and saw the falcons both before and after, so that their reactions on the tall cliff were less uncertain.

The wind was soft from the west. The falcon spent most of the afternoon perched on the cliff. The situation of earlier weeks was reversed. Then I had sat hours with the tiercel and seldom saw his incubating mate. Now she and I watched and listened for the tiercel. He brought prey frequently, every hour or so; he had hungry eyasses. The falcon several times went into the valley, once to bring prey that she had caught.

I saw the tiercel take gentle circles after one food exchange. He revolved on straight wings, slowly, and tilted them when he turned. He let the breeze lift him until, tired, I took my eyes away, and then couldn't find him again in the blue.

The falcon watched Dave during all his climb over the talus slopes. She started the stoops and cackles as he reached the rope end. Dave was almost on the ledge itself when the tiercel returned. Both were stooping over him, falling, falling to within fifteen feet of his head. When Dave almost had fitted the covering and was fussing with the inside of the blind, the falcon touched briefly on the ledge. Although the tiercel never landed at that ledge and although he sometimes passed east to circle over the far part of the cliff, he did rise higher and stoop lower than his mate, he was a graceful defender.

Dave went quickly to the scrape; then one of those hidden eyasses raised its head up high and watched him leave. The whole ledge visit lasted seventeen minutes.

Both falcons soon landed near the cliff top. The canvas, barely smudged with brown mud, shone. While the tiercel soon left the cliff area, the falcon dropped into flight and skimmed three times before the ledge, until she landed at its east end. She glared at the blind, waddled to the east side of the scrape, still glared. Next the tiercel brought food. He had nervously taken to his hunt, but the prey posed a dilemma for the falcon, who relanded at the scrape, dropped the body

to look at the canvas, but then instead of feeding picked
the prey up and departed.

She landed on the grassy cliff top. She left the body behind
as she flew back to her eyasses. The tiercel delivered more
food, which the female ate on an east cliff ledge. But after
an hour she returned to the same grassy top of cliff, and picked
up that body to return to the scrape.

The eyasses were agitating in the scrape waiting for her and
food.

Before long the falcon was ignoring the blind entirely.
And the tiercel also at the fourth meal alighted without
hesitation. The eyasses fed, the falcon stepped over the scrape,
and settled. The little ones have shining white down. I
wondered if they stirred at all, muffled warmly beneath the
falcon.

I laughed when I returned to the tent and said to Dave who
was almost ready to sleep, "Now I know why the falcons
always cackle when you climb to the lookout, but stay quiet
for me. It's you that bothers them on their ledge."

"I must get a disguise," Dave answered.

"How many eyasses were there?"

"Four." The littlest one still lived!

"Everything's fine."

We waited another two days for the watch in the blind.
I would take the first turn, for most of a day.

*　　　*　　　*　　　*

The falcon flew when we reached the rope end. I remembered many of the handholds, and for the rest, I examined
the dirt and rock, feeling rock cracks with sensitive fingers.
Dave already was in the blind to make last arrangements in
its construction. Soon he called to me.

I was standing over the scrape. It looked messier now
than at my first visit, with feather remains and broken pellets,
and the bare dirt space less evenly edged. Many flies hovered.
The eyasses huddled in the scrape, except one who sat upright
in the middle.

Into the blind. Dave closed and weighted the cloth

behind me. Only a shadowy, quiet light within. There was a damp odor of soil. Dave had placed a flat stone midway up the sloping back for me to sit on, and I had room to position my feet comfortably, to sit upright. Dave was at the scrape with a brief look to distract the falcons, and then he stepped carefully across the blind's front, and I no longer heard his boots.

Within minutes the falcon voices ceased, but still they were circling because several times the falcon passed so close that I heard her wings rush. The upright eyass had vacated his central position to crawl a yard toward the blind. The other three eyasses sat up and hissed with small voices.

With a soft plump! the falcon landed on the ledge. All the eyasses quieted, and one by one they settled down flat on their bellies, their wing stubs relaxed out from their bodies. The youngest eyass lay at the outer scrape edge; it was noticeably smaller than the others. But it too had glistening white down, and coal eyes that remained open, briefly, as it crouched. The eyasses all had large feet that poked out from their bodies: their upper legs on the back sides had pink skin where the down didn't grow. These legs spread awkwardly on the ground—they grow before any other part of the eyass.

The falcon rested close to me. When I looked in the binoculars I saw all the feather edges, and her black eyes, and feathery legs, and flat-topped falcon head, far beyond, the out-of-focus hillside that was ordinary meadow. She turned her head. Her eyes gave her a predatory look, or else it was her hooked beak. I even saw the nostrils, and on the upper mandible, a notched point with which falcons snap the necks of prey.

The eyasses were still. Once only did they peep. Sometimes the falcon looked at the eyass who had left the scrape.

The tiercel called. It was a different sound than I had ever heard, distorted and thin, higher pitched; perhaps the rock face was catching his voice and magnifying it, for he grew louder and louder until the falcon flew. Quiet. I couldn't see the sky or the falcons. Then the female landed. She had no prey but walked to the scrape edge. The outer eyass noted her and peeped. The falcon walked to it and grasped it with her beak, I think by loose skin somewhere on its upper

Jim standing over three eyasses and one egg in First Eyrie scrape.

parts. She tried twice to raise the bulgy eyass into the air before carrying it back to the scrape and setting it down. Eyass wings stirred, of that eyass, and then of the others too that it touched and set in motion. They subsided.

The falcon hesitated low over the scrape, shrugged her feathers and settled. Rear end up again, breast still to the ground, she waggled her tail back and forth as she settled and muffled the eyasses comfortably beneath her. But she didn't doze.

Perhaps because the flies buzzed, I could move in the blind, and bumble into minor noises without her noticing. This blind worked well. Apparently she never noticed, or at least didn't care, that while two intruders climbed, only one descended. That didn't matter as long as the ledge appeared safe and empty.

What happened at so many eyries, that all eyasses did not survive to fly? Among the healthy peregrines, three or four eggs are laid at every cliff, yet even in these normal populations an average only of one and a half or two eyasses fledge.[29] What takes the other half? High cliffs are not secure protection.

Some eggs never are fertile. More addle before hatching time, in prepesticide times as many as one on average out of each clutch. Most of these chill, or broil in the sun, when the parents stay away too long because of disturbances at the cliff.[30] In the same way eyasses die when they are young.

Various accidents occur. Rain may flood an eyrie, or one of the adults die, or even a piece of cliff fall. There are nest robbers. In Greenland such predators are few, but these creatures cause the disturbances that create greater risk for eggs in the Arctic from chilling or overheating than do disruptions in the south. Ravens and glaucous gulls are the chief enemies. The Iceland gull will raid an unprotected ledge. And some curious people merely stay too long too close to the cliff; still others kill the adults with rifles.

But I was most wondering what extra risks an eyass runs

29. See Hickey and Anderson (1969), who cite an average of 1.5 young reared per occupied eyrie for 67 British and American locations. The average number of young per successful eyrie (not including eyries where no young fledge) would be higher.

30. Hickey (1942).

who hatches later than its fellows. For the older eyasses needed less brooding now, and each day the falcon left the scrape for longer periods. Was the littlest eyass ready? And would it clamor for food as eagerly as its nest mates when feeding time came, or would a stronger eyass get all at each meal? In many species the eggs in a nest hatch at different times always, so that when food is scarce not all the young starve, but the older survive.[31] With the peregrine, at least in temperate areas, the eggs hatch all together; but when by chance they do hatch at different times, wouldn't the effect be the same, the weakest, or youngest, dying?

Once I heard the tiercel's voice, and ravens croaking. Was there trouble? Later I heard him again, and almost immediately I saw him flying close by the ledge. The falcon looked up, then stood, but before she could fly, the male landed on the round boulder. She walked to him, her wings extended and held high, and took the dingy, plucked body with her beak. He flew.

She flew to the scrape. The eyasses were up and peeping, some of the noise hollow, some whistley. Their mother bent over the prey. They were bunched together and erect, heads alert and shaking right and left, beaks gaping, all white and motion at the scrape. The littlest eyass with palest down stretched directly before the falcon.

Those eight eyes never glanced at the prey, only at her. She tore a fragment so small it barely drooped from her bill. She leaned forward and touched it to an eyass beak. Gobble, it vanished. "Hiss Hiss Pip Pattle Hiss." Again and again she tore bits from the talon-grasped prey and held them to the eyasses. One eyass for each piece. They never fought, except in jostling with bodies and flopped wings to see parent better.

This continued only for two or three minutes, but I was noticing the tiercel's voice close before the eyrie, and at last he landed on the round boulder. He had prey in his talons. As the falcon ignored him he cackled. Then she looked over, briefly. He flew cackling, relanded. When the falcon did walk to him she hunched her back and crouched with wings

---

31. Lack (1947–1948).

held down to the sides. They cackled, beak to beak, then flew for an aerial exchange. The falcon landed elsewhere on the cliff with her meal.

When the falcon left them, the eyasses initially remained alert and hopeful, peeking out from the scrape. A large eyass crawled out and flapped upright again. "Huk-huk-huk-huk" it called, a miniature version of the parents' call. Then it took to preening, which it did quite well. On the wings dark feathers were poking out from the down. I knew why Bill Burnham affectionately called them downies.

For not only did the down standing give them fuzzy heads and body edges, their movements were clownish also. Most of that afternoon they lay on their bellies. Only energetic wavings of their wings and legs could raise them upright. They were bottom heavy, like fat, bulgy, bowling pins, and sat well balanced. But to move more than an inch they'd flop down, for they could support their weight only vertically or horizontally. Body horizontal, they'd plunge forward, at least their wings and feet would revolve like a swimmer's, only their progress was in double-slow motion. This was when they had clear ledge space. But usually the eyasses were together at the scrape. Then one eyass would stir up all his fellows, and all four would bustle so that I couldn't tell which was which, or where each ended, and after all the exertion and excitement they'd end in positions identical to where they began, all motion, no movement.

The falcon brought them several meals. The eyasses would line up. Often she gave one several bites in a row. All four wouldn't get to eat at each feeding. The littlest luckily got in front every time, and instead a middle-sized eyass in back would suffer. I doubt the falcon had special intentions; she merely reached toward the gaping bills.

The first three eyasses looked equally developed. If so, then the largest was a female, the others males. Even considering that the littlest eyass was almost a week younger, he was so much smaller he must have been a tiercel.

The eyasses lay still on their bellies.

*   *   *   *

Adult female flies into eyrie with food (a small passerine already plucked). Only the little eyass, which is two and a half weeks old, is in the eyrie; his sisters have wandered farther up the ledge.

Adult female feeds littlest eyass from the carcass of the passerine.

Immediately afterward, the female feeds littlest eyass from
ptarmigan body that had already been in the scrape.

The smallest eyass attempts to feed on a ptarmigan carcass.

Here the littlest eyass sat. I could see he was well fed. At feeding time the crops of eyasses extend as the young hawks gobble meat, bones, and feathers. Now the littlest eyass with his fat neck preened in the sun. Yet it was not thanks to me, who wanted so to see him that I had climbed the cliff and hid and waited in the darkness of the blind. The eyass might have broiled in the sun while we erected the blind, or his father might have abandoned him; instead the little one preened, safe.

But safe only for the fragile moment. The peregrines are predators of the wild, but look at these bits of down, and the adults hardly larger; see the endless tundra, how easily the falcons live or die. The fierce eyes of falcon and the warm eyes of prey suffer alike. We can't fend off death from what we love. I do not hate to see the talons and notched beak, but the little, captured birds recall the general cruelty and dying; it is that ever-presence I hate.

Danger that hung low in the sky beyond the cliff, destruction for small birds, wrapped the steep rock also. I could not see the south horizon from the blind. But all the birds fly that way in August. The small ones in flocks. The peregrines solitary drift down the long American coasts and river valleys, eat winter prey fat with American insects or American seed.

Tundra peregrines now carry the organochlorine poisons.[32]

Despite the many natural deaths—eggs addled or young frozen, starvation the first winter, the steady slow passing of adults—always enough eyasses have fledged in summer so that the species has survived; more than that, it has thrived and spread. But the balance is perilous, and only a little more death causes the decline. What pesticides have done! What now was happening in Greenland? These eggs hadn't fractured prematurely, but what of other eyries? How many nest cliffs had Mattox found?

This wasn't at all the worst disaster for birds in evolutionary time. Yet at that moment it seemed to me, so full of peregrine and remembering all the other fish-, bird-, and insect-eaters, that this was the worst avian misfortune that humanity has witnessed, across continents, spread among many kinds of birds, so quickly. Bitterly, wasn't the witness responsible? Humans created and released the poisons. But each of us wants to deny responsibility.

It is easy to point at chemists, who discovered the organochlorines, or manufacturers, who profited from the sales, or farmers, who protected their vegetables or grains or fruits. There were foresters, or civic leaders who loved elms; they wanted DDT to save trees. And doctors, who wished to curb disease. But how were they to know that DDT was dangerous?

Look then to individuals in the government agencies, those who license use of pesticides. Why didn't they demand to know more before licensing? Or legislators, local or national, why didn't they demand we know more? And on, and on . . .

But this pointing of blame is useless, meaningless. Inextricably mixed with pride, greed, corruption were courage, love as well as ignorance and short vision. And who ultimately benefited from and desired cheaper, better food, full-leafed, spreading trees, health? Each human. Him. Her. You. I. And there is not one of us in innocence who could not have

32. Cade, White, and Haugh (1968); Lincer, Cade, and Devine (1970).

done more than he or she did to forestall the disasters. We were all bound together in this.

Not always have humans been so thoroughly joined. There are now vast multitudes of people, and collectively we have great needs. Humanity has grown so wise and powerful and needy that efforts, fortunes, disasters must be united, whether any one of us wishes it or not. An individual's private innocence has become a lost luxury. The cruelty and dying in the world involve us all. We breathe with the prey, with the predators. Destruction as well as life pass around us and within us.

Insects were in the blind with me. Among their buzzes I heard a dryer rattle, like a dying fly. One of the big brown spiders that I had recently seen at the bottom of the blind had climbed to the top. He grasped a fly that whirred while still the spider was poisoning him. No webs. These spiders must rely on their quickness and stalking. I offered a piece of cheese to another spider whose head poked round the frame edge. But it dodged away.

Later I heard the tiercel calling. I couldn't see him. The falcon had left the ledge. Soon Dave would come to the scrape to distract the falcon when I left the blind.

A mad redpoll was chuttering below. Still I would feel sharp pity for the prey, but my ears had changed; the wild and I seemed less separate.

Part V.

Eyasses

Dave and I wanted to watch more than one falcon pair at its eyrie. For our purpose was to learn about the behavior of tundra falcons generally, and the falcons at different cliffs presumably differed in their actions. We needed to know what characteristics this pair shared with all other peregrines and what distinguished this pair. Therefore, at the beginning of summer we had planned to alternate our observations between two, or even, if possible, three eyries.

We hadn't known how much time study of one eyrie would require. Nor did we have any idea of all the mountains, lakes, rivers in Greenland that made hiking difficult. Rivers in particular do not have the proper significance in civilized areas like New Hampshire that have bridges. Black Cliff Eyrie stood only two miles from our tent; yet we could never reach it because of the river in between. Nor could we hike around all the way to the base where a road bridged the river before it widened to meet the fjord. Upstream the river split; Black Cliff was on an island between swift ice waters and the ice cap.

Instead we had asked the two Bills about the northern eyries. The closest of these was miles away, but Dave and I decided to visit it. Thus one drowsy morning we sat waiting for the two Bills to arrive. I hadn't seen them since our trip down the fjord, more than two weeks earlier, but Dave had met them on his day at the base. They would watch our falcons the three days we were away.

Burnham reached the tent before Mattox. "I see you've got the blind up!" he exclaimed.

Mattox soon followed. "It's hot today!" He looked up at the cliff. "Have you watched the falcons yet from the blind? What do they think of it, or of you two coming?"

Dave and I had our questions. "Bill, what have you found?"

"Only one more eyrie." Only one in two weeks work!

"Oh, have we hiked. Burnham's going to need new boots. We've hiked everywhere as far north as we can go from

Terrain north of Isortoq River

the base, before we get to rivers. The new peregrines are near the ice cap. It's a three-hundred-foot cliff with a pond below it—we didn't climb to the eyrie.

"Jim, did Dave tell you of our trip out from the red cabin? That was terrible. I don't want to see that Taserssuaq again for a long time. It's high altitude, still frozen mostly. And we couldn't walk along the shore, all up and down around hills and cliffs. Barren. No bushes. And the snow. One day we just stayed in the tent."

"Your tent here is nicer than a two-man, in the wind," added Burnham. "You should try it."

"And both of us seemed to take up more than half the tent."

"So you don't think there are any peregrines around there?"

"No. Even if they could stand the cold, there's no prey."

"We got a helicopter to take us north of Isortoq River. There were cliffs but no eyries. Except perhaps along the river."

"We just couldn't get to them. Miles of rock with the water right below. We saw a female peregrine fly by—there must be a nest. The helicopter picked us up after four days. And that's our three trips—the one out from Musk Ox Eyrie, this one north of Isortoq, and the one to Ice Cap Eyrie."

"What's Musk Ox Eyrie?"

"Oh, I mean the Taserssuaq trip. We call that eyrie Jim and I found Musk Ox. Burnham names all the eyries."

"There's plenty of time during all that hiking."

What's the name of the one we're going to?"

"Ring Sø."

Mattox was looking up at the ledge and blind. "It's been a long time. Since I climbed an eyrie. When I was an undergraduate at Dartmouth I'd visit the eyries in spring. I knew of more than twenty in Vermont and New Hampshire."

Dave and I hoisted on our packs. "Good luck," I said to Bill and Bill.

Soon as we walked Dave remarked, "It's good to be moving again."

       *   *   *   *

We hiked without pause, for our way was mostly level or downhill. At the air base, airmen and Danes sat inside eating pastries, with beer before them. There was radio music. But we continued north. We climbed up over ridges and were soon wet with sweat.

Sø means lake in Danish. Ring Sø was a nearly round lake. Mattox hadn't been sure which shore had the eyrie, but he had marked our map generally. "You'll know it when you arrive."

We looked at the map and considered the lakes and ridges we had passed. Dave pointed northwest. "It must be this way." But he pointed straight toward a wearying hill. We decided to pass out of our way to our right and avoid it. When we got over the slight rise we had a long view north. Now we turned left. But a mile to the right stood a little cliff.

"Mattox said it was small."

"But that's the wrong way."

Dave loudly cried, "Yip!" But the cliff was a mile away.

To the astonishment of both of us, we heard a far, high voice, the peregrine answering. "That's it!"

We marched to the right. The peregrine continued screaming. But we hadn't even walked half way, the cliff was a half-mile distant, when the peregrine came out from his cliff, all the way out to us, and circled over our heads. We looked at each other. Peregrine cackling is terrible at any time, the cries echo; but how could we observe peregrine behavior if they reacted so strongly to our presence? This far away!

I think it was the tiercel. But we only looked at his wings quickly. We hurried forward because it served nothing to stay still. Suddenly we discovered a steep valley before us. We walked down the steep turf, and in doing so dropped out of sight of the cliff. At the same time the peregrine stopped his calling and winged ahead of us, vanishing toward his eyrie.

We waited several minutes to allow the peregrine time to settle. We tried sneaking out beyond the far side of the valley, but soon the top of the peregrine hill appeared and then the cackling rose and the peregrine came out over our heads.

We stood up straight. What should we do? For this was a major disturbance, and now the falcon also was flying and cackling, above the cliff. We kept walking but I was about to suggest we return to the narrow valley and camp there. Now we weren't far from the cliff. We had a swift stream to cross, then a knoll that dipped before the rock itself.

"See that flat spot beyond the stream? It's near water. It's out of sight of the cliff. Let's get down there and see what happens."

At the stream the water roared so well we couldn't have heard any bird scream. But the peregrines did leave us. And as we crept up, just past the water sounds, we knew they had quieted also. It was late. We set our tent close to the stream.

We wondered at the falcons' odd aggressiveness. What difference did it make when we dropped out of sight of the cliff? That the falcon would cease to worry, with us out of her view, did not surprise us. But this tiercel overhead could see us just as well. Perhaps the falcon's silence calmed the tiercel.

We liked our campsite. Ferns and mosses grew by the stream.

We understood pleasantly why the Bills tried to camp near eyrie cliffs, even if it meant stopping their work early that day. The beauty becomes more personal at these halting spots. We listened to the spilling water, and slept.

Dave got up early next morning and left the tent to try

watching the peregrines. Since he left the opening unzipped at the top some mosquitoes came in to bite me and I couldn't sleep. Several times I heard the peregrines. Then Dave came back.

"Well, that won't do any good," he said.

"What?"

"It was a useless hour. Every time I got where I could see the cliff the peregrines cackled. Even if I just poked my head out. I spent all my time hiding behind rocks."

We thought about this. I suggested, "Why don't we use the tent as a blind? We can move it out where we can see the cliff, and watch from inside."

This plan worked. We packed and climbed back up the hill south of the stream. Quickly we walked until we were opposite the cliff's middle, although 250 yards away. We set the tent, Dave had the telescope, and I walked away so that he could watch while my activity distracted the peregrines. The tiercel followed me a short way, but as I advanced north and away he returned to the cliff.

I walked, sat, walked for four hours. But, at the beginning, when I still could almost see the cliff, I stopped momentarily. I was hearing an occasional raven croak. Then abruptly the bird choked with hoarse and frantic rattles. It had wandered too near the cliff and the peregrine was stooping on it up down up, up down, while the shifty raven dodged. It headed straight for the nearest, cover, which unfortunately was the cliff itself. The angry tiercel hit it solidly in the back several times; feathers flew. When it reached the cliff I couldn't see it, although the peregrine appeared at the top of each stoop.

Then I saw nothing for two minutes. What had happened to the raven? It dodged back into sight high on the hill. Out rushed the peregrine. He assumed a pendulum motion with the raven at the bottom of every stoop. It managed to flip its feet just before each impact, surprisingly, desperately agile, and warded off the blows. Sometimes the tiercel would strike the raven from underneath as he rose in his strength out of the stoop. The raven dropped and cowered between rocks.

The tiercel was floating above. He had never made a

sound. The wind from the west was holding him over the raven, and he pointed his wing tips far into gentle currents. He dipped them, turned, and vanished before the cliff.

The raven didn't move for ten minutes. Then he walked a step forward, turned, a step back, peering around the boulders and up, and crouching. Then he jumped up into flight and winged low with wings almost touching the ground, directly away from the cliff.

Otherwise the hours were quiet. There were many lakes. I hiked in a circle to reach the tent as unobtrusively as possible. The only warning, several long, quiet calls from the cliff. Dave lay with his head at the tent opening.

"The tiercel is away."

"Let me in."

We lay on our bellies, looking out around the telescope toward the cliff. "It's real hard to watch from here. If I use the scope I can only see one adult at a time. If I just use my eyes, I can hardly see them against the rock; they keep disappearing."

"Where's the eyrie?" I asked.

"I just figured that out. . . ." It took him a minute to teach me the proper ledge, a triangular protrusion of rock, like a pulpit, with a flat top that was low on the cliff. He pointed the scope for me. A rock and dirt ledge edge, with an oval stone surrounded by grasses. That was all.

"A little while ago you could see the falcon, sitting up in the scrape."

"Has the tiercel brooded at all?"

"I don't think so."

Dave soon left.

I found it difficult to watch a new cliff. The ledges and points of rock formed unfamiliar patterns. We faced the cliff head-on, so that the adults would never be outlined by sky except in their highest flight. It was a short cliff, about 120 feet at its highest part. There, the stone was black and had huge mute splashes. The white blended with even larger patches of the orange lichen Caloplaca. White, orange, and black in the sun.

The falcon stayed at the scrape. Several times I saw white through the grasses. She was looking out, and I could see her dark head. She covered the eyasses. Later I saw wings in the air near the ledge. The telescope revealed the tiercel, and the falcon waddling out to meet him. Prey passed beak to beak: a little plucked bird.

Later I located the tiercel on a perch. He looked like a tiercel—even at that distance—and I was amazed that I knew. It was not the falcon, no, not with . . . perhaps it was that I recognized his upright posture, or the gleaming white of his chest, the small level head that turned side to side. I did not see him leave.

He brought many meals in, at less than hour intervals. These meals were more frequent than at our first eyrie, oddly, because the first pair had four growing eyasses. But once the falcon returned to the ledge a minute after a food exchange—I had lost her location before the rock face—without the prey. She couldn't have eaten it so quickly. At another meal time I watched her drop from the ledge, and beat low before the cliff, into the wind without effort, to land at a weak, crumbling ledge. She was motionless; then she peered at the back of the ledge, glanced intently out, back suspiciously at the ledge, and then placed her food in hiding. A cache, and apparently this was the second of the afternoon; while in all our watching Dave and I had seen a cache once only at First Eyrie.

In the later afternoon the falcon came out on the ledge several times, but only once did she leave for another perch, over the white splashes. The eyasses she cared for must be younger than our four.

Whenever she moved out from the grasses I became alert for a food exchange, and indeed she would drop into flight then close with the suddenly appearing tiercel for the spirals and exchange. I knew the ritual. But he returned silent, totally noiseless, no announcement for his coming. Thus the falcon was alerted only if she looked out at the proper times and saw him in the distance.

When Dave returned in the evening we cooked supper

Ring Sø eyasses in 1973.

over our noisy stoves. When the air was dusky and the sky deep
blue I wanted to find the tiercel at his night watch. The
falcon was not visible. All little birds slept. I looked over
the ledges and points for his white breast, or a dark shape that
might be his back. By day he often had failed to perch on
the cliff itself but had risen over it to the hilltop where
he rested on shallow ledges or rocks almost level with the grass.
The qualities of cliff did seem to influence the peregrine's
behavior. The first tiercel never paused near his eyrie except
on the inaccessible cliff. But this small fortress hadn't the lofty
view down upon all the landscape; nor did its perches overlook
far distant lakes and meadows; the tiercel sought the less
enclosed hilltop.

Now I wanted to see him. Tiercels at night seemed to
delight me; rather, the first tiercel at his quiet hours had filled
me with images. I missed him. Somewhere, here and at
a score of eyries, all the neighboring tiercels must be at their
similar guards. But I scanned all the hilltop perches in vain.
This tiercel remained hidden.

*   *   *   *

In the morning I took the first watch while Dave walked.

The sun that had risen in early hours at the northeast had swung round to hit the south-facing cliff. Still shadow lined the uneven rock but already at 8 A.M. the scrape lay in sunlight.

The two Bills had told us that all the eyries faced generally south. In cold Greenland the exposure determines a large portion of a ledge's suitability for eyasses. Climate threatens here, but the south-facing cliffs meet the sun when it is strongest, highest in the sky. Yet ledges most open to light are most vulnerable to wind and rain. At both Ring Sø and First Eyrie cliffs many cliff points but not the eyries were lighted in the chill evening or still morning before most birds sang. The sun had left Ring Sø scrape at 5:15 P.M. the day before. First Eyrie, which lay toward the southwest, not southeast, was lighted from 11 A.M until after 8 in the evening.

That morning the tiercel continued his silence. Not once had he called except at our first approach, when he screamed over our heads. The falcon's conversation shrilled in contrast. Twice I saw a new pattern to the echoing food exchange. Always before when the peregrines had climaxed their spirals, wings frantically beating, I thought I had seen the falcon beak reach toward tiercel talons. It happened swiftly. But at Ring Sø in the morning the falcon beat up under her mate, and then she flipped. Flipped upside down in her ascent, grabbed with her talons, fell forward, fell. An hour later at the next rising, screaming exchange she flipped again for that touch. Had I missed the motion all these times at Ring Sø and at First Eyrie? I felt like a blind witness.

This eyrie had the clothesline rope. It did not stretch straight down the cliff but climbed from the eyrie ledge like a snake from point to point to end below the cliff top. Who had set it here, with what intent?

Dave returned at noon for the last watch. We would return to First Eyrie that night. It was my turn to wander free. I climbed to the hilltop west of the tiercel's hill and sat down upon a rock, remembering how eagerly I had looked out for the tiercel on his night perch.

What had I wanted to feel?—the tall tiercel and I—feel that we both watched while all other animals and the growing tundra or the ground itself slumbered? Did that join the tiercel and me? Was I then really a part of the wild? Did I wish, did I as he tingle with the breadth and strength of the north, did the throbbing move me also, the sky bursting life and death and terror upon us?

Why did I come to Ring Sø, the perfect lake shaped like an oval mirror? I had left the First Eyrie peregrines for this second pair, that I might find a falcon who sat upon the scrape exactly as my first falcon did, or watched or preened above the landscape with the same expression and poise, who dropped into flight exactly as I knew she would. And another valiant tiercel who played on and mastered the playful wind so like, so like, it was the same as I remembered, the same tiercel, so like, it was a dream repeating. I wanted the same peregrine, that presence dotted over the north all falcons brooding, all tiercels guarding.

Yet at that same time I loved the first pair alone. I came to Ring Sø and found that my first peregrines were unique. I found that this second pair had its differences, subtle and great. I found that this pair touched with a barely lower spiral before their lower cliff. I found that an angry falcon seized this vulnerable rock with its rope; we had found an angry tiercel rushing out to meet us, not secure like the first pair on a greater cliff.

Mattox missed this intense uniqueness of each peregrine. He wandered too much, visiting many mountains, many eyries.

Almost always humans are individuals. Animals are not. To us they are simply interchangeable members of a species. Yet when we do see the unique animal, that one tiercel or those certain eyasses, delight opens, now possibilities for caring and for loss.

It was time to leave the hill. I returned to the tent the long way around, and the falcon made no noise at all.

"Is the tiercel gone?" I asked.

"Yes," answered Dave.

But after we took the tent down, and packed, and started up the first hill south, there was an outburst of noise high in the sky. A white-winged gull appeared, and the tiercel

Ring Sø cliff from a distance.

peregrine, at last calling again, "ka-ka-ka-ka-ka-ka." And the gull
cried too, a desperate two-noted croak that had a fish quality,
it twisted at the tiercel's stoops, and swirled its white wings,
its feet and head stretched in terror. Struck, struck, out
it would flip its feet, and it rushed for shelter, the cliff itself.
"Kak-kak-kak-kak." It sought the cliff top exactly over the
eyrie; the falcon too rushed out, frantic. It could not dodge both
peregrines; they struck again and again from above and below.
The falcon. She seized it, the two fell fifteen, twenty-five
feet before the eyrie. Released, still flying, the gull fled the cliff,
and the peregrines pursued. No pendulum swings, but
towering ascents wings churning, pause, and the dives two
hundred feet toward the gull. At the bottom, at the upturn,
the air whistled.

When the three reached the next valley the falcon returned
and cackled from the eyrie ledge. The hill blocked the gull
from sight, but we saw the tiercel at the top of each rise; then
he vanished also.

The end of our encounter with the Ring Sø pair. Dave and
I hiked south.

The Return

In our return to First Eyrie we passed without rest or
conversation along the long lake. I realized that a month earlier

we would have had a hundred creeks and marshy rills to cross.
The season was changing. The wetness of spring and high
summer—when the ground and snow still were melting—the
wetness had gone, or crept into the meadows and grass
tussocky hills that now were pale green, a lone flush of color
for the far north. I didn't see as many white and yellow flowers.
The little birds now skulked low to ground, and the males
joined the females in shyness and silence. The male longspurs
who had lost their black hoods warily cried, "kew! kew!"
but did not sing.

Dave slept early. I lay dozing on my cot with the tent
flaps still open. Two young, absolutely dark brown foxes came
up together so close before the tent that I opened wide my heavy
eyes. These foxes had chubby faces. One came closer, peering
inside with his black nose, until he caught scent of our dish
scrubber on a rock at his feet. It was greasy. The fox nipped
at its head, then hurried away a couple yards. I raised my
head. He snuck round the bushes to spring forward for a second
nip. Did he like the taste, the smell, or did he want a toy?
When he snapped the third time and retreated scarcely a foot,
I realized we might lose our scrubber. I roused myself and
hissed, "Sookie!" He looked up and rushed behind the
far cub. The two tussled together, wandered vaguely up the
hill, I believe, already I was falling into dreams.

Early the next morning Dave woke me. I groggily heard
a raven croaking; the mosquitoes hummed outside but the sun
hadn't yet warmed the tent. Very soon Dave would accompany
me to the blind, where I would stay the morning. He would
watch in the afternoon.

The falcon was watchful as we approached the rope end.
Her cries rose, and soon the tiercel's voiced joined hers. The
rope ascent was speedy and I hurried into the blind while
Dave stood over the scrape. The falcons still called from time to
time, but soon I heard the last of Dave on the rope. The
solemnity of the morning returned.

Three of the eyasses still lay flat, but one in their midst
had raised himself upright. His poise lasted a minute until
he dropped among his fellows. The adults still were calling from

Young arctic foxes.

the east part of the cliff. Not until a half hour had passed
did I hear alarm notes, as the falcon landed on the ledge,
facing her young and the blind. The eyasses were peeping, and
one piped, "hik-hik-hik-hik," his version of the adult cry.

The falcon bobbed her head at the passerines below. She
flew briefly, and the eyasses rattled at her return. On that hot,
lichened rock she was warming in the sunlight. She stretched.
All on her left side. The wing reached far out over the
ledge, its feather ends separated. She also raised her left leg
and extended it under her wing. While between wing and leg
she twisted her tail, stretching not behind but to the side,
and spread it, and arched her wing so that it drooped over the
rock. She held this pose for a half minute then repeated it
on her right side.

Later she walked to the grass hump by the scrape. The
largest eyass had sat up, grass stems extending from its beak. The
falcon looked at this eyass particularly. I don't know whether
it was the peculiar flatness of her headtop, and the notched
beak, or the intensity with which the eyes pierced, but she

looked fierce and perilous even over her own young. What sharp dagger-angers boiled within her, her life. She gently touched the eyass with her beak.

Generally that morning the eyasses lay flat. Sometimes, though, they would bustle, more energetically than before but without much effect. When the wings stretched I saw they had black of half-formed feathers on their edges. Tail feathers also were appearing. With wings they would push against each other, and struggle in movement, slow to subside, into stillness that lasted for many minutes.

When the falcon came to the scrape all the eyasses sat up and peeped. They were hungry. The littlest eyass looked very little, and delicate. The older eyasses had blue-gray bills now and the falcon anger, but the youngest had a pale, almost pinkish bill and vaguer, open eyes.

The falcon had flown and I heard both adults calling in the distance. Then I heard them closer and knew they were flying before the cliff, and their voices became more excited, broke: I knew there was a food exchange. Then the falcon called alone but the minutes passed and she didn't return with the food. So little could be seen from the blind—the scrape and ledge and a sliver of sky.

The morning passed. The sun fell full on the scrape. The eyasses and I waited for a feeding.

It is remarkable how little we know about the creatures around us. It is not remarkable, for their lives flow quite smoothly past ours, and all or most of what they possess or enliven isn't our practical concern. Our passions miss theirs. Yet perhaps for this reason their secrets charm us—how the eyasses spend the morning or what the mockingbird eats on rainy afternoons.

Occasionally I heard an adult cry; it was the tiercel's voice. The blind was dark, and I hadn't the peregrine view. But I sensed the splendid drop before me, saw how the ground under my legs rushed to the ledge brink. Blinded, how secure I was from any human's approach, with falcon guards and the rock. But in that quietness I warmed and stretched toward human images.

I thought especially of one man, G. Harper Hall, who was born in Scotland in 1874 and went to Canada as a young man, had various hobbies including wood-carving, insect-collecting, photography, and bird study. He worked for the Canadian Pacific Railway in downtown Montreal. And because he had an opportunity for observation, and seized it, I had been reading about him in my tent in Greenland.[1]

In 1936 two birds appeared in the middle of the city. They remained throughout most of the summer, particularly flying about and alighting on the tall building that served as the head office for the Sun Life Assurance Company. Some few of the people in the streets four hundred feet below knew they were peregrines. Mr. Hall watched them, from within the Sun Life Building itself, or across Dominion Square from the top floor in the tower of Windsor Station.

The following year the peregrines returned, while in spring of 1938 five of their eggs were discovered in various places, mainly in the rain scupper surrounding the twentieth-floor level. These eggs could not be incubated because rain water covered them at times and they addled.

Hall began to watch these birds because he liked peregrines, and this persistent pair drew his interest. They were the first known members of the species to attempt nesting in the middle of a city. But the falcons had nowhere safely to lay their eggs on the Sun Life Building. Two men, Mr. Pfeiffer and Mr. Luck, set wood boxes over the rain scupper at twentieth-floor level. These held gravel in which the falcon could hollow a scrape to hold the eggs.

The falcon took to the boxes, and in 1940 two eyasses were successfully reared. This falcon was clearly marked by a dimple or depression among her breast feathers; she wore immature plumage that first year at Sun Life; and laid eggs in one or the other of her boxes from 1940 until 1952. During that time twenty-two eyasses fledged. She had three different mates; but when she did not return in 1953 the eyrie location was abandoned.

---

1. Hall (1955).

Mr. Hall did not fear heights and climbed out onto the narrow ledges by the nest boxes to photograph the birds. He maintained he ran little risk of falling, but did respect the falcon's threat. The tiercels never attacked, but the falcon struck on occasion and once captured Mr. Hall's hat.

The skyscrapers of the city apparently substitute for natural cliffs. Myriad starlings and pigeons provide food.[2] The city's rich source of prey had long attracted peregrines in winter. Thus Montreal had peregrine visits many years before 1936. Philadelphia had wintering falcons also—Mr. Delos Culver watched them from his office—and peregrines lived in Boston, in Shanghai.[3]

The falcons found it more difficult to nest than to winter. They had long been attracted to man-created fortresses in quiet rural places for eyries—ruins in Spain, crumbling German castles, or a stone bridge pier in Pennsylvania.[4] Probably few peregrines can tolerate human noise below them. And some persons will attempt to destroy the peregrines.

The managers of the Sun Life Building sheltered the falcons, and the birds were liked by those in Montreal who knew of them. But in New York City, where as many as sixteen peregrines once wintered, the falcons were labeled cruel pigeon slayers. The second pair ever known to nest in midcity lived there, hatching eleven young from 1943 to 1948. Not one was allowed to fledge.[5]

Similarly in Philadelphia an eyass was threatened; an adult pair had chosen City Hall for their eyrie. One day two men appeared on a roof above the eyrie, and reached down with a long rod to push the eyass off the ledge. The rod wouldn't reach, and they fetched a longer one. Again in vain. By this time Mr. Horace Groskin, who watched the pair, was able to shout at them, and the men abandoned their attempt.[6]

Mr. Groskin was another businessman who worked in

---

2. Herbert and Herbert (1965).
3. Hall (1955); Culver (1919); Wilkinson (1931).
4. Hickey (1942); Hickey and Anderson (1969).
5. Herbert and Herbert (1969).
6. Groskin (1952); see also Groskin (1947) for an account of the Philadelphia peregrines.

midcity and watched nesting peregrines from an office window. All of these men in offices were astonished by the city peregrines. When the falcon took Mr. Hall's hat she let it fall to the ground.

When he climbed in through the window, he must have said to the secretary, "I'll be back in just a moment. I must get my hat."

And possibly, just possibly, a man stood by the punctured hat those hundreds of feet below. Mouth open, motionless, eyes skyward. "I saw it. That fast bird. Where has it gone?" he might have stammered.

While Hall smiled. "My hat. The peregrine."

Probably not. But some persons on the city streets must have noticed the falcons and wondered. Either on their own, on absent strolls, or after they saw the photograph and caption in the newspaper. These peregrines in the city, what a strange wildness, weren't they, untouched, violently out of setting. Did women below stop in their stride? Strange creatures whose fierce circles, wound among the civilized, wakened doubt and awe.

Strange to breathe, to sound that city air with shrieks.

The ill-shaven, sharp-chinned man, he isn't listless now. He smiles. He has seen the peregrine.

Of all the North American hawks the peregrine alone entered the city successfully. Now that is over, unless the peregrines survive and restore their numbers. How odd their arrivals must have been—I wonder if they voyage still to Nairobi or Shanghai or other cities.[7]

*   *   *   *

The quite unique eyasses in the scrape before me still waited to be fed. Then the first falcon landed at the scrape. I glimpsed her prey for an instant—it looked longer than a passerine, perhaps a phalarope—before the eyasses crowded round. The older ones did bulk over the little eyass, but he as before had reached the front row. They all were screaming

---

7. Brown (1961) discovered nesting peregrines in Nairobi.

while the falcon tore the meat into pieces that she held to their beaks. But the largest eyass snapped at the body several times for special bites. The littlest one snipped at it also, and the falcon gave him several pieces. When the largest pulled for meat at the same time as the falcon, the adult noticed and dragged the body twelve inches away. All the eyasses pursued her, waggling about madly, hungry and grown more boisterous in their clamor and gestures. One middle-sized eyass seized one leg of the prey, pulled, and the leg stretched long—it was a phalarope—still so firmly held beneath the parent's talons that he got nothing for his effort. But when the littlest eyass got a massive bite, his large sister seized the drooping end of it and took most or all.

When the feeding was over the eyasses still peeped madly. The falcon looked at them, then flew.

Three minutes later and suddenly she was back again with a small body partially plucked. The riot of feeding repeated. The eyasses swarmed as before, the littlest in front, and the falcon held pieces out to them. Again the female eyass tried to take the littlest one's large morsel. But the little tiercel wouldn't let go and as the female eyass reached from the rear he got pulled back and under, squashed between the gesticulating medium eyasses and the falcon eyass. He emerged, minus his bite and looking quite dizzy, at the west end of the scrape. Apparently he would receive no more food, not from this bad position. But soon one of the older eyasses got into a tugging match with the falcon over the body. She jerked the prey away to the left and resumed feeding directly before the littlest eyass, a lucky coincidence that the littlest took advantage of, swallowing several more bites.

The falcon looked at the eyasses when the feeding ended. They soon quieted, satiated. The littlest still was healthy, his crop bulging. The falcon glared over the tundra. Then something or someone caught her attention.

Soon she looked away. But her eyes turned less randomly over the earth, and always she looked back. The enemy was moving up the grassy slopes, I could tell by the direction of her eyes and tilt of her head. She gave the other objects

quick glances only, she shifted reared on her feet. It was
Dave coming to relieve me at the blind. I heard a stone rolling
below. The falcon gaped her beak.

A moment more. Another. She was looking toward the
rope. "Gak-gak-gak-gak-gak." The morning was broken.

In the hurry of the cries and the stooping falcon, Dave
spoke to me from without the blind. I answered, "I'm ready."

We changed places. "Good luck" and I left.

*   *   *   *

At evening I released Dave from the blind. He was stiff
from the motionless watch, but quickly paced the ledge to
descend. I stood over the messy scrape a moment. The eyasses
all reared and rattled at me. The largest flapped her wings, while
the littlest looked from me to his siblings. I picked up pellets
and left. At the rope top I looked down.

Dave was glaring at me from below. "Hurry up."

A trembling took my knees as I descended. My steps
were clumsy and hard. I clutched the rope. When I reached
ground Dave stared at me. Then we were running, Dave's
heels beside me then before me. He stopped abruptly. "You've
got to be faster."

I didn't pause, and we ran all the way to the tent.

"Well," said Dave. "The tent looks clean. Are you packed?"

"Yes. Let's go."

We closed the tent and raised our packs. Still we were
hot, my glasses wet, and Dave set an even, rapid pace toward
the long lake. I saw all the steps he took because I followed
directly behind him, and saw pieces of mud and grass cling to his
heels. Until my glasses became wet again, and all over I was
sweaty.

He was silent for a mile or more. Then abruptly he accused
me, "Have you been thinking about what conclusions we
can make?"

"Yes. Have you?"

"I don't want to have pages and pages of endless notes when
we go home."

"You're right."

"Why do you write down everything you see? You take

a page for just one feeding, and I don't want to know how one eyass looks at another."

"I do."

I followed Dave for several hundred more yards.

"I'm sorry, Jim. But we do need to think how we're going to write this up, while we're here and have time."

"Are you planning to go around the left side of the lake?"

"Of course."

"Well you do that. I'm taking the right side. See you in five miles."

I marched straight to the shore. To my right I noticed an intrusive tent. Unlucky. When I came to the lake I stepped onto the watermost rock and stared at ripples and waves on the water. I had come the wrong way and stood on a peninsula's end. Now just behind me a paper wrapper lay, some chocolate name on it. And farther a plastic bottle slit almost in two. Damned litter.

Not even this lake was sacred or safe. I would have to walk around the marshy bay, past the tent itself if I wasn't to turn out of my way. I walked the shore. The tent was pure white. A woman saw me and came out to meet me.

"Good evening."

"Hello."

"Would you like some tea or coffee?"

She was perhaps fifty, with brown hair gray-streaked. I was speechless and looked away.

"Yes, come and have something to drink." This voice was higher and softer. A much younger Dane stood at her companion's side. Both were smiling.

"Yes, I will, thank you."

They led me to their campsite, where I set my pack down and held my hands out over embers of their fire. They had collected willow twigs that burned with a slight rustle. It warmed me. The older woman saw the rubbish in my fist.

"Will it burn?"

I gave her the plastic and put the rest on the fire. The girl stood beside me and watched the black and red edges of the paper. She placed a kettle on the coals.

"Is that your tent up there?"

"Yes."

"Then you are watching Vandrefalken—how do you say it? pelgin?"

"Peregrine. How did you know?"

She laughed. Musical. "I work at the hotel. Steen Malmquist told me I might find you. Two Americans watching birds."

"Yes. What are you doing here?"

"Heating your tea. Isn't it beautiful this evening?"

"Do you want tea or coffee?" the older woman asked. She stood by the white tent that looked as if it had been washed in rain.

"Tea," and, "Do you also live in Søndrestrøm?"

"No. I am come from Denmark. I have been here four days." She looked at the sky. "I am not used to its being blue in the night."

"At midnight the clouds look as if sunset were just over. And the tundra has subtle colors and shadows. Come out of your tent then, and see."

"Is that what you do?" she asked.

"Yes."

She poured my water into a white cup with teabag. "Will you have some more?" The girl nodded.

We sat down on rocks. The woman asked me about the peregrines, and I told her what I had seen that day.

"There, there on that cliff!" she exclaimed.

Now the cliff was half-shadowed, and the scrape dark and the falcon must have been brooding the eyasses. I told them these things, and the way the tiercel now held guard, and what he was.

Now that tea was the best of temperatures, and I felt it falling down in my throat and chest. I had no wish to be anywhere else and groped for what could somehow express my feeling. The rock in my pack.

"I like your tea and chocolate."

I stepped gently to my pack, and in the top pocket the rock lay.

"Look what I am taking home. See the orange. It is a

lichen, Caloplaca." I laughed at the explanation. "The peregrines whiten the cliff with their excrement. It nourishes Caloplaca."

The woman turned the rock over in her fingers. The top with the lichen had a dark color, and roughened texture. The bottom was paler. "How long will the orange remain? Will it fade?" She handed it back to me.

The girl took it with a contented chuckle and carried it as if she loved the touch of small objects, close to her eyes, so that all the orange bumps were apparent, and the depth of the rock.

"What is it called?"

"Caloplaca."

"It will last well enough." She touched it in her hands with her fingers for five minutes. I was standing speechless, trying to feel these things, to share that youthfulness.

When she looked at me but didn't yet return the rock, her eyes didn't match the rest of her, I imagined griefs remembered (maybe she wasn't so young), from the air base, or when she lived in Denmark, perhaps reborn here too on the tundra, these she . . . suppressed, she looked down at Caloplaca again.

"Birds," and, "In little ponds. Do you know Odinshane—how do you say it?—Odin—the god-king—I can't remember what it is." Lightly.

"Odinshane?"

"They are little birds with long legs. I like them best."

"In Greenland?"

"Yes. They chipper, and swim in circles. What is the name? Some sort of chicken?" She looked at the woman.

"Phalarope!" I felt the same way about them.

"Phalarope. Male chicken. Rooster!"

"Odin's rooster."

"Yes. Do you know there are some very near here?" She pointed to the left shore.

"I've seen that one too. I like the name you have for him."

"Odin is a great, terrible god like the Arctic. That is where these little roosters live."

The Dane handed the rock back to me. I hesitated.
I returned it to the pack.

"I don't know how long the orange remains. How long?"

Then I continued, "Remember to leave your tent late tonight and see the clouds. I still must walk to the air base."

"Good-bye," they said.

When I had gone around the marshy bay I looked back at the white tent, and they saw me. We waved.

Like moths my emotions were hovering beautiful and fragile. No, they were like the fierce peregrines wind hoisted and shrill, I was feeling my own spirit, that is a vague colorless thing except when it catches me, I rub against it in some individual encounter; some creature must embody it, give it substance for me to experience. All these struggles of mine, of ours on the tundra this summer, were somehow the same desire, to sense our own full blood and spirit. And thus my breath caught, when, many times, when that snowy June day the tiercel spun, rolled, circled, soared, ascended over the wind, he had hung for a moment above me before he vanished where the ridgetop blocked the sky. I sucked my breath, gasped, by the edge of the lake, no tiercel near. The solemnity of the moment.

The silence without human or redpoll. The water lapping. I was filled with thought. My solemnity. And that was what I felt leaving the Danish tent, life that throbbed in me and trembling I was hoping I had left that with the women. This wish was what I had, to leap, to fly. Not alone, but together with others.

Quietly, late, I came to the lake's end. Dave sat there. I think he was looking at Sol Gryn and the other mountains that still had sun. I stopped at the water edge.

"Thank you for waiting."

Peregrines at the Coast

We had briefly left First Eyrie to help Mattox and Burnham with their survey work, which was requiring considerably more time than they had expected. The following night the four of us lay in our small tents on meadows by the

Low clouds and mist hang over Holsteinsborg; modern apartment buildings can be seen at left center.

coastal town of Holsteinsborg. We had traveled by helicopter to this home for three thousand people, second largest settlement in Greenland. We lay within sound of a running river and waves from the inmost, shallowest reaches of the harbor. Huskies were barking in the town, and we heard children's voices until we slept.

Out of the more than three thousand square miles Mattox had originally hoped to survey, the two Bills had covered six or seven hundred square miles. They had carefully planned their remaining time, to explore as much more land as possible and still visit all the discovered eyries to count eyasses and band them. We had worked only in the inland part of the sample area. Because the small aircraft were grounded, the Bills had seen nothing of coastal cliffs. There, the various ocean birds would make up an important part of the falcon's diet. Their maritime foods as well as their migrations, distinct from diets and migrations of redpolls or longspurs, might expose them to pesticides in a very different way. The present status of breeding coastal peregrines could differ significantly from inland falcons.

We had four full days to search for falcon cliffs near the sea. But a drizzly, gusty rain rose that first night. All the days following were dark with storms. Mists hung low over the mountains and we waited restlessly in the town.

207

*   *   *   *

One morning only did the clouds lift sufficiently to expose the cliff surfaces. We crossed the river by a wooden footbridge to climb hills to the north.

The first mile of tundra from the buildings was sadly decorated with glass and paper and assorted trash. Plodding uphill with Dave, I wondered at the smiling, friendly Greenlanders who lived still in a hungry, swallowing nature that hadn't ends or bottoms. The harbor was thick with garbage. These people were careless and brave; for them the stores glinted with wares that were wonderful, that defied the northern wild and eclipsed winter thoughts.

I could hardly imagine their view of the tundra. And the Danes here also had eyes different from mine. They came for tax-free wages, but with a mission, to open forbidding Greenland and develop modern joys for the people. They came for action and change. Holsteinsborg would become wealthier. Transportation would be more dependable. The Greenlanders would be happier.

Now in our climb we had to use our hands as well as feet. And we negotiated around and over two streams that ran together. I waited to accompany Mattox silently while Bill and Dave wandered ahead. As we climbed we felt a boost to our steps, for an air torrent was sweeping high off the sea from the southwest and funneling up the stream cleft. It supported us, it pushed at our backs. When we turned to see Holsteinsborg and the white waves and skerries, our eyes watered. Half the horizon in watery motion. No birds stirred near us and the wind made me doubt that any could nest here. Perhaps other days were milder.

Then we reached a small lake. Ice bobbed on the roughened surface, and we had no shelter from the wind. Beyond a long bank of hardened snow lay on the hillside. Burnham kicked steps into it with his heavy boots while the rest of us followed behind and I balanced with my arms. We mounted all the false ridgetops to reach at last the crest itself. Mattox shouted, "Let's go a little farther out of the wind."

At last we all sat on the north side of a great boulder. All the swirling gray and gray-white shapes of clouds were before us. I gave up any hope of finding peregrines. For there were range upon range of stormy mountains with snow and rocky arms and proud peaks that would probably break our courage to cross if we were to try. Between them, arms of the ocean ran with living water, a dull green-blue. The ground fell before us, its descent broken by rock pinnacles until our peninsula ended in the deep fjord. I looked at Dave, and he was smiling.

Mattox said, "We won't explore this."

The midafternoon lull soon ended. We struggled and fought the wind on our way toward Holsteinsborg. We couldn't see. We hurried. At the bottom we hesitated, the valley extending out of sight left, the town to our right.

"Let's go up the valley," I suggested.

We turned left. The vegetation here was different than Søndrestrøm's hills. There were fewer clumps of bushes, and their branches followed the ground. There were grasses, but especially soft mosses that cushioned our steps, like on the north-facing slopes inland, because this area had less sun and more rain. Because of the cold and the low vegetative cover I guessed that passerine prey would be sparse. There were no willow thickets for the redpoll homes. Peregrines could not be frequent on the coastal barrens, where shadowed snow remained in late July.

Salomonsen in his 1951 book stated that he had observed peregrines near the large colonies of seabirds. These are the rock islands or inaccessible points of land where thousands, sometimes tens of thousands, of water birds nest on the ledges with their irregularly round eggs that roll in circles. In flatter areas, the white arctic terns congregate. They have long, pointed beaks and pointed swift wings, and the adults mob a falcon when the predator steals one of their young. A gyrfalcon is greatly disturbed by such chases: it hides. Salomonsen says the peregrine easily dodges or outpaces the terns.

No one knows if peregrines inhabit the coastal valleys

Stream rushing down rocks at Holsteinsborg, barren
mountain slopes behind.

away from the open sea. It is natural that the peregrines that
people have discovered live with sea birds, for humans
visit these cliffs (like the falcons, for food) much more frequently
than other cliffs. The rugged coastal terrain requires painful,
chill hiking.

About three miles east of the town the narrowing valley
curved northeast out of sight. In the early evening we reached
the corner where we could look far ahead. Brown cliffs
lined both sides as far as the mists would reveal. Only three
miles away one cliff was splashed with white.

"That could be peregrines," I said.

Even here we saw litter, including red of shotgun shells.
"I doubt falcons could survive this close to Holsteinsborg,"
Mattox said. "Every Greenlander has a gun and uses it. The
falcons are too noisy."

"But we should check it. Who knows?" Yet it was growing
dusky and now there were drops of rain. Burnham didn't
want to try climbing on the slick, wet rock.

"Tomorrow," Mattox said. We turned back toward town.
But the next day mists and rains returned to blot out

the mountains. This was our last day, ending hopes of discovering an eyrie.

Falcons and the Tundra

Our helicopter was the first to enter Holsteinsborg since the day of our arrival. It appeared low below all the clouds, barely clearing the rocks upon the tall mountain slopes, to whir over our heads, hovering, dropping, landing. During the next hour I had another shifting view of the tundra as we flew a line eighty miles inland. I saw the shores of lakes and rivers, wandering, muddy caribou trails, cliffs, miles of sloping grassland. This was home for many animals. I wondered again about this northern land; what role did the scattered, hidden peregrines play?

What difference would it make among the other wild animals, if the peregrines vanished? Questions lead to more questions and we remember the extent of our ignorance.

As the peregrine population is not a significant food source for other animals, its interactions with its neighbors fall into three types that apply to the anatum falcons equally as well as to the tundra populations. The peregrine competes with some species for nest locations (cliffs); it defends the vicinity of its eyrie against certain other large animals; it preys on many small birds.

In Greenland the other large cliff nesters are gyrfalcon, white-tailed sea eagle, and raven. Is it possible that the presence of peregrines at some cliffs prevents the use of those sites by the other species? As a result, are fewer pairs of those species able to nest and produce young?[8]

Ravens are not particular about their nest precipices, taking mere ledges of rock, and therefore have a multitude of nest sites. It seems unlikely that peregrines affect their numbers in any serious way. But both gyrfalcons and peregrines demand tall rocks with prey-rich valleys nearby. Neither species tolerates another falcon's presence. Yet the two species

8. See Cade (1960) and White and Cade (1971) for discussions of interactions among cliff-nesting predators in Alaska. Salomonsen (1950–1951) describes the habits of the Greenlandic cliff-nesters.

are not simply equivalent in nest-site requirements. The gyrfalcon is limited by its need for ledges that are thoroughly sheltered to escape snow in May. And because of the differences in their diets, each species may prefer a different part of the tundra.

Gyrs choose their eyries before the peregrines arrive in spring. Peregrines cannot drive them away from their established cliff territories. But we shouldn't conclude that the gyrs therefore take the best sites and prevent the peregrines from using them. Traditions of use at the cliffs may be strong enough to mark some sites as peregrine, others as gyr, year after year.

We do not know whether gyrfalcons would increase if peregrines vanished. Various tall cliffs are unoccupied by either species—are they unsuitable for some as yet unknown reason? Perhaps the falcons aren't limited by their competition for cliffs.

Very few eagles nest in Greenland. We never found their eyries, which generally occur well south of Søndrestrøm. Most eagles nest on steep hillsides.[9] Even where eagles and peregrines prefer similar cliffs, it is questionable whether falcons could take a location the eagles wanted.

In Greenland the peregrines defend their eyrie territories primarily against the same species that also nest on cliffs. Gulls wandering away from their colonies and the large bodies of water are also threatened, but these are a negligible force on the tundra. In Greenland, in addition to competing for nest sites, the vigilant peregrines protect small pockets of tundra from visits of other predators. If, as Tom Cade suggests, peregrines defend only the immediate vicinity of their nests and not the whole of their hunting territories, this effect is very local indeed.[10]

In more temperate areas of the peregrine's range, such as Colorado or France, there live many other species of predators that the peregrines stoop upon and drive from their eyries. Because the peregrines nest at such wide intervals,

---

9. Salomonsen (1950–1951).   10. Cade (1960).

whole populations of the other predators would scarcely be affected by this limitation in their movement. The effect would be upon the predator-prey interactions at the limited collection of cliff sides.

More clearly than competitor or defender of cliffs, the peregrine acts as predator in the ecosystem. In past years human beings have simply labeled predators as beneficial or harmful, according to our own shortsighted interests. But natural systems do not work in such convenient ways.

Generalizations about predator-prey interactions have been drawn from observations in a wide variety of situations.[11] Presumably these principles apply to the peregrine, although we have no such data for the peregrine and its prey. Exhaustive study of predation requires years of observation of many species of animals.

The predator can affect its prey in three ways.

First, it can alter distribution or abundance of certain prey species. It may depress population levels below numbers that would be present if the predator vanished. The peregrine, unlike some predators, lives at great intervals—at cliffs—and large areas of country in between are never hunted. Thus the species's effect must be considered a local one—the peregrine does not touch total populations of a prey species throughout the land. Furthermore, the peregrine generally preys upon a wide variety of birds,[12] its effect is diffuse and not significant for any one species.

The second predator effect may be to alter the balance or degree of competition that exists between various prey species. For the prey species do not live in isolation, but one interacts with another. They both may seek the same food, or drive each other from the home territories. If numbers of one change, numbers of the other may also. If a predator preys on one species, the competitor may be able to increase, and this may make it even harder for survivors of the first

---

11. Keith (1974); I have talked with Dr. L. B. Keith about predator-prey interactions and am indebted to him for some of my ideas in the following paragraphs.

12. Cade (1960); Ratcliffe (1962).

species to thrive. This sort of predator-prey interaction is less common than the first type, and considerably more difficult for scientists to perceive. We have no such proven examples with the peregrine. It preys on many species, not a few; perhaps in some areas one of two competing species is particularly vulnerable to the aerial pursuit.

Third, predators can be strong agents of natural selection. Within a given prey species all individuals are not identical. Nor do all individuals run equal chance of death, but the differing qualities of the individuals render them more likely or less likely to survive. Predators are more likely to catch weak or unhealthy animals. This has long been cited as a benefit to the prey species population, which no longer will carry unfit or diseased animals that will consume food, take mates and territories with poor reproductive success, or pass unfavorable genetic qualities on to their offspring. Thus which individuals within a species are taken as prey is as significant as which species are taken. A mere tally of the species of predator victims ignores the selective effect. In Greenland many of each of the peregrine's prey species live, and the peregrine takes many of each of these few species. The hunter is probably much more important as a selective agent than in depressing abundance of any one species.

The effect of predation on a prey species is endlessly complicated. The continuance of each prey species depends much more upon successful reproduction than upon its total number of individuals. Among animals, more individuals are born than will ever reproduce. Many immatures die through the winter. Their deaths by predation will not affect breeding, except that peregrines may selectively take unfit individuals. Even in breeding season all individuals may not reproduce. Among red grouse in Scotland, a surplus of adults exists, and their loss to predators does not harm the population.[13] We do not know to what extent surplus adults exist in other species that the peregrine frequently takes. Always in questioning the effect of predators on prey populations,

13. Jenkins, Watson, and Miller (1963).

we must ask how reproduction is affected. Again tallies fail.

Large predators, including the peregrine, will take smaller predators as food, and this complicates their overall effect on smaller prey species. The smaller predators, some of which are removed, may eat the same sort of prey or different prey than the falcons. The peregrine's habit of driving hawks and ravens away from the eyrie has the same impact on the local area, freeing it of much nonfalcon predation. Without peregrines, other raptors would appear. There is no simple relationship between presence and absence of peregrines, or any other species, and populations of the prey species.

The complexity of interactions between animals makes assessment of one animal's impact a monumental task. Inaccurate assessments come treacherously easily. But this same complexity gives an ecosystem a stability it would otherwise lack. One animal does not directly control the fates of many other species. If it decreases, the others adjust, but not in catastrophic ways that in turn alter other animals and plants, and disrupt whole landscapes. Each animal is a subtle part, and the many small roles it plays may be shared among other creatures.

One species cannot be separated and valued apart from its fellows. Not because the task is difficult, but because it distorts the natural world. We do not need a landscape containing only "beneficial" species. Human interests are inseparably bound to the workings of healthy ecosystems that are diverse, stable, and adjusting. We constantly alter our surroundings. We do so for limited, focused reasons and are unprepared to cope with many of the unforeseen disruptions that our initial changes can create. Because we will continue to make changes, the capacity of an ecosystem to adjust is extremely important to humanity.

We do not know the impacts of the loss of the peregrine. Clearly, eastern North America has not suffered major and visible consequences. What we assume is that without the peregrine, the ecosystems are by that degree less complex and diverse in their interactions, and more vulnerable to change. This is a negative effect, whether great or small. In

snowy Greenland animal species are few; on the tundra a handful
of prey species lives, four predators. This system is less complex
and therefore less stable. Presumably—we do not know,
and that increases our risk—the peregrine's disappearance
would have more repercussions than it did in the south and
leave the arctic tundra yet more vulnerable.

For ecosystems generally, human beings must also consider that if the peregrine disappears, it does not suffer or
fall alone. The peregrine is most sensitive to the hydrocarbons
that we assumed would vanish into the vastness of the world.
But to varying degrees the other hawks follow the falcon. One
predator may be a small blow to an ecosystem, but less
so the group of avian predators with all their shared roles.
And the peregrine points out the fates awaiting the fish-eating
birds, from pelican to kingfisher, gull to loon. Or certain
of the fish. And to the mammals also, the chemicals are
dangerous.[14]

Peregrines are a sensitive dial we must watch—one that lives
across most of the world. We dare not ignore the warnings.

The Littlest Eyass

Our helicopter came to a gentle landing at Søndrestrøm
where the sky was fair and blue. Dick Graham had returned
from the United States. We passed that evening happily
discussing all we had done in Greenland since his departure in
June. The next morning all five of us hiked out to the First
Eyrie. At the long lake's end Mattox and I stopped to look
at a chittering Odinshane. But the white tent was gone.

Next morning we saw the still blue sky—it would
be another warm day. Once the falcon flew out to spin high
over our heads and return to the eyrie ledge. She watched
us from the brink, and two white eyasses came and crouched
beside her. Soon I noticed the tiercel. He winged south past Tent

14. Peakall (1967); testimony of R. W. Risebrough and C. F.
Wurster, Jr., at the Wisconsin DDT Hearings (1968–1969); Hickey
(1969); Anderson and Hickey (1972); Schreiber and Risebrough
(1972); Snyder et al. (1973).

Lake over the hills, beginning one more hunt on the green meadows, and he never knew that Dave and I climbed to the eyrie and I hid in the blind for my last time.

Dave left, the voices of my friends on the talus slope faded. The blind was dark and cool as it had been before. I hid as I had before but the eyasses had grown and two looked alertly about, squatting upright like penguins. The largest was at the ledge brink. She preened and peered down at small bird noises. I saw the darkness in her wings, the extending feathers; her tail was mostly dark also. The other sat outside of the scrape; but after several minutes he stirred his wings and took heavy strides to the remaining two eyasses. In a moment the three were sprawled upon the dirt, cool in the shade.

The falcon landed and stayed on the far round boulder. I spent the next hour watching her. When the littlest eyass rose briefly from the huddle I saw that he too now had bare skin showing in the face and a darkened beak, no longer pink. He too had become rather bulky and bulgy. His effort to rise stirred the other two eyasses. They bustled, and one extended its wing. They subsided.

Something new was happening during this watch that I was slow to perceive. The eyasses had grown more active. The largest even bobbed her head at the passerines as the adults did. When the young moved, they might extend their wings, especially if they hurried the wings would flap, and if all shifted at once they cut visibility on the ledge considerably. Thus the adults, who at intervals landed on the ledge's east end, were difficult to see. The eyasses would all hiss and scream and rush for the parent. Indeed, they were hungry and I began to wonder for I saw no feeding.

Once I heard and glimpsed the tiercel by the cliff. The falcon joined him for an aerial exchange (I was certain by their screams) and the falcon briefly landed again at the ledge. I could see no prey through the eyasses, and after a motionless pause she departed. An hour later the tiercel dropped onto the ledge. The eyasses charged and he was gone. The eyasses still called and moved in among the high grasses at the far part of the ledge.

Jim and Dave feeding the little eyass.

The near grasses had all been trampled by the falcons
or plucked out by Dave and me. We should not have removed
grass, the eyasses' shade. That morning as the sun hit all
the scrape they were panting, and now gladly sat in the undisturbed grass.

But the falcon on her next return landed directly at the
scrape. She dropped so abruptly that a moment passed before
the startled eyasses rattled and hustled toward her. She looked
out from among them and leapt into flight, as if to get out
of their way. Three eyasses moved out onto the outer
ledge, turning toward their parent who had again alighted at
the round boulder. Another foodless incident? But look,
the fourth eyass stayed at the scrape, and hefted a small body
with his beak, held it between talons, tore off pieces, ate. He ate
the whole body.

Twenty minutes later, alert, I saw the next feeding, where
one eyass hurried to the east end of the ledge, took the
prey from the falcon's talons, and ate alone, unmolested,
until only a long phalarope leg remained, hanging from its
mouth. At neither of these later feedings was I certain
which eyass took the meal, except that it wasn't the littlest.

Banding a peregrine eyass at Ring Sø in 1973.

I had warning that my watch was ending when I heard the adults cackling before the cliff. I heard the rush of their wings and, some moments later, human voices by the rope. My friends stood by the blind. To my surprise all four had climbed.

"We decided to do the banding," Dave said.

We had all been waiting for this. During the last month it had seemed this would be a high point, a climax, a recognition of the eyasses. We had not yet touched them.

"Stay back," Burnham said. "Don't startle them."

No longer did we fear the eyasses chilling or broiling—they were old enough to maintain their body temperatures—but with their flapping wings and energy one might tumble off the ledge if we were clumsy. They all sat on the narrow east part of the ledge, perhaps eighteen inches wide. While the rest of us waited, Burnham crept out onto it until he took the closest eyass up in both his hands. Carefully he passed it back, held with Bill's body between the eyass and the brink, back to Mattox, who set it in the scrape and also shielded it with his body from the rock edge. Then the second eyass. The third. And after retrieving the farthest, last one, Burnham retreated. The two Bills sat at the scrape with the eyasses between them.

Mattox took the largest eyass up in both his hands so that she couldn't flap her wings. The early feathers have blood in the shafts and are easily broken. She snapped at his hand several times, without reaching his skin, until as he turned her upright and held a leg out with his finger ends, she snapped her beak on his thumb. Mattox laughed. "Lucky I've got both her talons."

Only with her talons free and braced could she tear his skin. Mattox felt only a pin pricking. Burnham placed a metal band around the fully grown leg and with pliers squeezed it shut.

"Next," said Burnham.

Mattox set the largest down and took one of the tiercels. The eyasses bustled and hissed. "Watch his beak, Bill," he said to Burnham. "Oh, too late."

Then the third was banded and set down. The littlest eyass remained, crouched against Mattox's leg. Bill and Dick changed places, so that Dick banded the littlest.

"We better get going," said Dave.

The eyasses all sat in a row watching us. The adults flew overhead and I was noticing details, of the sky also, and ledge and rising cliff, the wind on our faces. The others would remain in Greenland two more weeks. But tomorrow would be my last full day.

I looked at the four men's faces as they passed me on the ledge, each with its different smile, and I remembered their expressions as I walked to the rope, and later as I sat among the talus.

These four wanted the peregrine to continue. By the cliff they had a special light in their eyes that was reflected in the faces of other people, across the world, through time, scattered persons whom the peregrine delighted in different ways. Mr. Groskin and Mr. Hall, Tom Cade out of Alaska, seamen, the vicar at Salisbury Cathedral, the woman who had cried, "Peregrine, peregrine!" as I stood on the beach long ago, and the falcon turned away in its flight.

Bill Burnham and Bill Mattox banding an eyass at First Eyrie.

The peregrine is one part of its ecosystem, and complex and poorly known are the effects of its loss. The species is a wealth of information, many formed in many lands; the falcon may lead scientists to many secrets. But clearer still was that light in my friends' faces, the energy peregrines sparked in humans.

Look at the descending peregrine, about to alight. Do not miss it!

For the falcon is sensitive to the full air and wind, and touches each current with its long feathers and soars and glides and draws ever-changing patterns.

For its wings are strong, to carry it beyond sight among clouds, rush on high and plunge swiftly down in the thunder stoop.

And it is furious in its pursuit of prey, and takes the swiftest fowl, nor can the swallow outrace it or twitter unafraid when the hunter appears.

And its voice is like the wind, thin, carrying to the distance, and proud with all strength and speed, it is a cutting, wailing sound, it holds the open country.

For its cliffs are tall and steep, they are wide-scattered

with the prince's view, the lone eyries secure and guarded like fortresses.

For the tiercel clutches rock, he glares with powered eyes and hooked, notched beak, fiery, gray and white and helmeted, upright he perches, always watchful.

And the raven cowers when the peregrine screams, and all the wide valley knows and stops and crouches, the falcon guards her home, she threatens croaking gull and the mighty eagle.

For each year in spring the falcons return, each spring the pageants are repeated at the cliffs, where old watchers feel young once more, and the young feel ageless.

Yet the peregrine strays across the earth, it is named the wanderer, where human travelers meet it in all the strange corners, where it is recognized, remembered, but transformed.

While on the high seas ships sail and no haven appears day or night but the falcon lands upon the highest mast.

While in the cities where the cars roar and humans never see the green meadows or woodlands, even here the falcon hunts and guards its concrete eyrie.

And solitary men capture eyasses and each raises his bird, the two wander far together because the falcon has learned to hunt in the human presence.

But the peregrine will never be important to all people. In many lives there is no chance to meet the falcon. Or it is luck where both human and falcon visit the marsh on the same afternoon. And for the human one day is not like another. On Tuesday he may leave the farm for the open lands, and his visions that day he'll hardly remember in a week. But Wednesday if he leaves home instead, his life may be transformed. The state of the human makes the difference, a mood that leaves him open to what he sees. If he boils too full of grief or else eagerness and a hundred businesses, he won't have time or emotion for the falcon.

An innate or deeply printed quality in humans leaves them sensitive to certain experiences. The wild calls some. Others respond most to curling plants, less to creatures. Some love the hunter, others the gentle soft rabbits first. Many look only to people and their creations.

What we value in our high experiences are the excitement and fullness of emotion that overflows. But we are mysterious. We do not understand what moves us. Therefore, it is best we surround ourselves with brilliant creatures, plants, objects. Sparks of different sorts that flame experience. For our different moods and vitalities. For the different humans.

It is not that the peregrine alone calls us into the world. Without the peregrine we will meet bear, caribou, the shrew and kestrel. But each creature has its own places and times and ways. Peregrine moments will be gone. All of them. By that degree the richness of our home will be diminished, and so too the echoing of our spirits.

I left my boulder perch. Down the talus slope and grass Dave was talking to Mattox.

Dave was saying, "We're going to do a night watch."

And Mattox, "Do you want some help?"

"No, Jim will take the lookout until early morning, when he'll get me up for the last hours."

"But really Dave, that's awful. . . ."

"No," I said, "It's what I want to do. The night watches are the best part."

*   *   *   *

So they were, and so once again I witnessed the thinning sunlight and extending shadows. I heard the voices of my friends distant from the tent and saw their last trips to the stream before they slept. And I had been hoping the tiercel would be sitting where I could see him well. He was.

There he perched, in the gloom and dark rock, everything silent but the south stream. He perched upright, white spot on rock directly above the eyrie. He faced me.

Our campsite seemed empty, as it had most of the summer, with Dave alone rather than four companions. I could imagine that we were in the fresh bloom of summer. But it was not quite the same. Oddly, despite the unmoving landscape, I felt that the tiercel and I were the still constant elements, all else revolving, passing in time to pull us apart. We both guarded the cliff. The twilight almost was night. The west looked far later than a sun-setted sky for the reds and roses had deepened to soft purples, when owls would hoot in the south. The shadow was heavier. I heard strange noises—perhaps young foxes—but the small birds were voiceless in their skulking and moults. A bright evening star rose in the east.

The falcon did not brood upon the scrape, as she had nightly since early June. The eyasses were not in the scrape either. I could not see them. I thought they must have all passed to the ledge's east end and squatted in the grass. Was the falcon on her own cliff perch?

The hours passed. No creature moved. I was endlessly content. For half an hour about midnight the tiercel's head was craned round and up out of sight on his back. I could scarcely see more than the white of his breast. He slept.

Imperceptibly at 1 or 2 A.M. it seemed less after evening than before morning. I could hear soft rattles and hisses. The invisible eyasses called. Unseen, the tiercel left his perch.

Later I thought the east grew less dark. Later I heard the eyasses again.

I heard a far "kaaa kaaa kaaa." The tiercel was winging home and he landed unanswered on the eyrie ledge's east end. With a small body. The largest eyass leaped out from the grass and grabbed the prey. "Kak kak kak kak kak." The tiercel's voice rang and drowned the eyasses' peeping. The littlest left the grasses, but the big falcon had the whole meal in her talons. She took it into cover, while the little one pipped before his parent. The tiercel answered but had no food.

Would the littlest be fed anymore? It hadn't captured a bite during all my watch at the blind because the falcon no longer divided the food. The larger eyasses all were aggressive and greedy.

The little one followed the largest into the grass. Now grew his greatest danger of starving. Even if he were old enough to feed himself he was not strong enough. He was an extra eyass. The big eyass's head showed from among the stems. It huffed out its wings and charged at the tiercel, its parent. He fled! He flew and relanded west of the scrape. "Kak kak kak kak."

I hadn't seen the falcon in six hours. Now it was 3:05 A.M., and sun bathed the southernmost hilltops.

Later silently the falcon landed at the scrape with a large, large body primarily white—ptarmigan or oldsquaw. Then the two excited eyasses rushed over and pulled at the prey. But the falcon kept it from them. She tore the flesh into pieces as had once been her custom and held them for the eyasses to take. I was grateful she judged this prey too large to deliver unsevered and torn. After the first minutes the littlest eyass in his turn was gorged and safe. With such hunts of the falcon he would survive.

It was a seventeen-minute feeding. The falcon took the body still half remaining and flew to the east cliff end near the base. I think she ate some of the meat—I couldn't see because my eyes watered and hurt from squinting through the telescope—before she dropped gliding into the valley.

During all this the tiercel hadn't moved. He perched some dozen feet from the scrape, where the eyasses remained. Unexpectedly this new morning I had another puzzle—where were the two middle-sized eyasses? No eyasses would stay in the grass through all that noise and feedings. I couldn't understand it. They couldn't have fallen? They certainly weren't able to fly. All white with down.

I remained at the lookout, because the tiercel remained and called occasionally, the two eyasses had vanished, and I had an endless, motionless feeling.

I did at last pack and descend. I looked back puzzled many times. I remember the dryness of the hillside.

"Yes, yes, that's white. It's fluffy not whitewash or quartz." Facing the cliff, I remembered the eyrie ledge didn't end by the round rock but slanting into a ramp rose past that short ledge we once thought was the eyrie, past into grasses and rocks. One, two eyasses sat there, where they must have crept in the evening. One high, but the other descending even as I watched, back toward the scrape and food.

The tiercel did depart, just as I reached the tent and soon would shake Dave, "Wake, wake up, Dave."

*   *   *   *

I slept only until the others came rummaging about the tent for breakfast. Then I was placing all I had into my pack and duffel bag. Only on our first days in Greenland had I climbed to the ridge top. I would take a walk. Just before I left, Dave came down from the lookout.

"Wait a minute," he said. "I'll go with you."

We both took cameras. We set out due east as we had separately that first afternoon. "I'm going to try getting caribou pictures," Dave said.

He got ahead of me as usual. Near the spur's crest I called as loudly as I could, "Dave . . . I'm going north. . . . See you."

I climbed alone to the ridge top, camera in hand. Near-sighted caribou blundered near me, to tempt me into photographs at long range, and I found yellow flowers I wished to remember. There, there, here was the tip top cresting boulder over the cliff. I turned to have all the tiercel's view. I sat to examine the tundra.

What was I doing this last day? Making word pictures of the landscape. Tilting my camera this way and that. Trying to memorize sights and feelings. These feelings were fleeting; I didn't want the adventure to leave, I didn't want to leave. Thus I had my notebooks, the feathers I had taken, even a pellet or two I kept separate from those for the museum. I wanted to hold on.

Let me keep this best thing.

How absurd that the value of everything material and real, all of nature and humanity's creations, should ultimately be measured by the transient and intangible human experience. How could the value of the peregrine be subjective? Must we defend it thus? I cling to these delicate pleasures and still they slip away.

How long will it last, the girl had asked me by the lake shore. She hadn't only meant the Caloplaca orange. Already I was forgetting our fragile meeting.

Mattox, or Dick, or Burnham didn't desire that the peregrine continue because of its various human-centered values. Rather they felt the peregrine was a treasure that should be preserved for its own sake. Its survival needs no other justification.

I continued walking as far north as I needed to look down on the north river, bound by the regular curving Black Cliff. Now the river filled all its wide bed, no trickle in August; I heard its churning currents and saw the white of its waves. Late July and early August are the height of the ice cap's melt. Along its half horizon it stretched, pocked and darkened with the dirt its melting ice had left. My previous afternoon here this had seemed the edge of the world.

Dave was waiting for me at the tent. "Mattox decided we should come get him early." Mattox, now in the blind, would photograph us with the eyasses, and then we would pack the camera equipment down. Today all five of us were returning to the base.

We climbed quickly. Only the falcon cackled before the eyrie. Mattox was ready. But the eyasses were all out of sight east on the ledge in the shade.

Mattox said, "They were here when I arrived. One by one they left when the sun got hot. Let's see if I can reach one."

He crawled along the ledge as Burnham had done, although more slowly. He stretched both hands and grasped an eyass. It was the littlest. Back at the wide scrape Dave and I sat with the downy peregrine between us. He stared at Dave with beak gaping. Dave picked up the disgruntled eyass, who broke into "hik hik hik hik" calls, haggard screams in miniature.

I noticed I nearly sat upon a ptarmigan body. "Try feeding him," said Mattox.

I tore a piece of flesh off and drooped it from my finger tips. I proffered this morsel before the eyass as I had watched the falcon do; gingerly, for these eyasses had grown greedy. The little one who still loudly was objecting to Dave, abruptly quieted, leaned forward and took the bite. He made no

A banded male eyass at another cliff; it is nearly ready to fledge.

more noise, and accepted additional pieces. I fed the eyass whose health and fate I had been watching since hatching. And so also I felt it was a climax when I took the eyass while Dave fed. Its down was soft in my fingers and the firm body vibrated, moved in my hands. It was as close an encounter as I could have with a wild peregrine.

"Well, Dave," I said. "I guess we should go."

"We better, Jim."

I set the littlest eyass down. It shrugged one wing and looked somewhere straight ahead, toward my boot or the distant valley.

And Mattox said when I reached him on the ledge, "You'll remember this. I'm glad."

We climbed down. I remember all the footholds and near rock shapes from this last descent. And that last part of that last afternoon all the valley—the caribou paths, the redpolls, the wind-stirred grass in hummocks, and holes made by foxes—all impressed me, all details were marvelous. I felt this world was a good home for people. My delight.

No, our spirits are not free or infinitely buoyant. They are stirred, released from within and also from without. The peregrine family quickened me.

We shared the solemnity. Without the brilliant images we as well as the world are impoverished.

Rarely had I been so filled with life and movement. I clung to the feeling and wished to hold it. Graham and the Bills were walking toward the lake. The sunlight was weak, near sunset.

"Are you coming?" my friend Dave asked.

"Yes." I wanted to hold on, hold on at least to the memory of the eyass touch. I watched the cliff. As if the loons had laughed; sometimes when they laugh you are paralyzed. Some people seek to save the peregrine because a species can be saved. The race can continue to survive. Even if life and movement always elude us. Would the struggling tiercel come before I left? Yes, that one moment was right, I heard the thin, high voice, the voice that gradually grew and above me the tiercel sped, he cut the air with his pointed, silver wings while the falcon rushed out deep-voiced and beat up under him with her crooked wings, and the two spiraled in the sky.

Afterword

The Outcome

When I left Greenland, less than two weeks remained
for my companions to complete the population survey.
The eyries we had found stood in scattered directions above the
tundra. All but First Eyrie had to be visited so that the young
could be counted and banded. My friends also hoped to
explore new stretches of tundra. It was August 5; very soon
the eyasses would begin to fledge.

Because the breeding season neared an end, Dave joined
the other three as they completed the survey. The four
journeyed first to the four eyries between Søndrestrøm, the
ice cap, and Isortoq River. These were Ice Cap, Hut, No-name,
and Ring Sø eyries.

First at Ice Cap they banded three eyasses. Hut Eyrie
had the tallest cliff we had found with falcons. Both adults
screamed overhead, but Burnham and Dave climbed all over
the rock, without finding white downies. They stood at
last by an empty scrape that had feathers of prey at its edges and
peregrine down. No young could have fledged for the two
adults still wailed at the cliff, and we would not know what
had happened to their brood. At No-name Eyrie grassy
ledges broke the cliff into sections, and middle parts of the
cliff could be climbed without a rope. Only one eyass waited
on a ledge; Burnham banded it.

The short Ring Sø cliff had held four eggs at the end of
June. Still the valiant tiercel defended his home; but only one
eyass survived on the exposed ledge. Its feathers were hardly
growing because it was still young, late, and it looked sickly
as if it might die.

After this trip Bill Mattox and Dave took one direction
while Burnham and Graham chose another. Bill and Dave
had talked with the Dane who knew the tundra, the man I
had met on the Air Force cruiser. Following his directions they
discovered the symmetrical round hill that overlooked the
fjord, and they called it Dome Eyrie. Two branched
peregrines screamed with parents on the cliff. They flapped

Looking east from the base of Hut Eyrie to the ice cap.

their wings and flew beyond reach. Dave and Bill crept down a crack in the vertical face of the rock, across rotten, crumbling ledges to the cavelike scrape. And a third eyass cowered before them and hissed; they banded him.

A helicopter flew Bill Burnham and Dick across the rushing river, so that at last we learned about Black Cliff. It also had dangerous, crumbling rock; it had treacherous overhangs, and a fall directly into the river current. But the pair had raised three angry eyasses, and these were banded.

So too, the Musk Ox Eyrie tiercel and his mate had raised three eyasses. Already they had fledged.

The eyasses were flying sooner than we had expected. It was August 12, too late to begin journeys to tundra remote from Søndrestrøm. My four companions made a last trip to First Eyrie and dismantled our camp. That ended their work in Greenland.

On foot we had surveyed approximately 800 square miles, discovering eight nesting pairs of peregrines (and an unmated female at a ninth cliff). Thus the sample area held a breeding density of one pair per 100 square miles. The average distance between neighboring eyries was 6.2 miles. We saw eighteen eyasses, thirteen of which we banded. The eyries therefore produced an average of 2.25 young, or (if Hut Eyrie is excluded) 2.57 eyasses per successful eyrie. As most of the eyasses had not yet fledged, we could not calculate a fledging rate, although we estimate that an average at least of two flew from each eyrie.[1]

The breeding success and density of this Greenland population compare favorably with peregrine reproductive success and density in other parts of the Arctic or with populations in more southern areas when the peregrines were unaffected by pesticides.[2] I laughed with relief when Dave's first letter arrived with the survey results. The First Eyrie pair was not simply isolated and lucky with their young. The Greenland peregrines still were healthy and seemingly untouched.

But we had collected eggshell fragments from seven eggs of four different females. These and the shells of two addled eggs—that had remained unbroken and dead in Musk Ox and Ring Sø eyries—were measured for thickness. Shell thickness had decreased 14 percent from the average thickness for Greenland shells collected before 1940.[3] In failing populations peregrine eggs begin to break when their thickness is reduced by about 20 percent.[4]

Contents of the two addled eggs were analyzed for DDE and PCB concentrations. The DDE concentrations (364 and 300 ppm lipid) were somewhat higher in these eggs than in several other northern peregrine populations, but by no means the highest concentrations yet measured. PCB concentrations had not previously been determined in eggs from

---

1. Mattox et al. (1972).

2. See Hickey (1942), Cade (1960), and Hickey (1969).

3. Walker, Mattox, and Risebrough (1973); D. W. Anderson measured the eggshells and provided the comparative data on the pre-1940 Greenland shells. As eggshell thickness varies over a species's range, thickness measurements can only be compared for a given area. Data from healthy quail and chickens indicate that eggshells become somewhat thinner as incubation progresses (Kreitzer, 1972). Similar thinning probably occurs in the peregrine and could account for a portion of the 14 percent decrease in thickness that Anderson detected. Nevertheless, events in subsequent years appear to confirm that in 1972 Greenland peregrines already were gravely threatened by pesticides.

4. See Berger et al. (1970); Ratcliffe (1970, 1972); White and Cade (1971); Enderson and Craig (1974); for other species see also Milstein, Prestt, and Bell (1970); Porter and Wiemeyer (1969); Anderson and Hickey (1972); Snyder et al. (1973).

the Arctic, but levels in our two eggs (403 and 210 ppm lipid) were comparable to those of DDE.[5]

This Greenland population was perilously balanced. While peregrine numbers were intact, the species could vanish quickly from the tundra. The species would vanish, if DDE concentrated still more heavily within the falcons.

And thus, most urgently if the peregrine is to survive, humanity must stop dispersing DDT, dieldrin, and the other hydrocarbon pesticides. The Greenland falcons cannot continue to absorb them during their migrations and winterings through North and South America. Fortunately the Environmental Protection Agency in 1972 banned use of DDT in the United States. Nearly all uses of aldrin and dieldrin have also been suspended. Canada and a number of European countries have taken similar action against DDT. Residue levels of the organochlorine pesticides appear to be subsiding in North American animals, and some previously threatened birds are now having improved reproductive success. But the new and strict laws should not be weakened nor riddled with exceptions for special applications of the chemicals—in the United States several emergency DDT permits have been issued since 1972. In the countries of the tropics, DDT still is widely spread for crop protection and disease control. Heavy demand for the chemical is likely to continue.[6]

In these countries people are threatened by insufficient food and by malaria. Yet the choice is not whether we use DDT for humanity's sake, or not use DDT for one animal's sake and human detriment. For the peregrine's survival is an index of a general environmental health. As the eyries fail, we know that populations of other fish- and bird-eating predators sicken, as well as fish species, while in little-understood ways mammals, perhaps people as well, are harmed. The hydrocarbons are widely dangreous. With effort and foresight, ways alternative to releasing hydrocarbon poisons can be exploited. Where we do not like the available alternatives

5. Walker, Mattox, and Risebrough (1973).
6. U.S. Department of Agriculture (1973, 1975, 1977); Goldberg (1975); Newton (1976); Peakall (1976); Chancellor (1977).

we have the responsibility for discovering new means.

Beyond maintaining an environment safe for peregrines, the nest locations require protection. Eggs and young easily die, and at the eyrie the far-flying adults are most vulnerable. The adults may abandon the site if humans disturb the cliff area. Rock climbers on nest cliffs will threaten any falcon family. In many areas parks are placed about cliffs, because the precipice is spectacular and its top offers wide views. But visitors to the parks will walk about the rock. Human use of the eyrie areas need only be avoided during the nesting season. Known eyries should be quiet and secure during the spring and early summer—if humans watch them, it must be from a distance. New eyries should be identified so that disturbances can be prevented.[7]

American peregrines can no longer be taken from the wild for falconry without endangering the wild population. Now it is illegal for falconers to catch peregrines, either eyasses, passage birds, or adults, in the United States.[8] For the present this must remain law.

Beyond guarding the eyries with rules, signs, wardens, and secrecy, persecution or disturbance of peregrines at the eyries and elsewhere (some peregrines still are shot) can be lessened by informing the public about peregrines. More people must recognize and like the falcons. Education and art can help protect peregrines. But also in opening human eyes the species will bring more delight to humans. Insofar as we preserve the peregrine because it touches people, art will multiply the species's value.

But even with these measures the peregrines will be slow in returning to their wide range in North America. As a part of its ecosystem, the species should be represented by a healthy population and not merely by last survivors. Moreover, the species is subjectively rich only as pairs are present for humans to witness.

In recent years many individuals have tried to breed peregrines in captivity, primarily falconers who held birds and

---

7. Hickey (1942, 1969); Hickey, personal communication.
8. U.S. Endangered Species Act.

worried about the species.[9] Captive breeding has three goals. First, to obtain a stock of peregrines for use in research on pesticides, falcon behavior, and physiology. Second, so that falconers may fly peregrines without taking them from the wild. And third, with hopes that captive-bred birds can be reintroduced into the landscape. Healthy peregrines would inhabit the old cliffs. Only in this way will the Massachusetts or Hudson eyries soon be reoccupied.

Many falconers encouraged their falcons to breed. But successes were few and unpredictable. The lone, fiery peregrines did not easily mate in their restricted pens. The two adults might fight until perhaps the falcon killed the tiercel. The two might tolerate each other but not mate. And even when copulation occurred and the female laid eggs, the eggs often were infertile.

In most cases peregrines captured as haggards and even passage birds proved too intractable to reproduce successfully. Peregrines held since they were eyasses and the few born in captivity were less disrupted by their human keepers or enclosures. But if young were to be raised on a large scale, methods of handling the falcons had to be developed so that reproductive success could predictably occur.

One of the largest facilities for the breeding of peregrines has been built at Cornell University in Ithaca, New York. Tom Cade, the Alaskan researcher, directs this program. In 1972 fertile peregrine eggs were obtained from one pair. These remained viable until just before hatching in an artificial incubator; but the advanced embryos died, perhaps because temperatures were too high. Then the summer of 1973 brought major success. Twenty-two peregrine eggs hatched. These were from three pairs of the falcons who were induced to lay additional clutches of eggs by removal of the first clutch. Only two of the eyasses died. The three pairs successfully raised full sets of eyasses, while foster parents, including

---

9. The following paragraphs are based upon conversations with R. A. Graham and J. J. Hickey, as well as Nelson (1971), Cade (1973), and Clement (1974).

an unmated white gyrfalcon, cared for the extras.[10]

The Cornell peregrines have produced increasing numbers of young. In 1976, 25 females laid eggs and 69 young were raised.[11] In 1977, 31 laying females yielded 96 young.[12] Also in 1977, 38 peregrine young rewarded efforts at a second breeding project, run by the Canadian Wildlife Service in Alberta.[13]

Varying methods of managing the birds have resulted in successful reproduction. Because sexually performing females outnumber males, artificial insemination has been an important procedure, although so difficult that its success largely depends on the intuition and sensitivity of a small number of the human keepers—among them, Bill Burnham, who now runs a second Cornell breeding facility established in Colorado in 1974–1975. Tom Cade believes captive propagation is an art, with each peregrine pair each season providing its own challenges. The process will never be easy, inexpensive, or automatic. Yet the breeding programs have demonstrated that, with adequate funding, availability of young peregrines will not be an obstacle to reintroduction to the wild.[14]

Many uncertainties remain about reintroduction. First, the environment must be safe for the peregrine's return. As long as hydrocarbons are not used in a region, the levels of the chemicals will gradually drop. No one knows how great a level of environmental contamination the falcons can survive, or how long we must wait. In the eastern states, where no native peregrines remain, eyasses must enter the wild, learning to survive, without care or help from parents and without the evident presence of humans—or else the falcons may become too tame.

For the last four summers, Cornell personnel have been working out release techniques by freeing a portion of their captive-bred eyasses. Once again, the falconers' knowledge of how to handle their birds has proved invaluable. A pro-

---

10. Cade (1973).
11. Cade and Dague (1976a).
12. Cade and Fyfe (in press).

13. Cade and Fyfe (in press).
14. Cade and Fyfe (in press).

cedure called "hacking," which enables young falcons to strengthen their flight muscles, has been modified for use with Cornell peregrines. Traditionally with this technique, the falconer has allowed his captives to fly free before the birds know how to capture prey for themselves. They must return to a particular location—a platform of boards or a tree stump—to obtain food the falconer has set out. The birds are recaptured before they learn to kill wild food.

At Cornell, this last step is omitted. Four-week-old eyasses are placed in boxes either upon cliffs traditionally used by peregrines, or on artificial structures in areas without suitable cliffs but with abundant prey and small risk of human interference. These eyasses previously have been cared for by captive adult peregrines, thus getting exposure to their own species. The chicks, now alone in their lofty eyries, are fed without seeing people. Soon they are testing the wind with their wings, and gradually they gain the flight skills in company with their siblings. Interaction with other young peregrines has provided sufficient stimulus for the birds to develop the behaviors they will need for life in the wild. Their human caretakers, watching from a distance, have marveled to see the fledglings stoop upon, and finally catch, their own prey.[15]

The first release, in 1974, ended abruptly. Two healthy eyasses learned to fly from the top of the Faculty Tower on the campus at New Paltz, New York. Shortly after they began to pursue prey, they disappeared. Someone found a young peregrine wing—the two birds had probably been shot. In 1975, eyasses were placed in secrecy at five sites where the birds could be well protected. All fledged and after a time of practice flights and hunts, twelve small peregrines scattered across the empty anatum range.[16]

The parents of these birds came from the far north, where peregrines are highly migratory and winter in the tropics. Would the Cornell releases do the same? If so, not only

---

15. Cade (1975); Zimmerman (1975).
16. Cade (1974, 1975); Kaufman (1976).

would they run the risks of an arduous migration, but for a good part of the year they would live where organochlorines still are heavily used. The released birds wore numbered blue leg bands that could be read through binoculars at a distance. Reports the winter following the 1975 release indicated that 4, possibly 6, of the peregrines wintered within 50 to 100 miles of their release sites. They were behaving not like their arctic kin, but like the sedentary anatum peregrines native to the Eastern States. Apparently local environment heavily influences their migratory behavior.[17]

A total of 83 peregrines were freed in 1976 and 1977. Sixty-six of them, more than 80 percent, lived to become independent hunters.[18] But even 66 falcons may never find each other to mate and nest. For mortality is high the first year. And the falcons will not be ready to breed until two years or more pass. They have half a continent to wander over.

In many species of birds, the young tend to return to their birthplace to nest.[19] If this were true of the peregrine, the Cornell birds would reappear at or near their release sites in following summers. These prominent locations would serve as beacons to bring the scattered hunters together again. Five yearlings did return in 1976. And in 1977, as many as ten falcons revisited their release areas. One two-year-old male even acted paternally toward the 1977 eyasses, actually carrying prey to the release box.[20]

Annual releases of young peregrines are planned. Very soon, both mature male and female may come to the same eastern eyrie and raise their own wild eyasses. With success of the breeding and reintroduction projects, we may replace what humanity has destroyed. Yet remember that life is not restored but only replaced. In the Arctic the ancient traditions and lineages native to their landscape are maintained. In the Eastern States this continuity is forever broken.

---

17. Cade and Dague (1976c).
18. Cade and Dague (1976b); Temple (in press).
19. Hickey (1952).
20. Cade and Dague (1976c, 1977); S. A. Temple, personal communication.

*   *   *   *

Peregrines continue to decline across America and Europe. By 1975 most American arctic populations had shrunk to about half their maximum recorded size. The population along the main portion of the Colville River in Alaska retained 35 percent of its former numbers, and its reproductive success of less than one young per pair appeared insufficient to maintain breeding numbers. All boreal forest populations have declined. In the vast areas south of the boreal forest, at least 62 eyries were occupied in 1975, mostly in southwestern United States and Mexico. These anatum peregrines have been most closely studied in the Rocky Mountain region. In 1973 and 1974, eggshells were 20 percent thinner than normal. In 1973, only 3 eyasses fledged from 14 occupied eyries. In 1975, only 9 pairs occupied cliffs, probably producing 5 young in total.[21]

Although in some areas data are inadequate to demonstrate population changes, nowhere in North America have peregrines shown signs of recovery following restriction of DDT use. The Peale's peregrines of the Pacific northwest are the only substantial population stable in recent years.[22]

At both the Cornell and Canadian Wildlife Service breeding projects, researchers are attempting to prevent further losses among the last remaining anatum peregrines. If pairs can survive just a few years longer, while environmental contamination subsides, reproduction may improve enough to allow a slow population recovery. Work here has involved selecting pairs that in past years have failed to reproduce and replacing their eggs with dummy eggs. The peregrine eggs are hatched, if possible, in artificial incubators where risks of breaking the thin shells can be minimized. Later these eyasses or else offspring of captive birds are returned to the wild pairs. The adults have accepted the chicks, successfully rearing them so that new peregrines have joined the wild population

---

21. Enderson and Craig (1974); Fyfe, Temple, and Cade (1976).
22. Fyfe, Temple, and Cade (1976); see White, Emison, and Williamson (1973) for a discussion of the status of *Falco peregrinus pealei*.

from eyries that, without human help, would have been barren yet another year.[23]

In Great Britain the peregrine population has shown continued slow recovery between 1971 and 1975, with marked improvement at last even in Wales.[24] But elsewhere in Europe, the situation remains grim. In 1975 the peregrine as a breeding species was extinct or practically so in Austria, Belgium, Denmark, and Hungary, with populations in Norway, Sweden, and elsewhere barely existent. Peregrines have shown drastic declines across the Soviet Union. Unless present trends change, the species may utterly vanish from continental Europe.[25]

I returned to Greenland in 1973 and camped near the Ring Sø peregrines to compare their nesting behavior with the First Eyrie pair.[26] I also assisted my companions with the breeding survey. The same eight eyries all had pairs, and young fledged at each cliff, while the lone falcon of 1972 had a mate and eyasses as well. In all, we counted 24 eyasses, for an average of 2.67 at the nine successful eyries.[27]

My friends have also worked in Greenland each summer since 1973. In 1974 and 1975, only 5 out of 9 eyries produced young. In 1976, only three eyries were successful; and in 1977, only four. Musk Ox and No-name cliffs have not held a breeding pair in any of the four years. Ring Sø stood abandoned in 1976 and gyrfalcons took it over in 1977. Apparently there are no adult peregrines to fill vacancies at the eyries.[28]

My friends have not found young at First Eyrie. The three eyasses Burnham and Clement banded in 1973 may have been the last for the cliff.

I did not accompany my friends on that rainy day. Instead on a sunny afternoon I hiked alone to the mountain. I

23. Cade and Dague (1976b); Fyfe (1976).
24. Prestt (1977).
25. Bijleveld (1974); Chancellor (1977).
26. Results of this research on peregrine behavior appear in Harris and Clement (1975).
27. Burnham et al. (1974).
28. Mattox (1975); Mattox, personal communication. Burnham (1974) describes in detail much of the Greenlandic peregrine research for the years 1972–1974.

Four eyasses in scrape; they are two to three weeks old;
adult female looks out from eyrie.

remember standing among the birch bushes at the stream,
dazed and a little slow-minded because this quiet spot of tundra
seemed like home. Here was the level space where the tent
stood, here the whitened pile of five antlers I had collected a
year earlier, here the caribou path toward the lookout. Up
the grass and talus I walked. I recognized my path on the rocks.
At this place I had sat on lookout. I sat. I remember a white
spot on the cliff, the white front of the peregrine. It hadn't
called during all my progress about the valley. She flew, she had
the falcon's wings, and her voice. She dropped to a far
ledge and bent briefly behind the grasses—eyasses lay hidden
in the scrape.

I remember the second letter from Dave: "We went to
first eyrie. Three eyasses had fledged. I'm sorry, Jim, but the
littlest was dead at the scrape. I guess the adults stopped dividing
the meat. He starved."

I remember the falcon returned to her high perch. Her
voice was a painful, thrilling sound. But far, far away, the
wind, I heard a thinner voice. The falcon flies before the cliff
until both now are flying. He has silver underwings, hers
are brown and the sun shining. She beats up under him as he

rises until they meet once, she drops, beats up again and at the last instant—so quickly I hardly see the motion—she flips to seize the prey with her feet.

She dropped to the new ledge. The brilliant tiercel gradually soared higher and higher to leave the cliff behind, the tiercel was a hardly visible speck and then he was gone.

This was the same falcon and the same tiercel. The tiercel would never be seen again—during the following four seasons a falcon has watched her cliff alone. I knew I could not stay with them that afternoon. All my stirrings of hope and grief soared. It felt like a huge and paralyzing task, to preserve the peregrines at their eyries. But as large as the sky was, as little as I, somehow I would act upon my caring. That is the only beautiful response for any poet. Beyond feeling, each one of us must act, must try as he or she can for sake of the life all around us.

Literature Cited

Conclusions from other students' work should not be presented without a listing of sources so that the details of method and data can be examined. Therefore I have included notes on the sources for my material on the peregrine falcon and the other animal species. The reader may wish to explore more extensively certain of the topics I have briefly introduced.

Four articles describe aspects of our 1972 and 1973 peregrine research in Greenland: Burnham et al. (1974), Harris and Clement (1975), Mattox et al. (1972), and Walker et al. (1973).

Anderson, D. W., and J. J. Hickey. 1972. Eggshell changes in certain North American birds. *Proceedings of the XVth International Ornithological Congress, the Hague, 1970.* Leiden: E. J. Brill, pp. 514–540.

Beebe, F. L. 1969. Passenger pigeons and peregrine ecology. In J. J. Hickey (ed.). 1969. *Peregrine Falcon Populations, Their Biology and Decline.* Madison: University of Wisconsin Press, pp. 399–402.

Bent, A. C. 1925. *Life Histories of North American Wild Fowl (Part 2).* United States National Museum Bulletin 130, 376 pp.

———. 1927. *Life Histories of North American Shore Birds (Part 1).* United States National Museum Bulletin 142, 420 pp.

———. 1938. *Life Histories of North American Birds of Prey (Part 2).* United States National Museum Bulletin 170, 482 pp.

Berger, D. D., D. W. Anderson, J. D. Weaver, and R. W. Risebrough. 1970. Shell thinning in eggs of Ungava peregrines. *Canadian Field-Naturalist* 84(3): 265–267.

Berger, D. D., and H. C. Mueller. 1969. Nesting peregrine falcons in Wisconsin and adjacent areas. In J. J. Hickey (ed.). 1969. *Peregrine Falcon Populations, Their Biology and Decline.* Madison: University of Wisconsin Press, pp. 115–122.

Berger, D. D., C. R. Sindelar, Jr., and K. E. Gamble. 1969. The status of breeding peregrines in the eastern United States. In J. J. Hickey (ed.). 1969. *Peregrine Falcon Populations, Their Biology and Decline.* Madison: University of Wisconsin Press, pp. 165–173.

Bijleveld, Maarten. 1974. *Birds of Prey in Europe.* London: Macmillan, 263 pp.

Bond, R. M. 1946. The peregrine population of western North America. *Condor* 48(3): 101–116.

Brodkorb, Pierce. 1964. Catalogue of fossil birds: Part 2, *Anseriformes* through *Galliformes. Bulletin of the Florida State Museum* 8(3): 195–335.

Brown, L. H. 1961. The peregrine falcon comes to town. *Country Life* 129(3352): 1280–1281.

Brown, Leslie, and Dean Amadon. 1968. *Eagles, Hawks and Falcons of the World,* 2 volumes. New York: McGraw-Hill, 945 pp.

Burnham, W. A. 1974. *Breeding Biology and Ecology of the Peregrine Falcon (Falco peregrinus) in West Greenland.* M.A. thesis, Brigham Young University, Provo, Utah.

Burnham, W. A., D. M. Clement, J. T. Harris, M. A. Jenkins, W. G. Mattox, and F. P. Ward. 1974. Falcon research in Greenland, 1973. *Arctic* 27(1): 71–74.

Cade, T. J. 1960. Ecology of the peregrine and gyrfalcon populations in Alaska. *University of California Publications in Zoology* 63(3): 151–290.

———— (ed.). 1973. Captive breeding—the 1973 season. *Peregrine Fund Newsletter* 1: 1–4.

———— (dir.). 1974. Captive breeding—the 1974 season. Introductions to wild begin. *Peregrine Fund Newsletter* 2: 1–3.

————. (ed.). 1975. Restoring peregrines to nature. *Peregrine Fund Newsletter* 3: 1–3.

Cade, T. J., and P. R. Dague (eds.). 1976a. Captive breeding—the 1976 season. *Peregrine Fund Newsletter* 4: 3.

————. 1976b. Establishing falcons in the wild. *Peregrine Fund Newsletter* 4: 3–5.

————. 1976c. Our falcons come home. *Peregrine Fund Newsletter* 4: 1–3.

————. 1977. Parental duties. *Peregrine Fund Newsletter* 5: 4–5.

Cade, T. J., and R. Fyfe. 1970. The North American peregrine survey, 1970. *Canadian Field-Naturalist* 84(3): 231–245.

————. In press. What makes peregrine falcons breed in captivity? In S. A. Temple (ed.). In Press. *Endangered Birds, Management Techniques for Preserving Threatened Species.* Madison: University of Wisconsin, pp. 251–262.

Cade, T. J., C. M. White, and J. R. Haugh. 1968. Peregrines and pesticides in Alaska. *Condor* 70(2): 170–178.

Cahalane, V. H. 1947. *Mammals of North America.* New York: MacMillan, 682 pp.

Chancellor, R. D. (ed.). 1977. *World Conference on Birds of Prey, Report on Proceedings, Vienna 1975.* London: International Council for Bird Preservation, 442 pp.

Clement, R. C. (ed.). 1974. *Proceedings of a Conference on Peregrine Falcon Recovery.* Audubon Conservation Report No. 4, 38 pp.

Cochran, W. W. 1975. Following a migrating peregrine from Wisconsin to Mexico. *Hawk Chalk* 14(2): 28–37.

Culver, D. E. 1919. Duck hawks wintering in the center of Philadelphia. *Auk* 36(1): 108–109.

DeWitt, J. B. 1956. Toxicity of chlorinated insecticides to quail and pheasants. *Atlantic-Naturalist* 1956(3): 115–118.

Enderson, J. H. 1969. Peregrine and prairie falcon life tables based on band-recovery data. In J. J. Hickey (ed.). 1969. *Peregrine Falcon Populations, Their Biology and Decline.* Madison: University of Wisconsin Press, pp. 505–509.

Enderson, J. H., and J. Craig. 1974. Status of the peregrine falcon in the Rocky Mountains in 1973. *Auk* 91(4): 727–736.

Enderson, J. H., S. A. Temple, and L. G. Swartz. 1972. Time-lapse photographic records of nesting peregrine falcons. *Living Bird* 11: 113–128.

Fyfe, R. W. 1976. Rationale and success of the Canadian Wildlife Service peregrine breeding project. *Canadian Field-Naturalist* 90(3): 308–319.

Fyfe, R. W., and H. I. Armbruster. 1977. Raptor research and management in Canada. In R. D. Chancellor (ed.). 1977. *World Conference on Birds of Prey, Report of Proceedings, Vienna 1975*. London: International Council for Bird Preservation, pp. 282–293.

Fyfe, R. W., S. A. Temple, and T. J. Cade. 1976. The 1975 North American peregrine falcon survey. *Canadian Field-Naturalist* 90(3): 228–273.

Goldberg, E. D. 1975. Synthetic organohalides in the sea. *Proceedings of the Royal Society of London, Series B, Biological Sciences* 189 (1096): 277–289.

Groskin, Horace. 1947. Duck hawks breeding in the business center of Philadelphia, Pennsylvania. *Auk* 64(2): 312–314.

———. 1952. Observations of duck hawks nesting on man-made structures. *Auk* 69(3): 246–253.

Grossman, M. L., and John Hamlet. 1964. *Birds of Prey of the World*. New York: Clarkson N. Potter, 496 pp.

Hagar, J. A. 1969. History of the Massachusetts peregrine falcon population, 1935–57. In J. J. Hickey (ed.). 1969. *Peregrine Falcon Populations, Their Biology and Decline*. Madison: University of Wisconsin Press, pp. 123–131.

Hagen, Yngvar. 1947. Does the merlin sometimes play a role as a protector of fieldfare colonies on the fells? *Vår Fågelvärld* 6(3/4): 137–141. (Norwegian with English summary).

———. 1952. *The Birds of Prey and Game Management*. Oslo: Gyldendal Norsk Forlag, 603 pp. (pp. 88–126 translated by W. G. Mattox).

Hall, G. H. 1955. Great moments in action: the story of the Sun Life falcons. Privately printed, Montreal, 37 pp. Reprinted in *Canadian Field-Naturalist* 84(3): 209–230.

Hansen, Kjeld. 1977. The Greenland white-tailed eagle. In R. D. Chancellor (ed.). 1977. *World Conference on Birds of Prey, Report on Proceedings, Vienna 1975*. London: International Council for Bird Preservation, pp. 73–74.

Harris, J. T., and D. M. Clement. 1975. Greenland peregrines at their eyries. *Meddelelser om Grønland*, 205(3): 1–28.

Harrison, H. L., O. L. Loucks, J. W. Mitchell, D. F. Parkhurst, C. R. Tracy, D. G. Watts, and V. J. Yannacone, Jr. 1970. Systems studies of DDT transport. *Science* (Washington, D.C.) 170 (3957): 503–508.

Henny, C. J., and H. M. Wight. 1972. Population ecology and environmental pollution: red-tailed and Cooper's hawks. In *Population Ecology of Migratory Birds: A Symposium*. U.S. Department of Interior Wildlife Research Report 2, pp. 229–250.

Herbert, R. A., and K. G. S. Herbert. 1965. Behavior of peregrine falcons in the New York City region. *Auk* 82(1): 62–94.

———. 1969. The extirpation of the Hudson River peregrine falcon population. In J. J. Hickey (ed.). 1969. *Peregrine Falcon Populations, Their Biology and Decline*. Madison: University of Wisconsin Press, pp. 133–154.

Herren, Hans. 1969. The status of the peregrine falcon in Switzerland. In J. J. Hickey (ed.). 1969. *Peregrine Falcon Populations, Their Biology and Decline*. Madison: University of Wisconsin Press, pp. 231–238.

Hickey, J. J. 1942. Eastern population of the duck hawk. *Auk* 59(2): 176–204.

———. 1954. Survival studies of banded birds. *United States Fish and Wildlife Service Special Scientific Report*: Wildlife No. 15, 177 pp.

———. (ed.). 1969. *Peregrine Falcon Populations, Their Biology and Decline*. Madison: University of Wisconsin Press, 596 pp.

Hickey, J. J., and D. W. Anderson. 1969. The peregrine falcon: life history and population literature. In J. J. Hickey (ed.). 1969. *Peregrine Falcon Populations, Their Biology and Decline*. Madison: University of Wisconsin Press, pp. 3–42.

Hickey, J. J., J. A. Keith, and F. B. Coon. 1966. An exploration of pesticides in a Lake Michigan ecosystem. *Journal of Applied Ecology*, 3 (Supplement): 141–154.

Jeffries, D. J. 1973. The effects of organochlorine insecticides and their metabolites on breeding birds. *Journal of Reproduction and Fertility*, Supplement 19: 337–352.

Jeffries, D. J., and I. Prestt. 1966. Post-mortems of peregrines and lanners with particular reference to organochlorine residues. *British Birds* 59(2): 49–64.

Jenkins, M. A. 1978. Gyrfalcon nesting behavior from hatching to fledging. *Auk* 95(1): 122–127.

Jenkins, David, Adam Watson, and G. R. Miller. 1963. Population studies on red grouse, *Lagopus lagopus scoticus* (Lath.) in north-east Scotland. *Journal of Animal Ecology* 32(3): 317–376.

Kaufman, John. 1976. Soaring free again. *National Wildlife* 14(2): 4–11.

Keith, L. B. 1974. Some features of population dynamics in mammals. *XI International Congress of Game Biologists, Stockholm, Sept. 3–7, 1973*: 17–58.

Kelsall, J. P. 1968. *The Migratory Barren-Ground Caribou of Canada*. Ottawa: Roger Duhamel, Queen's Printer, 340 pp.

Kreitzer, J. F. 1972. The effect of embryonic development on the thickness of the egg shells of coturnix quail. *Poultry Science* 51(5): 1764–1765.

Lack, David. 1947–1948. The significance of clutch-size. *Ibis* 89(2): 302–352; 90(1): 25–45.

Lincer, J. L., T. J. Cade, and J. M. Devine. 1970. Organochlorine residues in Alaskan peregrine falcons (*Falco peregrinus* Tunstall), rough-legged hawks (*Buteo lagopus* Pontoppidan) and their prey. *Canadian Field-Naturalist* 84(3): 255–263.

Linkola, Pentti, and Teuvo Suominen. 1969. Population trends in Finnish peregrines. In J. J. Hickey (ed.). 1969. *Peregrine Falcon Populations, Their Biology and Decline*. Madison: University of Wisconsin Press, pp. 183–191.

Lockie, J. D., and D. A. Ratcliffe. 1964. Insecticides and Scottish golden eagles. *British Birds* 57(3): 89–102.

Lockie, J. D., D. A. Ratcliffe, and R. Balharry. 1969. Breeding success and organo-chlorine residues in golden eagles in west Scotland. *Journal of Applied Ecology* 6(3): 381–389.

MacQueen, J. 1953. Cooperation between butcher-birds and falcon. *Emu* 53(4): 330–331.

Mattox, W. G. 1969. The white falcon: field studies of *Falco rusticolus* L. in Greenland. *Polar Notes* 9: 46–62.

————. 1970a. Banding gyrfalcons (*Falco rusticolus*) in Greenland, 1967. *Bird-Banding* 41(1): 31–37.

————. 1970b. Bird-banding in Greenland. *Arctic* 23(4): 217–228.

————. 1975. Bird of prey research in West Greenland, 1974. *Polar Record* 17(109): 387–388.

Mattox, W. G., R. A. Graham, W. A. Burnham, D. M. Clement, and J. T. Harris. 1972. Peregrine falcon survey, West Greenland, 1972. *Arctic* 25(4): 308–311.

Mayr, Ernst. 1970. *Populations, Species, and Evolution, an Abridgement of Animal Species and Evolution*. Cambridge: Harvard, 453 pp.

Mebs, Theodor. 1969. Peregrine falcon population trends in West Germany. In J. J. Hickey (ed.). 1969. *Peregrine Falcon Populations, Their Biology and Decline*. Madison: University of Wisconsin Press, pp. 193–207.

Merriam, C. H. 1889. A hawk bearing a legend. *Auk* 6(3): 276.

Milstein, P. Le S., I. Prestt, and A. A. Bell. 1970. The breeding cycle of the gray heron. *Ardea* 58(3/4): 171–257.

Moore, N. W., and D. A. Ratcliffe. 1962. Chlorinated hydrocarbon residues in the egg of a peregrine falcon (*Falco peregrinus*) from Perthshire. *Bird Study* 9(4): 242–244.

Morres, A. P. 1882. The peregrines of Salisbury Cathedral. *Zoologist* 6(61): 18–20.

Nelson, R. W. 1970. *Some Aspects of the Breeding Behavior of Peregrine Falcons on Langara Island, British Columbia*. M.S. Thesis, University of Calgary, Calgary, Alberta. 306 pp.

————. 1971. Captive breeding of peregrines: suggestions from their behavior in the wild. *Raptor Research News* 5(2): 54–82.

Newton, I. 1976. Raptor research and conservation during the last five years. *Canadian Field-Naturalist* 90(3): 225–227.

Peakall, D. B. 1967. Pesticide-induced enzyme breakdown of steroids in birds. *Nature* 216(5114): 505–506.

————. 1975. PCB's and their environmental effects. *Critical Reviews in Environmental Control* 5(4): 469–508.

————. 1976. The peregrine falcon (*Falco peregrinus*) and pesticides. *Canadian Field-Naturalist* 90(3): 301–307.

Pettingill, O. S., Jr. 1970. *Ornithology in Laboratory and Field*. Fourth Edition. Minneapolis: Burgess, 524 pp.

Porter, R. D., and S. N. Wiemeyer. 1969. Dieldrin and DDT: effects on sparrow hawk eggshells and reproduction. *Science* 165(3889): 199–200.

Postupalsky, Sergej. 1975. Current status of some Michigan raptors. *Jack-Pine Warbler* 53(2): 76–77.

Prestt, Ian. 1977. A review of the status of birds of prey in Great Britain. In R. D. Chancellor (ed.). 1977. *World Conference on Birds of Prey, Report on Proceedings, Vienna 1975*. London: International Council for Bird Preservation, pp. 114–118.

Ratcliffe, D. A. 1958. Broken eggs in peregrine eyries. *British Birds* 51 (1): 23–26.

————. 1962. Breeding density in the peregrine *Falco peregrinus* and raven *Corvus corax*. *Ibis* 104(1): 13–39.

————. 1967. Decrease in eggshell weight in certain birds of prey. *Nature* 215(5097): 208–210.

——. 1969. Population trends of the peregrine falcon in Great Britain. In J. J. Hickey (ed.). 1969. *Peregrine Falcon Populations, Their Biology and Decline*. Madison: University of Wisconsin Press, pp. 239–269.

——. 1970. Changes attributable to pesticides in egg breakage frequency and eggshell thickness in some British birds. *Journal of Applied Ecology* 7(1): 67–115.

——. 1972. The peregrine population of Great Britain in 1971. *Bird Study* 19(3): 117–156.

——. 1973. Studies of the recent breeding success of the peregrine, *Falco peregrinus*. *Journal of Reproduction and Fertility* Supplement 19: 377–389.

Rice, J. N. 1969. The decline of the peregrine population in Pennsylvania. In J. J. Hickey (ed.). 1969. *Peregrine Falcon Populations, Their Biology and Decline*. Madison: University of Wisconsin Press, pp. 155–163.

Risebrough, R. W., G. L. Florant, and D. D. Berger. 1970. Organochlorine pollutants in peregrines and merlins migrating through Wisconsin. *Canadian Field-Naturalist* 84(3): 247–253.

Risebrough, R. W., P. Rieche, S. G. Herman, D. B. Peakall, and M. N. Kirven. 1968. Polychlorinated biphenyls in the global ecosystem. *Nature* 220(5172): 1098–1102.

Salomonsen, Finn. 1950–1951. *Grønlands Fugle, the Birds of Greenland*. København: Ejnar Munksgaard, 608 pp.

——. 1966. Den gronlandske fugleringmaerkning. *Feltornithologen* 8(3): 88–99.

——. 1967. *Fuglene-på Grønland*. København: Rhodos, 343 pp.

——. 1970. Birds useful to man in Greenland. *Proceedings of the Conference on Productivity and Conservation in Northern Circumpolar Lands*. Morges, Switzerland: International Union for Conservation of Nature and National Resources, pp. 169–175.

Schrieber, R. W., and R. W. Risebrough. 1972. Studies of the brown pelican. *Wilson Bulletin* 84(2): 119–135.

Schriver, E. C., Jr. 1969. The status of Cooper's hawks in western Pennsylvania. In J. J. Hickey (ed.). 1969. *Peregrine Falcon Populations, Their Biology and Decline*. Madison: University of Wisconsin Press, pp. 356–359.

Schröder, Horst. 1969. The decline of tree-nesting peregrines in the German Democratic Republic. In J. J. Hickey (ed.). 1969. *Peregrine Falcon Populations, Their Biology and Decline*. Madison: University of Wisconsin Press, pp. 217–224.

Sick, Helmut. 1961. Peregrine falcon hunting bats while wintering in Brazil. *Auk* 78(4): 646–648.

Simkiss, K. 1961. Calcium metabolism and avian reproduction. *Biological Reviews of the Cambridge Philosophical Society* 36(3): 321–367.

Snyder, N. F. R., H. A. Snyder, J. L. Lincer, and R. T. Reynolds. 1973. Organochlorines, heavy metals, and the biology of North American accipiters. *Bioscience* 23(5): 300–305.

Spofford, W. R. 1969. Hawk Mountain counts as population indices in northeastern America. In J. J. Hickey (ed.). 1969. *Peregrine Falcon Populations, Their Biology and Decline*. Madison: University of Wisconsin Press, pp. 323–332.

Temple, S. A.. In press. Reintroducing birds of prey to the wild. In S. A. Temple (ed.). In press. *Endangered Birds, Management Techniques for Preserving Threatened Species*. Madison: University of Wisconsin Press, pp. 355–363.

U. S. Department of Agriculture, Agricultural Stabilization and Conservation Service. 1973. *The Pesticide Review 1972*. Washington, D.C., 58 pp.

―――. 1975. *The Pesticide Review 1974*. Washington, D.C., 58 pp.

―――. 1977. *The Pesticide Review 1976*. Washington, D.C., 42 pp.

Vaurie, Charles. 1961. Systematic notes on Palearctic birds, No. 44, Falconidae: the genus *Falco* (Part 1, *Falco peregrinus* and *Falco pelegrinoides*). *American Museum Novitates* 2035: 1–19.

Voous, K. H. 1961. Records of peregrine falcons on the Atlantic Ocean. *Ardea* 49(3/4): 176–177.

Walker, Wayman, II, W. G. Mattox, and R. W. Risebrough. 1973. Pollutant and shell thickness determinations of peregrine eggs from West Greenland. *Arctic* 26(3): 255–256.

Ward, F. P., and R. B. Berry. 1972. Autumn migrations of peregrine falcons on Assateague Island, 1970–71. *Journal of Wildlife Management* 36(2): 484–492.

White, C. M. 1968. Diagnosis and relationships of the North American tundra-inhabiting peregrine falcons. *Auk* 85(2): 179–191.

―――. 1969. Breeding Alaskan and arctic migrant populations of the peregrine. In J. J. Hickey (ed.). 1969. *Peregrine Falcon Populations, Their Biology and Decline*. Madison: University of Wisconsin Press, pp. 45–51.

White, C. M., and T. J. Cade. 1971. Cliff-nesting raptors and ravens along the Colville River in arctic Alaska. *Living Bird* 10:107–150.

White, C. M., W. B. Emison, F. S. L. Williamson. 1973. DDE in a resident Aleutian Island peregrine population. *Condor* 75(3): 306–311.

Wilkinson, E. S. 1931. Peregrine falcon in Shanghai City. *Ibis* 1 (Thirteenth series)(1): 89–90.

Wisconsin DDT Hearings, Transcript of the. 1968–1969. Held by the Wisconsin Department of Natural Resources, Madison, 2811 pp.

Wood, C. A., and F. M. Fyfe (trans. and ed.). 1943. *The Art of Falconry, Being the De Arte Venandi Cum Avibus of Frederick II of Hohenstaufen*. Stanford: University of Stanford Press, 637 pp.

Wurster, C. F., Jr. 1969a. Chlorinated hydrocarbon insecticides and the world ecosystem. *Biological Conservation* 1(2): 123–129.

―――. 1969b. DDT goes to trial in Madison. *Bioscience* 19(9): 809–813.

Young, H. F. 1969. Hypotheses on peregrine population dynamics. In J. J. Hickey (ed.). 1969. *Peregrine Falcon Populations, Their Biology and Decline*. Madison: University of Wisconsin Press, pp. 513–519.

Zimmerman, D. R. 1975. That the peregrine shall live. *Audubon* 77(6): 38–49.

Index

Accipiter, 122–23

Aircraft: use in peregrine studies, 24–25

Alaska: peregrines contaminated by DDT, 21–22; methods for peregrine studies, 74. See also Colville River

Aldrin, 13, 14. See also Organochlorine pesticides

Anatum peregrine. See *Falco peregrinus anatum*

Assateague Island, Maryland, 103–4

Austria, 10, 242

Banding, bird: description of, 96–97; use of mist nets, 98–99; recovery of peregrines, 101, 105; peregrine mortality studies, 105–6; of gyrfalcons in Greenland, 119–20

BHC, 14, 15. See also Organochlorine pesticides

Blind, observation: use and construction of, 158–60; response of peregrine to, 164, 170–71, 172; used with First Eyrie peregrines, 171–76, 195–97, 200–202, 217–19

Bunting, snow, 130–31, 152, 155, 156

Cade, Tom, 74, 156, 237–38

Calcium: metabolism disrupted by DDE, 18–19

Caloplaca (lichen), 25, 189

Canadian Wildlife Service: peregrine management, 238, 241–42

Captive breeding: of peregrine, 158–59, 236–38

Cedar Grove, Wisconsin, 103, 104

Colville River, Alaska, 21, 156, 241

Cornell University, New York, 237–40, 241–42

DDT: use of, 13, 14, 235; contamination of peregrines, 13, 15, 19–22, 101, 104, 234; characteristics of, 15–17; role in decline of peregrine and other birds, 15–21; metabolized form, 16; contamination of peregrine prey, 16–17; restrictions on, 235. See also Falcon, peregrine—pesticides; Falcon, peregrine—population status; Organochlorine pesticides

Denmark, 68, 97, 242

Dieldrin: use of, 13, 14; contamination of peregrine, 13, 15, 104; impact on golden eagle, 19; induces liver enzymes, 19; lethal to falcons, 20. See also Organochlorine pesticides

Eagle, white-tailed sea, 112–13, 212

Enderson, James, 105–6

Estrogen: affected by DDE, 18–19

Evolution: and species change, 144–46

Extinction: biological significance of, 144–45

Eyrie: traditions of occupancy by peregrines, 11; gyrfalcon and raven, 120; protection from disturbance, 236. See also Falcon, peregrine—breeding sites

Falco peregrinus anatum: range and status, 45; differences from *tundrius*, 48–49; migration of, 101, 104. See also Falcon, peregrine

Falco peregrinus pealei: range, 45; population stability, 241. See also Falcon, peregrine

Falco peregrinus tundrius: range and status, 45; differences from *anatum*, 48–49; timing of migration, 104. See also Falcon, peregrine

Falcon, peregrine: range, 8, 105; subspecies of, 45, 48–49; voice, 91, 92, 131–32; migration and winter, 101–5; fledging of young, 102; behavior as yearlings, 107–8; behavior at night, 135–37, 223–24; evolution of, 144–45; impacts of decline on other birds, 211–16

—and humans: persistence despite disturbance, 11; falconers' names for, 49–50; disturbance affecting clutch counts, 84–85; peregrines inhabiting cities, 198–200; special management programs, 235–40, 241–42; needs for protection from disturbance, 236

—sexes, behavior of: physical differences, 51–52; pair relationship, 52; courtship, 52, 106–7, 144; differences in flight, 83–84; sex roles, 91–92, 142, 148

—breeding sites: traditions of occupancy, 11, 107; occupation by solitary birds, 36; occupation by immatures, 36, 107–8; description of scrape, 59; artificial sites, 70, 71; site requirements, 70, 71; defense

color variation, 113–14; in winter, 118–19; banded in Greenland, 119–20; breeding sites, 120, 211–12; hunting, 146; and arctic terns, 209

Hall, G. Harper, 198–99
Hawk, Cooper's, 122–23
Hawk, sharp-shinned, 122–23
Hawks: in North America, 121–24; other birds nesting near, 156–57
Hepatic enzyme induction: caused by DDT, 18–19
Heptachlor, 13, 14. See also Heptachlor epoxide; Organochlorine pesticides
Heptachlor epoxide, 13, 15, 20. See also Organochlorine pesticides
Herbert, Kathleen, 9–10
Herbert, Richard, 9–10
Highlands of Scotland, 14, 15
Hickey, Joseph, 8, 10, 11
Hudson River, New York, 9–10
Hunting habits: affected by flight patterns in raptors, 83, 123; and vulnerability to pesticide contamination, 123. See also Falcon, peregrine—hunting; Gyrfalcon

Longspur, lapland, 32, 153, 155

Massachusetts, 10, 11
Merlin, 49, 156
Montreal, 198–99
Mutes: staining eyrie cliffs, 24–25

New York, 9–10, 199

Oldsquaw, 154–55
Organochlorine pesticides: and peregrines, 13, 14–15, 20, 235; effects on birds, 19; and accipiters, 122–23. See also Aldrin; BHC; DDT; Dieldrin; Falcon, peregrine—pesticides; Heptachlor; Heptachlor epoxide

Palisades Interstate Park, New York, 9–10
PCBs: threat to birds, 21; contaminating peregrines, 104, 234–35
Peale's peregrine. See Falco peregrinus pealei
Phalarope, northern, 154, 155
Polychlorinated biphenyls. See PCBs
Prey: methods for determining, 147–48; safety near raptor nests, 156–57. See also Falcon, peregrine—feeding
Ptarmigan, rock, 127, 155
Puffin, common, 97, 115

Ratcliffe, Derek, 12–15, 17–19
Raven, common: nest sites, 120, 211; and peregrines, 142, 174, 188–89
Redpoll, common, 29, 153, 155
Reintroduction: of peregrines to the wild, 238–40
Reproductive isolation, 43–44
Ring Sø Eyrie: behavior of peregrine pair, 185–94; breeding success, 232, 242

Salomonsen, Finn, 114, 209
Shooting: of birds in Greenland, 97–98; impact on white-tailed sea eagle, 112
Søndrestrøm Air Base, 26–27, 68
Species: definition of, 42–45; changes through time, 144–46
Subspecies: definition of, 42–45
Sun Life Building, Montreal, 198–99
Survey, population: in Greenland, 22–23, 232–34; analysis of methods, 71–76

Tundra peregrine. See Falco peregrinus tundrius

Wales, 14, 242
Wheatear, 151–52, 155

Young, Howard, 108–9